"This book is essential reading for anyone concerned about the truth of our embodiment as male and female and how to promote that truth in our confused era. The contributors are leading experts in their respective fields who write with authority and compassion, and the result is a one-of-a-kind, interdisciplinary defense of vital truths about the human person. My own research on this topic has benefited from many of the scholars who contributed to this book, and I will be recommending this new volume to others."

RYAN T. ANDERSON,
President of the Ethics and Public Policy Center,
Author of *When Harry Became Sally:*
Responding to the Transgender Moment

"The very first page of the Jewish and Christian Scripture proposes the key to making sense of the paradoxical unities of human life—matter and spirit, body and soul, male and female: 'The Lord God formed the man of dust from the ground and breathed into his nostrils the breath of life, and the man became a living creature' (Gen 2:7); 'In the image of God he created them; male and female he created them' (Gen 1:27). *Sexual Identity* presents these philosophical and theological concepts in a manner accessible to all, without losing any of the dignity, grandeur, and hope that they contain. Its interdisciplinary approach demonstrates the place of these age-old truths as the real foundation of modern scientific research and the necessary guideposts for medical and psychological treatment and care. It will be an important resource for all those who want to understand and care for the whole person and will allow even the casual reader to perceive the complementary identity of men and women as, in the words of Pope Francis, 'a great treasure. . . . Not only an asset, but a thing of beauty.'"

FR. PHILIP G. BOCHANSKI,
Executive Director, Courage International

"At a time when the 'hot-button' issue of sexual identity provokes more strident reaction and position-defending than patient and honest investigation, John Finley's edited volume is more than just a breath of fresh air; with its aim to get to the bottom of the matter in all its interrelated aspects, it is a reaffirmation of our humanity. The book is a thoughtfully composed whole, woven from the contributions of experts in distinct fields who collaborated with one another over the course of a year or more. The result is a comprehensive vision of what sexual identity is and what it means."

D. C. SCHINDLER,
Professor of Metaphysics and Anthropology at
The John Paul II Institute in Washington, DC

"*Sexual Identity* is an unassailable prophylactic and antidote to the transgender cult. The truth contained in this book about what it means to be human is needed now more than any other time in modern history. Parents, high school and college students, educators, health professionals, lawyers, and policy makers should give this book a close read. We live in a culture that feeds two dangerous lies to our youth: first, that some people are born in the wrong body, and second, that there are more than two sexes. This is not science—it is a false philosophy. It is a reformulation of the heresy of pagan gnosticism. When our youth today 'learn' that they cannot trust the objective reality of their own physical bodies to tell them who they are, it strikes a major blow to their entire system of reality-testing and leads many of them down a medical pathway resulting in permanent, lifelong sterility, emotional suffering, chronic illness, and physical harm. *Sexual Identity* is a book that will save lives."

MICHELLE CRETELLA, M.D.,
Executive Director, American College of Pediatricians

"It's unfortunate that the world has come to the point of needing thorough and scholarly defense of the fact that men and women are different. But thanks to the contributors of this excellent work, such a resource is now available. Drawing upon the theological, biological, philosophical, and psychological sciences, *Sexual Identity* charitably presents irrefutable evidence for the unchanging reality that God 'made them male and female.'"

JASON EVERT,
Author of *Theology of the Body in One Hour*

"*Sexual Identity* is the kind of book that is needed today as a sound criticism of those who argue for sexual ambiguity. I have also just edited a book with a related position, titled *The Complementarity of Women and Men*. Get both books and you have a 'one-two knockout punch' for defending the traditional and Catholic understanding of men and women."

PAUL C. VITZ,
Professor Emeritus, New York University and
Senior Scholar/Professor of Psychology,
Divine Mercy University

Sexual IDENTITY

Sexual IDENTITY

The HARMONY *of* PHILOSOPHY, SCIENCE, *and* REVELATION

Edited by JOHN DESILVA FINLEY

EMMAUS ROAD
PUBLISHING

Steubenville, Ohio
www.emmausroad.org

Emmaus Road Publishing
1468 Parkview Circle
Steubenville, Ohio 43952

Library of Congress Control Number 2021952731
978-1-64585-189-9 Hardcover | 978-1-64585-190-5 Paperback |
978-1-64585-191-2 Ebook

Cover design by Patty Borgman
Layout by Joseph Antoniello and Allison Merrick
Cover Image: Masolino da Panicale, *Temptation of Adam and Eve* (1425) Basilica of Our Lady of Carmel, Florence.

To Hilary

Contents

CHAPTER 2
Cara Buskmiller, MD
Paul Hruz, MD, PhD

CHAPTER 3
Andrew J. Sodergren, MTS, PsyD

CHAPTER 4
Patrick W. Lappert, MD

CHAPTER 5
John D. Finley, PhD

CHAPTER 6
Lawrence J. Welch, PhD

Acknowledgments

THANKS TO THE JOHN TEMPLETON FOUNDATION and its "Engaging Science in Seminaries" program for a grant that greatly assisted in the development of a course I taught at Kenrick-Glennon Seminary in 2017. That course featured guest lectures by the co-authors of this book and became its launching point. The grant also enabled most of us to meet regularly and discuss the project for over a year. Thanks also to Kenrick-Glennon Seminary for a sabbatical in 2016, during which I began work on the course, and another in 2019, which saw the bulk of the manuscript's completion. I am very grateful to Fr. Richard Conrad, OP, and the Aquinas Institute at Blackfriars, Oxford, for hosting me and my family on sabbatical in 2016. The intellectual and spiritual atmosphere there was conducive to many wonderful conversations. A heartfelt thank you to my co-authors: Cara Buskmiller, Paul Hruz, Patrick Lappert, Andrew Sodergren, and Larry Welch. Their expertise and dedication to truth have been a great inspiration. Dr. Shawn Welch, Mrs. Anne Hruz, Dr. Hilary Finley, Fr. Laurence Kriegshauser, and Dr. Dustin Baldridge provided many helpful contributions along the way. The programs of liberal education at Thomas Aquinas College and the University of Dallas stand behind much of this book's interdisciplinary vision. Finally, my loving gratitude goes to my wife, Hilary, whose encouragement, insight, and dedication to our children made the completion of this book all the more meaningful.

The Problem: Man and Woman as Incoherent

DESPITE LIVING AMIDST a World Wide Web of information, we have lost sight of ourselves. At a recent National Women's March some of the participants were asked, "How would you define 'woman'?" One participant could not answer the question, another said that a woman was whatever she defined herself to be, and a third responded that anyone could be a woman.[1] There is no reason to think men are better off. After all, the question "What is a man?" might not even be asked. For being a man likely has something to do with masculinity, which in its dominant form has much to do with "toxicity," and in its marginalized form is simply whatever *isn't* toxic.[2] Better put the question away and not embarrass those of us who happen to be male.

Granted, I am quoting a few people caught in front of a microphone and one recent phrase tossed around the media. Yet larger cultural movements show that these episodes are not outliers but vivid markers of an incoherence

---

[1] See the YouTube video "How Does the Women's March Define What a Woman Is?," live interviews at the National Women's March in Washington, DC, January 20, 2020, https://www.youtube.com/watch?v=ax-rB7ieV0o.

[2] See Maya Salam, "What Is Toxic Masculinity?," *The New York Times*, January 22, 2019, https://www.nytimes.com/2019/01/22/us/toxic-masculinity.html. Or the Colorado State University's *Women and Gender Advocacy Center* website, which defines masculinity itself as potentially problematic: https://wgac.colostate.edu/education/vocabulary/#1533847855504-b8ae849e-4caf.

that has worked its way deep into our daily activity and discourse. Consider: a woman marching for women finds herself caught when asked in public to say what a woman is. You would think it a great thing to announce the nature of women, especially at a march celebrating them. And yet to say what a woman *is* is also to say what she is not, and to say what a woman is not—a male, perhaps?—would be to discount the identity of a trans woman (a biological male who identifies as a woman). Or, to say that a man is one who can impregnate a woman but cannot himself have babies fails to capture the reality of a trans man (a biological woman who identifies as male).

Viewed in this light, speech itself starts to look like a failed enterprise.

In Plato's *Republic*, Socrates and his colleagues construct a city in speech for the sake of discussing the ideal city, supposing that it would show the human soul writ large. We, too, can take a closer look at our society to see something of ourselves, magnified, moving, like a giant drama dedicated to the topic. The protagonist is the rational animal, made for truth. The action reveals meteoric flashes of technological and economic achievement, but also faltering steps, stumbles, and gaspings. Rarely has the character and fall of human rationality been brought to the fore as in the twenty-first-century first world.

Note again the episode I began with. A question is asked concerning what something is. This is promising, for the central task defining human rationality, as distinct from animal sensation or emotional response, is to seek out the natures of things. Still, it is unusual for society as a whole to ask what a particular thing is. Usually specific questions fall to local constituents, like scientists, children, or college students. It must be something quite fundamental, universal, or urgent if society asks about it. And indeed, the question here concerns ourselves as men and women—realities we have heard about since Homer and have talked about since we hit puberty. The fact that we are asking *this* question as a society is an ambiguous sign. It may be reason's equivalent of a slur or a facial droop, indicating a deeper problem. The fact that we can't coherently answer the question is like a brain scan showing a stroke.

For vagueness is not just a different path from truthful speech, leading to a destination embraced on its own terms. Rather, it becomes a trap. A woman is to be celebrated, but no one knows what a woman is. A man is suspect in being masculine, but not if his masculinity defeats women in a sporting event while he identifies as one of them. Lived incoherence brings a kind of human demise. As one philosopher puts it, being untruthful is not just *a* way of failing at being human; it is *the* way, since in it we undermine the rationality that defines us.[3]

Incoherence leads to isolation and intellectual slavery. We act as if we know what things are, but we cannot define them, because doing so would deny another's right to define himself however he wishes. In such a state, nothing public or common can be asserted as true, though the individual's self-definition can compel common assertions in his favor. It is not just that transgender ideology makes us unable to speak coherently about man and woman.

---

[3]   Robert Sokolowski, *Phenomenology of the Human Person* (Cambridge: Cambridge University Press, 2008), 20–21.

It can also leave trans persons as ghosts of themselves, crippled in their bodily capacities for relations with others, fragmented in their own selves. And for men and women not so harmed, what does our sexual difference mean anyway? We barely need it for reproduction, given in vitro fertilization (IVF) and similar technologies. We don't need it for marriage, which has been redefined to include same-sex couples. We don't need it for pleasure, since the real-life encounter can be replaced with porn, more of which is available for our detached viewing than stars in the sky for shared wonderment. In all cases we risk more attention to the internet and social media than to our human relations, sexual or otherwise. Being man and woman is more and more like a tale told merely for the sake of nostalgia, but one that really signifies nothing.

A Response: The Aim of This Book

In the face of such confusion about a profound dimension of human existence, two sorts of response are needed. One is to counter: to show the confusion for what it is. Some books, thankfully, are doing that: Ryan Anderson's *When Harry Became Sally*, for instance, or Abigail Schrier's *Irreversible Damage*. The other sort of response is to shore up what has been fragmented, to show anew its truth, beauty, and goodness. This book takes both routes, but prioritizes the second. It asks the question "What is man and woman?" and seeks to offer something of human and divine wisdom in response.

To that end, this book is catholic: interdisciplinary and holistic. Common sense and everyday experience, irreplaceable as they are, will not by themselves suffice at this point. The attacks come from scientific, medical, psychological, and cultural quarters. In a culture of incoherence lies reason's fragmentation, which allows development through specialized research but lacks the deeper vision that can see parts in relation to a whole. Such vision used to come from philosophy, the most undone of the disciplines today. By recovering a philosophical tradition in which the branches of human knowledge flourish all the more as they form a living unity, this book wishes to speak coherent truths about man and woman.

Consequently, this book is unusual. A work by one or two authors would lack the competence to address the variety of disciplines whose voices should be heard. A large collection of essays by many authors would risk losing the unity in which each discipline's contribution is an integral piece. Here there are six authors, roughly one for each chapter, speaking to man and woman from the viewpoint of a distinct discipline. The authors are recognized experts in their fields. They have spent several years in communication with each other, reading and discussing works from their respective areas for the sake of a book whose parts will cohere more seamlessly.

We begin with philosophy as we seek a careful, non-technical articulation of our common experience as man and woman. We know much about ourselves but typically don't take the time to make our knowledge explicit. Chapter 1 gives us that opportunity and contextualizes the more specialized discussions to come. In chapter 2 we turn to a biological account of man and woman, which considers the male and female organisms at the anatomic, reproductive, genetic, and molecular levels. Chapter 3 focuses on sexual difference from a psychological point of view, considering the ways in which men and women perceive, think, respond, and behave. At this point the book's scientific view of man and woman is complete. Yet the argument we cannot ignore is the current objection: "Even if men and women are typically as you say, science and technology have changed everything. People go in for sex changes. A guy can become a very attractive girl." Chapter 4, then, is written by a plastic surgeon who discusses the details involved in hormonal and surgical "transitions." The analysis shows the threat posed to the distinctive identities of man and woman in transgender ideology, thus confirming the vision of the human person as examined in preceding chapters. Chapter 5 provides a brief excursion into metaphysics, commenting on the place of man and woman within the soul-body unity that is human nature. Finally, chapter 6 turns to the height of wisdom: God's revelation of himself to his creation. Man and woman are considered in light of their ultimate meaning as an image of God, a communion of persons at the heart of creation's integral ecology.

The chapters thus form a unity, from the everyday to the eternal. Still, for a given reader, each of the chapters is sufficient unto themselves and can be read on their own and in any order preferred. Our style is deliberately not academic. We have made every effort to preserve fidelity to our disciplines while speaking in a way that will appeal to a broad but thoughtful audience. Review points and suggestions for further reading are given at the end of each chapter. While we would argue that the vision we present finds its fullest expression in the teachings of the Catholic Church, the majority of this book relies on reason, not faith. It can be read and evaluated on its own merits by those who are neither Catholic nor Christian.

Without man and woman, the human race does not exist. Without the capacity for truth, we are not human. My hope is that this book strengthens its readers in wisdom concerning themselves, their loved ones, and their fellow men and women. We are all the protagonists; our story has been a good one from the beginning. May we speak it rightly, with coherence and affection.

CHAPTER 1

What Men and Women Mean to Us: A Philosophical Articulation

John D. Finley, PhD

THIS CHAPTER IS "PHILOSOPHICAL"—which means what, exactly? It might be enough to say that, without relying on religious doctrine or scientific studies, we'll think about what men and women are. How we do this, and why it's a crucial beginning, will be the focus of section 1. We will then consider the significance of men and women in human life, as well as the meaning of human sexuality, including its aspects of love, reproduction, family, culture, self-expression, abstinence, and privacy (sections 2–7). In conclusion we'll turn to contemporary urgencies (sections 8–9): What do we say about issues that could make the categories "man" and "woman" virtually meaningless, especially the transgender phenomenon? And what do we mean by "gender"? My aim is to reawaken appreciation for realities we've always lived with, and to help us think rightly about them.

I. KNOWING OURSELVES: DEVICES, SCIENCE, AND RELIGION ASIDE

All of us know men and women, and nearly all of us recognize ourselves as either man or woman, so we should be able to think about what men and women are and what kind of impact they have in human life. This is an exercise in self-knowledge, not just at the individual level ("Who am I?") but also in our familial and social contexts. The unexamined life is not worth living, writes Plato, by which he means that if we deliberately refrain from reflecting on ourselves, we are in some sense not-human.

But taking a step back to think about reality in a sustained way is not easy. (Try doing nothing but thinking about a single person—even your favorite person—for a mere fifteen minutes.) There have always been the usual distractions stemming from practical necessities of day-to-day living. In today's first world, however, where daily survival is no longer a matter of urgency, our distractions have been multiplied through technological forms of inquiry and communication that validate our least whims to get in touch with so-and-so or find out *x* about such-and-such. These outlets consume extraordinary amounts of time and attention precisely because they capitalize on our human tendencies to gain knowledge and communicate it with others. The problem is that our devices tend to crowd out the kinds of communication and thoughtfulness that get us to the heart of things.

In thinking about ourselves as men and women, an additional obstacle stems from the fact that, like many subjects, this one seems to require almost immediate entrance into advanced realms of science, like genetics, endocrinology, and psychology. Especially given the recent and rapid growth of transgender phenomena, many of us suppose that any serious consideration of human maleness and femaleness—anything deeper than stereotype, inherited prejudice, faith-based position, or hunch—demands knowledge of specialized fields of research. So, for example, I might begin life thinking that "men are men and women are women." Men act like my dad, brothers, and buddies, while women act like my mom, sisters, and their friends. But over time I realize that some of my thoughts, while true, are pretty vague (e.g., "men are men"). Other thoughts do not fit as many people as I initially supposed (some men do not act at all like those in my tribe). I am forced to take more seriously the questions "What is Manhood?" and "What is Womanhood?" Is there some way of acting that women have and men don't, or vice versa? Where do I look to find out what this is? Maybe textbooks in psychology or sociology?

Especially challenging might be physical conditions in which the very maleness or femaleness of the person is not evident. What about a baby born with the XY chromosome pattern typical of men but who has a vagina instead of a penis? Here I'd need to know a lot from the realms of biology and medicine just to understand what is going on at the bodily level. And if this is the case, maybe any serious pronouncements about the nature of men and women have to rely considerably on the sciences. So isn't it going to be a waste of time for us non-scientists to think on our own about what men and women are? Wouldn't it be far more effective to plunge directly into the sciences—or better yet, wait until we can read something or chat with someone who possesses scientific expertise?

In the face of this concern, we should consider two things. First, we can and should admit that many questions can be satisfactorily answered only with the help of specialized scientific research. This is why the sciences exist. Without the work of scientists, we would have never known that the earth orbits the sun (contrary to initial appearance), or that light actually has a rate of travel, or that what we call "matter" is not homogenous brute stuff but a structure of constituents that become somehow less real the more elemental they get.

For a person with a disorder of sexual development (for instance, congenital adrenal hyperplasia), science has made such enormous strides that this person who centuries earlier might have simply been labeled "freak" is now appropriately diagnosed with a medical condition. The person can even participate in sexual or reproductive functions with the assistance of medical technology. The benefits of modern science are central to our lives and yet so commonplace that despite their achievement, we tend to take them for granted. Because maleness and femaleness are deeply significant dimensions of the human reality, we should not be surprised to see that the sciences offer much regarding various aspects of our sexuality. Indeed, later chapters of this book display important findings from biology, psychology, and surgery as parts of a larger whole seeking to offer some wisdom about what it means to be man and woman. The sciences are crucial.

Still, and this is the second point, science and its accompanying technology are, on their own, partial. They are not the whole of human wisdom or even its most important parts. Science reveals aspects of the world, and technology enables us, with that knowledge, to change something in the world. But on their own, science and technology do not set the goals. Science does not tell me that my goal is happiness; happiness is already my goal. Were I setting out to pursue brain research, I would not approach neuroscience on the chance that neuroscience will tell me whether or not to be fulfilled, and if so, how. I pursue neuroscience because I already want to be fulfilled and I have decided that pursuing neuroscience will help me do so. My decision-making process relied on all sorts of considerations that do not stem from things like neuroscience but from sources of a more familiar nature: the advice of friends and parents, good teachers, stories of great scientists and their discoveries, contemplation of the human being, reflection upon my own talents, and so on.

If there is a problem with the sciences today, it is not something intrinsic to their own character, methods, and findings, all of which are undeniably fruitful. The problem, rather, lies in the fact that the sciences have become typically presented within a *scientistic* outlook, which regards as truth only facts that can be scientifically established. This mentality, in apparently elevating science, has actually undermined it by burdening it with an authority it cannot bear. After all, even the notion that truth equals what science can establish is a premise that science itself cannot demonstrate! In reality, science is one important piece of the integral whole that is wisdom, which also includes philosophy, great literature, and divine Revelation.

We need to recall that we are the originators of science and technology, that they exist to serve our goals, and that we find ourselves stunted to the extent that we accept scientistic conclusions that don't fit with what we recognize to be true. We are the only animals in the cosmos with full-fledged reason, language, art, and civilization; the only animals for whom living according to thoughtfulness and love *is* our way of life. Because we have been raised by other humans, we have learned quite a bit about the world around us; and in turn, we communicate this learning to others. Everyday life just would not be possible without this learning and communication. The very fact that people can get together to pursue science and build technological marvels in the first place depends on it. So nothing should stop us from returning to ourselves and considering more deeply who and what we are, the wonders of nature, and the persons in our lives.

II. A Threefold Primacy of Woman and Man in Human Life

Let us begin with some simple but crucial statements:

- A woman is a female human and a man is a male human.

- Humanness means animal life that is characterized by thought, deliberate love, and relations with others.

- A female is an organism that can produce offspring from within herself through receiving from a male in sexual intercourse. A male is an organism that can produce offspring outside of himself through giving to a female in that same activity.

Such statements, like most definitions, give us a foundation for further thought and discussion. Like most foundations, they are not especially impressive on their own, though without them further progress is impossible. Most of this book is dedicated to examining the implications of these statements. For now, though, let us simply note three ways in which man and woman are especially significant realities within human life.

Biological

Aside from saying that we belong to the species "human," we could, of course, say a lot more about each one of us. We possess countless individual features that help make us who we are: things like bone structure, height, eye and skin color, vocal tone, personality, family of origin, and talents and interests. In comparison with these traits, the male-female distinction reaches uniquely into us, since it involves distinct organs with distinct purposes. It involves a network of genetic, hormonal, and anatomical structures that undergird these organs. The human reproductive system actually spans two organisms: male and female. In this sense the male is a different sort of organism than the female, while two people with different eye color or temperament could well share the same organs and organ systems. Being male and female is our *only* organismic difference in this sense, involving purposive inborn diversity in an organ system and its related hormonal activities. We might expect, then, that our maleness and femaleness will affect us as persons in a more holistic manner than our eye color or body type would. The extent to which sex differences affect our physiology and behavior will be shown in the biological and psychological discussions of chapters 2 and 3.

For now, we can say that the reason for the prominence of the male-female difference is that the nature of our species demands it, and so it cuts evenly across the species itself: about half of all humans are male, and half are female. In contrast, the percentage of humans characterized by blond hair, low voice, or tall height could vary wildly from one time and place to another. Such characteristics don't matter a whole lot to the species itself, while man and woman are the very means by which humanness self-perpetuates from one generation to the next. So from a biological point of view, after humanness itself, male and female are our primary characteristics. Like humanness, they are so foundational that we often rightly take them for granted and focus on more individual characteristics: people's looks, mannerisms, likes and dislikes. But foundational things are, for all that, still foundations: we ignore them at our peril.

Personal

Unsurprisingly, daily forms of language, thought, and communication witness to the importance of male and female. Pronouns display the distinction (he/she/it), and personal conversation either takes it for granted or quickly seeks it out when ambiguity occurs. Imagine that a friend starts telling you in glowing terms about another person your friend recently met:

> You've got to meet my new friend!
> Yeah? Who's that?
> Rehs. Rehs is great. Went with me to that show the other day.
> Nice. How do you know each other?
> Rehs is a coworker. We just started hanging out.

You may be about to ask whether Rehs is a guy or girl, or you've already subconsciously presumed that Rehs is a particular sex based on the context of the conversations, connotations with the name "Rehs," or some other little tell. The point is that when we wish to get to know someone— and not just interact for a utilitarian purpose—perhaps the first thing we want to know is whether the person is male or female. This priority in personal encounter mirrors the built-in priority that male or female occupies within the person itself.

Historical

From another angle, is it surprising that we quickly, even subconsciously, seek out another person's sex, when probably the first and most influential people in our lives are marked by the man-woman difference? Mothers and fathers—whether biological, adoptive, step, or figural— are the persons we come from, the ones who have most radically made us what and who we are. The whole reason nature builds the male-female reality so deeply into our organisms is for the sake of human completion, both in the union of man and woman, and in the procreation of new humans who, over time, display the contours and possibilities of the race itself. There's a historical priority, along with the biological and the personal, that the man-woman reality occupies in human life.

III. Human Sexuality: The Obvious but Mysterious Intersection of Love and Reproduction

We are at a good point to ask more positively, what does it mean to be man and woman? What does the male-female distinction amount to in human life? I'd like to suggest as a starting point that our sexuality is the obvious yet mysterious intersection between two great human capacities: love and reproduction. The intersection is obvious, because everyone knows that sexuality concerns both an intense sort of love between people *and* the typical avenue for another human person to come into existence. The very phrase "safe sex" shows how aware everyone is of the two sides of the one coin that is sexual intercourse. Sex is "safe" when it can allow for one side of the coin—expression of mutual love—without the other side—a possible child.[1]

The intersection between love and reproduction is not just obvious, though; it is also mysterious. Think about the fact that a biologist can spend a lifetime doing excellent research on reproductive aspects of human sexuality without once needing to invoke intimacy, romance, infatuation, dating, flirting, break-ups, marriage, anniversaries, and a world of other things that couples in love so often think about. On the flipside, much romantic language, profound

---

[1] The alternative, presumably, is "dangerous sex," in which both sides of the coin are on offer. Is the possibility of another human dangerous? Undoubtedly: it uproots our comforts and expectations but increases our engagement with reality.

or trivial, doesn't mention procreation and might well lose its force in doing so. Consider Shakespeare's *Romeo and Juliet*, the Song of Songs, and most Valentine's Day cards. The realms of romantic love and reproduction can appear easily separable, at least in how we think about them. Indeed, through widespread acceptance of contraception, in vitro fertilization (IVF), and homosexuality, contemporary society considers it fairly obvious that romantic love and reproduction need not have anything to do with each other. So we can at least wonder, *Why* would these realms be joined in the one sphere that is human sexuality? Why does this joining make sense? Here is something mysterious.

Romantic Love

To pursue the mystery, we should consider more deeply the two things intersecting: love and reproduction. Neither will be intelligible without consideration of the sexual difference. Let's begin with love.

Love is such a powerful and fundamental reality in human life that it sometimes receives mention as a core item distinguishing us from other animals. To be sure, it's true that other animals love in some way: a mother's love for her young can be verified as dramatically in bears and orcas as in humans. But in bears and orcas, it's difficult to tell whether love is simply instinct; we have no communication from those animals as to what they think love is, which might indicate to us whether their love goes beyond instinct alone. In humans instinct is also powerful, but our love goes beyond instinct. We can choose to love or not to love, whom to love, and how to love. Still, the relationship between mother and young seems to be a primary embodiment of love in the animal kingdom as a whole, so that in this light, at least, the link between love and reproduction should not surprise us: it's one of the strongest and most manifest links in nature.

Yet if we had to identify the most iconic love relationship in our *human* experience, it would probably not be the mother-child but the romantic (erotic, or sexual).[2] Our literary record over the centuries attests to it. This is partly because of the mutuality in romantic love. A two-sided, conscious willingness pervades the romantic love between a man and woman, whereas the mother-child bond, though at times stronger, is weighted on the side of the mother. Mother-child love is a hallmark of the animal kingdom, humans included, whereas the human sexual relationship is much more unique. Even for those non-human species in which monogamy is normal, the sexual relationship seems to be nowhere near the momentous occasion in the life of the animal that it is for humans.[3]

Love in the human species recapitulates, elevates, and transcends love in the non-human animals. We preserve the mother-offspring relationship and elevate it through thoughtful concern for the good. We also bring to the equation a centrality to sexual love, which is at best

---

[2] For our purposes, these terms can be used more or less interchangeably.

[3] For a fascinating look at sexual difference in non-human animals, see Daphne Fairbairn, *Odd Couples: Extraordinary Differences between the Sexes in the Animal Kingdom* (Princeton, NJ: Princeton University Press, 2015).

imitated in other animals, and then only partially and in some species. That humans expect sexual love to be mutually desired, and that it is not subject to a mating season, are two facts showing a significant difference from the majority of other animal species. From the standpoint of the non-human animal, we could say that the very strong reproductive dimension of love, exhibited by the generational encounter of mother and offspring, becomes founded on another dimension in humans: the sexual, an encounter between equals and one that brings to bear in a new way the father-parent role.

From a reproductive point of view, the importance of the romantic love between mother and father has to do with the kind of being we humans are. The mere fact that a new human is brought into the world is hugely significant, of course, but being a parent means far more in the human realm than it does in the animal realm, given the kind of upbringing humans need. Becoming a mature human simply on the physical plane takes longer than it does in other species, and more importantly, emotional, moral, and intellectual maturity take even longer. The complete lifespan of a human being has been thought for centuries to be somewhere around seventy, maybe eighty, years (see Psalm 90:10). In other words, we imagine a whole human life to include woman or man being able to see their children and their children's children. Why? Because witnessing a successful reproduction of oneself involves seeing one's offspring as capable of successful reproduction in their own right. More than this: as grandparents know, parenting is never really complete. Since no human person can be known exhaustively or reach total perfection in this life, a parent's concern and responsibility never ends. For humans, then, those who are responsible for a new member of the species have a life-long project. Their sexual, personal relationship forms and is formed by this project. It is the origin and touchstone, in some way, for the unending challenge and adventure that is involved in the nourishment, support, and education of their child. Human reproduction, as a lifelong and personal task, is suitably exercised within a parental relationship that can be likewise permanent and intimate.

But how does erotic love in itself connect with repro-duction? What we deduce from the task of child-raising might be limited to the idea that parents should have a firm and, hopefully, lifelong commitment to mutual support and cooperation in their joint efforts to raise children well. This is a huge expectation, a feat to accomplish. Still, thinking in these terms alone would miss perhaps the very heart of romantic love, which is that a man and woman love each other for their own sakes, and not merely as significant others who might or might not cooperate in child-rearing. Romantic love, then, seen from the perspective of repro-duction alone, comes as something of a surprise or gratuity. It seems to go beyond what's strictly necessary for procre-ation and child-rearing. What can we say about it in itself, and how might this track into the realm of reproduction?

Although many kinds of love-relationship permeate human life (parent-child, friendship, admiration), only one of them involves people being "in love," as the expres-sion goes. Erotic love (sexual, romantic, spousal) holds this distinction because in it the love between two people man-ifests a greater wholeness than either person alone could achieve, and it does so at the level of the whole person,

body and soul. Being in love suggests that romantic partners participate in something not only greater than either
of them alone but also crucial to their personal well-being.
Erotic love thus shows most vividly one of the deepest
paradoxes of human life: that we are complete and fulfilled not so much in being ourselves as in transcending
ourselves. Parent-child love also reveals this paradox, but
more one-sidedly on the part of parents. Also, a potential
parent is not incomplete without children in the same way
that a woman or man is incomplete without the other.

The Sexual Difference

For what lies at the heart of romantic incompleteness is the
sexual difference. In some real way, as mentioned earlier,
men and women are different sorts of organisms. A difference in hair color, personality, or body type is never able
to signify incompleteness as sexuality does, because none
of those traits carries with it the ability to perform certain
kinds of actions and not others, or to have certain kinds of
experiences and not others. There is no *kind of action* specific to brunettes rather than blondes. Melancholics and
fast-talkers act differently than cholerics and the slow-of-
speech, but such differences are of degree rather than kind.

Women, on the other hand, can know what it is
like to be a female organism and have a baby human
growing inside of them. Men cannot. Men can know
what it is like to be a male organism and to impregnate
a woman.[4] Woman can experience and appreciate a man's

---

[4] What's involved in being a female or male organism is explained in

sexuality in a way that he or any other man never could, and vice-versa. Man and woman seek to possess each other, lacking what the other is. Yet what a woman experiences in a man's sexuality is not a vicarious or imitative way of being a man; quite the opposite, in experiencing the male, she experiences more of what it means to be a woman, because her sexuality is validated and fulfilled by his. (It is also validated and fulfilled in the way she, in turn, appreciates the male.) She experiences maleness, but not as he does, and not as herself becoming like a male, but as if making her more her. The same is true of a man experiencing a woman's sexuality. He seeks her since she is attractive and possesses what he is not, yet in so doing he experiences her not as though he were becoming female but as someone that makes him more him.

While we can speak of terms like "attraction, arousal, libido, and sexual" as applying to both men and women, clearly they do not refer to the exact same experience. Arousal in a woman-organism will feel and play out as something different from arousal in a man-organism. (The more psychological and interpersonal consequences of these differences account for much that is comic about human sexuality.) Sex itself, then, isn't even the same in man and woman; rather, it refers to this very difference, built deeply into the organism of each, by which the one, possessing, enhancing, and completing the other, is fulfilled.

The reason men and women are and always have been somewhat mysterious to each other is because the sexual

greater detail in chapters 2–3, which address biological, neurological, and psychological aspects.

difference grants to each of them possibilities for action and experience that are off-limits to the other, and yet very much *for* the other. The mysteriousness here is hardly one of mere difference or otherness, which tends to provoke fear, alienation, or lack of interest. Instead, the mystery is laden with interest, since men and women inherently validate each other, somewhat like the negative and positive charges in electricity, for they are fully what they are only in mutual, dynamic engagement.

Our nature is endowed with a diversity that reaches so deeply into our being that it underlies all other diversities, whether of race, color, creed, or expression. Such diversity does not demand sheer separateness or independence; it exists for the sake of an encounter similarly profound. The significance of this encounter is revealed in its enormous effects on people: it has united couples' lives throughout history, and has traumatized victims of assault in an indelible manner. When a man and woman realize they can pursue self-fulfillment by enhancing each other in this encounter, when such realization is mutually expressed and desired, we are faced with a new kind of human wholeness, a personal duality that can never be totally exhausted.

All forms of love-relationship involve a whole that is greater than any one individual: think of a group of close friends, a family, or a veteran military unit. Each of these unities is built on some distinctive bond, like common interests in the friends, blood kinship and shared upbringing in the family, or intense experiences of support in life-or-death situations for the army squad. Romantic love is unique in that it brings together the realm of thoughtful choice (characteristic of all friendships) and the complementarity of sexual differentiation. The biological structures of human nature call for the unity-in-difference manifested by sexual love, and because we're talking about *human* nature, this love is personal as well. All recognize that a sexual encounter sought by both partners is one of the most desired experiences in human life, while an unwanted encounter involves a tremendous violation of the person.

Given what we have said about romantic love and reproduction, we can perhaps see at this point why sexual love (and conversely, a violation of it) is so intensely experienced, unlike any other form of human interaction. In terms of romantic love, I experience this particular person of the opposite sex as somehow completing me, both at the level of sexual nature and through shared interests or personality. My sense of self is then somehow bound up with her, and so is my self-love. But at the same time, she remains her own self, and with an attractiveness that remains her own. Unless I disregard this and think of her as merely an extension of myself (which no one would consider romantic love), my own sense of self and self-love have become paradoxical, since they now somehow belong to another person. What can it mean to experience love of self for one who is in fact an other self, and who must remain so, and yet who sees her self as somehow for me? This is precisely what we experience in romantic love, and this accounts for its unique intensity. Built into this dynamic is the fact that I experience her not simply as completing me but as somehow beyond what I could have expected or come up with myself. This has to do both with her sexual nature, distinct from mine, and with her selfhood as truly her own. If I were able to design what I might consider my perfect complement, I would in fact not encounter another person but simply an (initially) attractive extension of myself. Doubtless, I would seek to change this extension as often as I desired or thought it necessary. In the end, I would be alone as ever.

Fortunately this is not our fate. As the great literary record of our past has shown, wonder, gratitude, and challenge surround the encounter of a man and woman in love. We are amazed to discover that the completion of ourselves turns out to be an organically different sort of self who willingly sees us in the same light. We recognize that we didn't come up with this surprise on our own. Neither the other person in her selfhood and attractiveness, nor the sexual distinction with its polarities and yearnings, are items of our own making. Nature and civilization have granted these to us, so that when people in love view the world itself as a better place on account of their beloved, more than rose-tinted sentimentality is at work here. The human realm, even if steward of the natural, is still part of it. The merging of nature and civilization is nowhere more vividly on display than in the love between man and woman.

Reproduction

Speaking of nature, reproduction's involvement in sexual love also explains the latter's characteristic intensity. We have seen how romantic love is built upon the reality of mutual incompleteness encountering in the unexpected person of the opposite sex the possibility of fulfillment. But the reason men and women are structurally incomplete on their own and suited for each other is that they become one, so to speak, for the purpose of bringing about another human being. This is the only action humans are fitted for yet cannot accomplish on their own. I can do everything I need in order to survive as my own self: breathe, walk, eat, see, think, and so on. The one thing I cannot do on my own is ensure the survival of humankind. I am the kind of thing that can reproduce another like myself, but only in union with the sexual other.

This sheds important light on the kind of incompleteness that characterizes romantic love. Men and women on their own are not incomplete in any realm connected with individual flourishing; if they were, they would need each other as desperately as they need food, air, and water. To the extent that a person's incompleteness in the sexual realm resembles this kind of neediness, that person is considered immature, unable to see the self or the other as selves in their own right. In such cases the gratuity of the other person can't be appreciated; he or she is reduced to a kind of life-support system serving the needy. Paradoxically, a couple is healthy in being free from neediness, yet at the same time they really are incomplete in some way and so really do fulfill each other. We can explain this paradox through the fact that the couple fulfills each other not by way of individual survival but by way of survival beyond themselves.

Reproduction can seem a dry and reductive notion, barely suited for robust exploration of human love. But we might think about reproduction of ourselves more broadly. Is it not something we are engaged in nearly all the time, in one form or another? Whenever I speak I reproduce for another something about myself: my thoughts, views, opinions, and reactions concerning the world (assuming I speak thoughtfully and honestly). An artist, filmmaker, or craftsman reproduces into a medium something of himself: a vision, idea, or plan. Teachers and mentors constantly reproduce their own insights and ways of acting into those for whom they are responsible. It is almost impossible *not* to reproduce ourselves in some way through daily interaction. Even the way we carry our bodies is typically an outward reproduction of something very much belonging to us: our sense of self-identity. The great works of genius, endurance, discovery, and virtue could all be considered partial reproductions of their authors.

In this light, the significance of biological reproduction and parenthood in general is evident. Here we are not reproducing an aspect of ourselves like an idea or way of acting; we come as close as possible to reproducing our actual selves—an entire human being. In reproducing the human itself, we bring about the kind of reality that can originate all other derivative and partial kinds of reproduction: art, music, speech, good conduct. This is reproduction in the most fundamental sense. As the author of every idea, artwork, and moral excellence, the human being is the greatest sort of thing that can be reproduced.

Just as romantic partners surpass each other's calculations, provoking a sense of joy, gratitude, and challenge, so the possibility of their mutual life surviving in the person of a child is the most radical surprise of all. Of course, I do not mean that couples are amazed to hear that they can reproduce. I mean that the reality of a new human being altogether surpasses his or her parents' expectations and calculations. Any parent holding a newborn for the first time can know, "I didn't come up with this myself. I couldn't have. Somehow the ability is in us, but the reality of this child exceeds what we could ever figure out or assemble." Procreation is so natural, such a part of the everyday for all life-forms in our world; conception and gestation occur quietly and hiddenly. We tend to take it as a matter of course until it enters our personal lives and we are forced to juxtapose our conscious efforts and actions with the actions occurring within us—within her, especially. We are and are not responsible for what has happened in procreation.

Because the child surpasses us but comes from us, we experience its gratuity in an especially striking manner. A couple finds new wholeness in the person of their child, who concretizes their own union but surpasses it in his or her new self. The dynamics that constitute romantic love—selfhood, otherness, incompleteness, fulfillment, gratuity, attraction, wonder, ongoing depth—would be strangely employed were they to end with the persons of the couple themselves. Love of oneself that is simultaneously love of another finds extraordinary, but fitting, resolution in a third that is somehow both.

Simply put, I cannot reproduce myself. Having joined with another in sexual love, as we have seen, I am in some way no longer "just myself." To then seek a replication of myself as though I were still simply my own would be somehow unjust to the situation. The child confirms this: I can only ever be partially responsible for its being, and the same is true for my wife. No one of us can ever make another in our image; rather, one is suited to contribute to the making of another only when one has become a "we."

This says much about who we are as human. How strange it is that reproduction, the hallmark of individual maturity and the natural goal of all individual organisms, is achieved in us only when I am no longer simply "myself," and not even an extended version of myself, but myself as found also in another who is her own self and likewise found in me. Self-fulfillment for humans comes through mutual self-transcendence.

Strangely, biological reproduction is at once both the highest form of reproduction and the most unconscious. While couples can attempt to have or not have a child, ultimately the process is beyond their direct control. They are the stewards, not the absolute creators, of their own offspring. The natural realm intersects with the human in delivering to the world its greatest reality: a human person. In fact, the reality of the child, surpassing its parents' abilities and calculations, testifies that it is not just the product of its parents but of all humanity, bearing in its DNA traces of ancestors throughout history. And in some real sense, all of humanity is still not sufficient to account for the child: if its immediate parents are unable to concoct it of their own devices, no set(s) of parents can. Something greater than humanity has given rise to the child—or better yet, humanity goes beyond itself in the person of every newly conceived child. If he or she is the image, the reproduction, of parent-humans, then what these parents are is something beyond their own knowing. For as we have seen, the parent is not simply himself or herself but a participant in the procreative unity wrought through sexual love, something that neither man nor woman on their own could create, a duality that neither on their own can bridge.

A child, then, is a gift to parents in much the same way a woman is a gift to a man, and vice versa. We might see better now why romantic love and reproduction are integrally united in human beings. It is ultimately because the human person naturally seeks what goes beyond his or her own brute survival. Whenever we look into reality, make art, tell a joke, drink good wine, or spend time with friends, we naturally and vaguely expect something that will in fact surpass our expectations. Strikingly, in the sexual distinction, our very organisms display this aspect of humanness. We are built, man and woman, so as to long for another who is like us and will complete us, yet is unlike us in a manner that delights and challenges us into greater fulfillment. Together we are built so as to seek a third who is like us two, coming from us and yet possessing his or her own self, and in this way marking a completion of us that is also a new beginning. Challenging, yes, but in the way that could only ever do justice to the sort of beings we are: our own selves, yet belonging to each other.

These successive gifts, of man and woman to each other and of child and parents to each other, are blends of vague natural expectation and wondrous gratuity, surpassing expectation. Sexual, or romantic, love is the form of human love belonging to the reproductive sphere, in which the man-woman union finds perpetuation of itself, in some sense overcoming the limitations of mortality; and on top of that finds it in an entirely new person, drawing attention away from self-perpetuation and toward the wonder of human life. The reproductive capacity shows something crucial about romantic love: that it seeks to go beyond itself and into another. *In loving mutually*, the couple can bring about an entirely new life. Conversely, the romantic capacity shows something crucial about human reproduction: that it is not just the physical arrival of another member of the species but an arrival that can and should be the outgrowth of love. Gratuitous love is the most fitting "rationale" for a human being. We are naturally capable of more than we know. With such realities at play, is it any wonder that sexual love should be characterized by a uniquely felt form of attraction and joy?

IV. We Are Familial: Biologically and Personally

The human person, then, cannot be fully understood as simply a singular organism but as something made by and for interpersonal communion. Built into our human structure are capacities for sexual and generative activity, our only capacities decidedly oriented toward persons. We noted earlier that these interpersonal capacities are also the only incomplete ones in each of us as man or woman. If they were sufficient unto themselves, like our capacities for breathing or eating, we would more easily regard persons of the opposite sex as mere objects that can satisfy our desires, like air or food. As it is, the interpersonal but also incomplete nature of the male and female capacities shows human persons as not meant for objectification. These interpersonal capacities can be fully used only in concert with others. If *all* of his or her natural faculties were brought to actuality, the human person would be a walker, talker, eater, drinker, breather, senser, and thinker—and also a romantic partner and a parent.

In short, the human person in its fullness is *familial* by nature.

The familial realm incorporates a twofold distinction among humans that lies at the heart of all history and civilization: man-woman sexual differentiation and the generational border between parents and children. Both differences are typically experienced as unbridgeable: as a man, I really don't know what it's like to be a woman, and as a son, I really don't know what it's like to be my parents.[5] The successive realms of extended family—grandparents, aunts, uncles, cousins—are natural consequences of familiality; these realms also receive their interpersonal forms from it. Typically, the ways I view my grandmothers, grandfathers, aunts, and uncles derives fundamentally from the way I view my mother and father. In turn, their treatment of me derives from the relationships they have had toward their own children. We could extend this reasoning further to claim that for society at large, male-female, generational, and peer relationships are in some way predicated on the natural relationships that define the human person: the relationships that make up the family.

---

[5] See two insightful works: One by Fabrice Hadjadj, *La profondeur des sexes: Pour une mystique de la chair* (Paris: Editions du Seuil, 2008), some central themes of which can be found in English in "Sexuality as Transcendence: An Interview with Fabrice Hadjadj," trans. Artur Rosman, *Ethika Politika*, April 14, 2015, https://ethikapolitika.org/2015/04/14/sexuality-as-transcendence-an-interview-with-fabrice-hadjadj/.

The other is by Margaret H. McCarthy, "Gender Ideology and the *Humanum*," *Communio* 43, no. 2 (2016): 274–98.

At this point we should note an important asymmetry in the man-woman relationship. As noted earlier, the sexes are not simply complementary parts that form a single whole. They are already personal wholes that naturally seek to form an even greater whole. They remain their own selves, paradoxically, while transcending themselves. This means that even sexual intercourse, which intensely unites them, is experienced differently in each.

One of the most striking aspects of man-woman asymmetry emerges from biology but affects families and societies. I refer to woman's capacity for pregnancy: conceiving, bearing, and nurturing a child. To illustrate through contrast with a vastly different life-form, consider the lowly sea urchin. Males and females of that species reproduce by releasing sperm and eggs into the ocean, which at some point unite, initiating Junior. Here we have the incompleteness proper to all sexual organisms: distinct structures belong separately to male and female, who respectively produce and release sperm and eggs. Yet the incompleteness of urchins is radically heightened, since the offspring is present to neither the male nor the female. Once reproductive release has occurred, sweeping tides account for the rest, irrespective of the parent urchins' proximity, consciousness, or even life. However, in most higher animals, including humans, the reproductive process finds its conclusion in the female. Following intercourse, a woman can conceive and see her offspring through to the point of readiness for life in the larger world. A man biologically initiates this process through intercourse, but in one sense he is like the sea urchin: the rest of the story can occur apart from him.

The woman is truly the nexus of humanity as familial, because her capacities, including her body's abilities, are dually oriented toward the sexual other (a man) and the generational other (a child). A man's capacities are also dually oriented, but only via woman. While his sexual function can be satisfied in intercourse alone, his biological generative ability cannot realize its goal apart from woman's conception and pregnancy. This means that women provide a connection between men and their progeny, and new communities form around human reproduction due to female sexual asymmetry. Here is a fundamental way in which women contribute to the origin and maintenance of civilization.

In this light, from the viewpoint of the species as a whole, men are more expendable than women. While the woman's generative capacity is more self-contained and interior, finding its realization in her body, a man's generative capacity is characterized by a kind of separateness, differentiation, and exteriority.[6] The male facet of this asymmetry has tremendous advantages for the human species: in being more exteriorized from reproduction, he is available to work on behalf of his mate and offspring.

---

[6] Walter Ong, in *Fighting for Life: Contest, Sexuality, and Consciousness*, focusing on masculinity, considers the male and female identities as distinguished in terms of externality/self-differentiation and interiority/self-possession, respectively (Ithaca, NY: Cornell University Press, 2012). Karl Stern, in *Flight from Woman* (New York: Paragon House, 1985), pursues a similar line of thought but focuses on the female and ultimately on the different "modes of knowing" that the sexes symbolize. Both authors discuss Christian revelation, wherein God and Christ, on the one hand, and Mary and the Church, on the other, respectively exemplify the masculine and feminine principles.

By providing the family with necessities for human living (survival, but also art, play, insight, and discovery), the male can contribute in his own way to civilization. From an evolutionary standpoint, it is no accident that the male's typical physical characteristics make him especially suited for protection and provision. Men are certainly capable of nourishing and raising post-natal children; likewise, women pursue all sorts of careers outside the home. But women possess generative abilities that men do not, and the exercise of women's abilities, by extension, calls upon men to realize their own potential as providers for human community.

From the standpoint of a child's personal growth, the same male-female asymmetry highlights two dynamics crucial for any kind of human development: affirmation and challenge. Owing to the unique biological ties involved in pregnancy and nourishment, a mother's sense of self can be more bound up with the child than a father's is. The mother knows the child in a manner that the father does not, by way of an intimacy, concreteness, and proximity the father can never have. Conversely, the father's knowledge of the child initially depends on the mother but is also more abstract. "Abstract" here is not a bad word; it does not signify just an inferior way of knowing. We realize throughout human life that it is important for us to be around those who know us more abstractly along with those who know us more concretely. The former, like many teachers and coaches, are able to challenge us from the outside, in a way that might be missed by those who support us from within.

A myriad of benefits accrues to children from the

asymmetrical ways in which their parents naturally know them. Mothers and fathers enlarge each other's knowledge of the child through complementarity: supplying what the other lacks and appreciating what the other has. We will consider this theme in greater detail in our psychological exploration of men and women (chapter 3).

In light of the preceding discussion, we can note that of all the differences between men and women, the most fundamental lies in their distinct capacities for relating to a potential child. A man can biologically initiate the process that leads to a particular conception of a new human being within a woman, who in turn can not only conceive, bear, and give birth but also nourish. Compared to hers, a kind of exteriority or otherness characterizes the man's role in procreation, contribution to familial well-being, and knowledge of offspring, while in woman these activities are more interior and intimate. To the extent that sexuality affects the human person as a whole, we might expect to find men and women subtly affected by this most fundamental difference, regardless of whether they actually have children or even sexual relations.

V. Sexual Identity: Development from the Womb to Personal Expression

Sexuality Is Developed

Becoming a man or woman is something developed in human life: over time, within the person, and in response to relationships with others. Physically, this development occurs most strikingly in utero and at puberty, but in many other ways it occurs through relationships, especially the familial.[7]

Our physical development is extensive. While the human being as a one-celled zygote typically possesses an XX or XY DNA, it would be strange to refer to an XX zygote in its mother's womb the day after conception by saying, "There's a woman inside of that other woman!" or, "How's your little girl doing?" There is something about "woman" and "girl" that isn't present in that XX zygote. The DNA pattern alone in a unicellular organism is the barest hint of full-fledged sexuality, male or female. Doubtless, it will typically result in a fully developed sex, but that is the point: sexual maturity is something the organism must realize. All sorts of physiological processes constitute the move from an XY zygote to a newborn boy, and from there to a fully developed man (more details on this in chapter 2).

Yet the process whereby a boy becomes a man includes

---

[7] More specifically, we might consider the different positions occupied by sons and daughters in the natural family structure. Sons are like their mothers in coming from them but unlike them in being male; while they resemble their fathers in maleness but do not come from them. In both respects, then, boys are suspended between mom and dad (recall the male note of separation, or differentiation). Daughters, on the other hand, both come from and resemble their mothers. They neither resemble nor come from their fathers. For girls, then, both intimacy from within and knowledge from without are more dramatically emphasized. What are the consequences of this male-female asymmetry among children and siblings? Again, we are here on the border of psychological dimensions in human sexual development. See chapter 3.

not only increased musculature and penis size but also profound emotional and relational developments. Is this male self-controlled? Can he engage other people, especially women, with respect? Here is the human difference from other animals: the sexual and reproductive realms are personal, not just physical (see chapter 3 for psychological aspects of sexual development).

Sexuality as a Whole-Person Reality

We can put it this way: in their mature states, being a man or a woman involves a person's bodiliness, mind, self-image, thoughts, desires, and relations with others. It is a whole-person reality, running through the entire organism and shaping its human life to some degree. This makes sense if we recall that being male or being female are the two fundamental ways of being human. Abstract humanity on its own never shows up; it typically exists in a male or female configuration.[8] Because humanness itself includes the aspects just mentioned—physical, mental, emotional, personal—so does manhood and womanhood. The fundamental aspect of one's sexuality is physical, since

---

[8] Some disorders of sexual development (DSDs) are so serious that one may never know with certainty whether a person is male or female. Indeed, various reproductive and sexual functions may be impaired to the point that for all practical purposes the person is neither a man nor a woman in the fullest sense of those words. Still, in these cases the person can self-identify and express as a man or woman in various spheres of life, including dress, social presentation, and certain forms of romantic interaction. See the brief discussion below, in section 8, and the more detailed biological account in chapter 2.

reproduction and sexual activity make no sense apart from bodiliness. But the bodily scope of sexuality runs through the organism itself as a distinct structure, affecting the person as a whole. (This idea is examined in detail in chapters 2 and 3, which focus on the biological and psychological identities of man and woman.)

Sexuality as Self-Aware and Communicated

To see better the whole-person impact of sexuality, we should note how important it is that human beings, alone among animals, know what they are and incorporate that knowledge into their own being. For example, it's crucial for my life not only that I *am* a rational agent capable of self-direction and relationships, but also that I am *aware* of it and *express myself* as such. Otherwise, I would be *practically speaking* non-human, like other higher-order primates who can enjoy life according to their own capacities. We can say something similar of maleness and femaleness. It's not enough for human living that I possess XY DNA along with male hormones, gonads, genitalia, and a host of other physiological and psychological traits that characterize human males. I also have to *know* that I am a male and somehow express it.

Perhaps this sounds obvious or even redundant—but imagine the alternative. Imagine a human male who really does not know he is male, which is to say, he really does not know what female is either. Imagine he meets another human, in fact a woman, and experiences feelings of sexual attraction toward this person. She may feel sexually drawn to him but will be quickly disconcerted to realize that he does not know he is male. He will be like a small child on a personal level and awkward on the physical level. Something analogous would be true of a man encountering a female unaware of herself as woman.

Of course, such scenes are implausible, and for good reason: our sexuality is physically and culturally significant enough to make the scenario rather hypothetical. It's important to our species that females, for example, know they are capable of being attractive to males, of being sexually intimate with and possibly impregnated by them. They need to know that conception, pregnancy, and baby nourishment are activities they alone can accomplish, crucial for the human race, challenging and fulfilling, in which they are greatly assisted by their mates. The very fact that a woman knows such things about herself will make her act in certain ways toward men, who in turn will view her—and only then view her—as a possible romantic partner. A mature human is self-aware and seeks a mate who is also self-aware. In other words, a significant part of being a woman is *knowing that* she is humanly female, incorporating this knowledge into her life, and expressing it as part of her personhood. The same is true for men. Otherwise, among other consequences, violation would increase while the bulk of human reproduction and romantic love would likely disappear.

We see here the importance of one's sexual identity (or what some call "gender identity"—an ambiguous notion that we'll discuss in section 8). A man or woman's sexual identity exhibits the fact that sexuality in the human being has its roots in the biological realm and naturally extends from there into the realms of the psychological, rational, and expressive. In the healthy, mature human, sexual identity is a culmination of sexual development, completing what began at the subconscious genetic level. As we have seen, biological sex without maturation into sexual identity lacks something distinctively human. Conversely, self-identification as man or woman without the corresponding biological sex lacks coherence. We will discuss the transgender phenomenon shortly.

The Importance of Culture

How does a woman make others aware of the fact that she knows herself to be a woman? To verbally inform everyone of her self-awareness would be tiring and awkward. Deliberately exposing the physical aspects of her sex would risk physical and social discomfort, objectification from men, and dismissal from other women. Fortunately, humans naturally cultivate a venue by which they can signal their sexual selves publicly, honestly, and gracefully: culture. Culture is not something accidental or superficial to human nature. Because we are social *and* self-conscious beings, we naturally foster things like words, actions, dress, and other signs—what we will call public or cultural "forms"— that enable us to communicate important realities about ourselves without having to think much about it. While specific aspects of culture change from one time and place to another, the presence of culture itself is a constant across the globe.

Because cultural forms are public, common to large groups and multiple generations, we typically enter into them easily, even subconsciously. We are born into and surrounded by them. Culture itself is not irrational, though forms of it can be and some people dwell in it unthinkingly. Much of an individual's maturation involves conscious and deliberate engagement with one's culture, through acceptance, rejection, or modification of various forms. For cultural forms run the entire gamut of human living: some express deep and abiding truths about human nature—like burial of the dead and rejection of murder. Others involve nuanced aspects of specific times, places, and previous cultural developments—like furniture styles or punctuation usage in text messaging.

One form we find in nearly all cultures is awareness and expression of the sexual difference.[9] Though the particulars will vary, humans naturally find it important to recognize maleness and femaleness in their bodily appearance, personal development, and social behavior. Like other cultural forms, those surrounding men and women range from the timeless to the transitory. That pregnant women, for example, are given particular kinds of attention stems directly from a universal, basic truth about femaleness, while hairstyles or clothing color manifest a cosmetic preference specific to one time and place.

Sexuality, more than other physical traits, creates a bridge between the individual human and his or her culture, since a person's sexuality involves activities at once biological and social: sexual intercourse, pregnancy, and parenting. Sexuality contradicts the idea that we are polarized between individual selfhood and extrinsic cultural

---

[9]   See Joyce Benenson, *Warriors and Worriers: The Survival of the Sexes* (Oxford: Oxford University Press, 2014).

artifice. In reality, our sexual nature shows that selfhood is naturally social and that selfhood asks for cultural context.[10] We see a natural contiguity between the human self, the familial realm, and the cultural, with certain forms expressing unchangeable truths about the person and other forms expressing more superficial preferences or tastes. The latter are rightly subject to change: after all, American men at one time wore pink.[11] The former, however, should be taken seriously as exhibiting and preserving fundamental human realities.

Marriage

One of the most important cultural forms is marriage, recognized and celebrated for most of human history as a public, lifelong commitment between a man and a woman (until the United States Supreme Court decided otherwise in the *Obergefell* decision of 2015). The nature of marriage as lifelong commitment perfectly suits both the romantic and reproductive dimensions of human sexuality. Romantically speaking, marriage affirms man-woman love as a mutual completion of the whole self through possession

[10] This link between the personal and the cultural is particularly visible in the cultures in southern Africa: at the heart of the African Ubuntu philosophy is the saying "Because we are, I am," a principle that most vividly refers to the familial realm and that expresses the truth of the self quite differently from Descartes' "I think, therefore I am." See Michael Battle, *Ubuntu: I in You and You in Me* (New York: Seabury Books, 2009).

[11] See Anna Broadway, "Pink Wasn't Always Girly," *The* Atlantic, August 12, 2013, https://www.theatlantic.com/sexes/archive/2013/08/pink-wasnt-always-girly/278535/.

and enhancement of the other. It recognizes that human persons are not transitory, replaceable parts but abiding wholes, worthy of love no matter what. Unlike a meal or movie that is consumed and finished, the person is not exhaustible. We can grow in knowledge and love of each other, in mutual challenge and development together, until we die. To the extent that my self is somehow completed in her, we remain one as long as we remain ourselves. The marriage bond is also deeply founded on our procreative capacity. As we have seen, parenthood is a lifelong project, involving the continued formation of children, with mutual parental love as the terrain in which younger life develops. Psychologically and morally, we don't simply separate from (forget about) our children at a certain point, like most animals do, nor do they so separate from us. To the extent that marriage is culturally weakened by no-fault divorce or polygamy, children and spouses become more easily seen as replaceable. In competing forms of union, like gay marriage, romantic love and reproduction lose their organic connection, and true sexual diversity is lost.

VI. Sex Is Not Our Whole Self

While being man or woman affects the whole person and contributes to the possibility of human culture, it is neither the fullness of the person nor even the most important part. Our sexuality is significant *on account of our humanity*, not the other way around. Our animal and rational capacities work together in many spheres, one of which is the sexual. As we saw earlier, the human person is a whole self in his or her own right: indeed, such wholeness is required for a healthy sexual relationship. Reproductive and romantic incompleteness may or may not be resolved, depending on the circumstances and choices of the person herself and of the sexual other.

On the one hand, since the sexual capacities are natural to humans, most will find a mate and expect the particular sort of fulfillment that romantic love and parenthood bring. At the same time, people throughout history have lived full human lives without having sex and without reproducing. In fact, for some people, deliberately choosing *not* to engage in a sexual relationship will be their path to fulfillment—if, for example, they cannot find a suitable mate or if some other work to which they are committed demands their time and attention. In this light, we see again the element of gratuity belonging to the sexual realm: it does not have to be exercised in order for human fulfillment to occur.[12]

Our culture's ads, media, and moral attitudes typically over-sexualize human beings by taking sexual attraction and pleasure as the height of fulfillment, without regard for mutual thoughtfulness, committed love, and procreation. In such an environment especially, we do well to affirm our identities as man and woman, while recalling that sexual activity plays a limited, even optional, role in human life. The goods of friendship, work, art,

---

[12] Similarly, reproduction itself is not a matter of our direct control. A couple may or may not have children regardless of their procreative efforts. Though this lack might be keenly felt, since the sexual relationship naturally tends toward reproduction, a couple can find fulfillment in their life together and in parenthood through other avenues: adoptive, foster, educational, and so on.

recreation, and discovery are available to all, regardless of engagement in sex. Motherhood and fatherhood themselves go well beyond the biological realm, as the bulk of these roles lies in educating and guiding children over the course of a lifetime.

VII. Privacy Is Crucial

We have seen why human reproduction and romantic attraction—both involving the mysterious desire to fulfill oneself through interpersonal transcendence—entail the strength and delight characteristic of sexual love. Now we are better able to explain another realm of experience that typically accompanies our sexuality: the need for privacy and even a sense of shame. While being male or female is only one of many organic features in our personhood, it is the one that most vividly depends on other persons for its fulfillment. A man, for example, not only comes to awareness of his manhood largely through recognition from others (male and female); he typically fulfills his sexuality in a mutually desired love relationship with a particular woman. Sexuality vividly marks an area of his selfhood that is biologically grounded yet dependent on conscious affirmation from others *and* dependent on his choice of a woman who in turn chooses him.

We do not simply own our sexuality, then. While it belongs to us in a profound way, evident in our organisms, it also relies on others and especially on a particular other. There's something strange and possibly terrifying about a dimension of ourselves that runs so deep in our being that it significantly configures our organism and yet is precariously at the mercy of other persons who must affirm us in it and choose us in light of it.

Add to this the fact that at a physiological level, we are simply not in total control of our emotions and bodiliness. This powerlessness is keenly experienced in the sexual realm, where our physicality does not always exhibit the restraint that we know ought to exist in the presence of the sexual other. Our bodiliness at times betrays our feelings and attractions, in blushing, body language, genital activity, and so on. These involuntary movements cannot help but manifest our incompleteness, even a kind of neediness, regarding another person. Being human involves our abilities to rationally *govern* instincts and appetite; but here, where the instinct concerns fulfillment in and through another human person, we do not exercise complete control. Any lack of control can be embarrassing, like a hiccup or a temper tantrum, but when it concerns our desire for fulfillment through another person, a particularly striking vulnerability comes to light.

Pervading our human sexuality, then, is a kind of deep call for modesty, not through prudishness but through the awareness that our selfhood is visible (not just spiritual), interpersonal (not exclusively our own), and still beyond our full control. It lies open, in some sense, to others. Thus we see the importance of cultural forms that respect the need for privacy, reserve, and even a natural sense of shame pertaining to our sexuality. Privacy and respect are warranted most of all for women, who are more physically susceptible to violation and whose sexual capacities include conception and pregnancy.

VIII. Are Man and Woman the Only Options? Intersex and Transgender

Everything we have discussed so far presupposes that man and woman are the only options: the two ways of being sexual. Yet public voices have recently challenged this assumption on two counts. First, biologically: in a number of rare but serious conditions, sex does not develop normally. Some babies, for example, are born with ambiguous genitalia, or with male chromosomes but genitals resembling a vagina. These intersex conditions, or disorders of sexual development (DSDs), have always existed. In their most serious forms, they constitute a great trial for those suffering from them. But only recently have people argued that in view of such "differences," biological sex should now be seen as a continuum, with male and female as the extremes and a countless number of other possible sexes somewhere in the middle.

This claim has surfaced in part because of the second challenge, which comes from a more subjectively personal realm. Some people possess normal biological sex yet identify themselves as belonging to the opposite sex on account of *gender dysphoria*, a condition in which they experience their own sex as foreign to their self, as "not me." Some of these persons may identify themselves as *transgender* and pursue paths of medical reinforcement, seeking through hormone therapies and surgeries to change their biological sex so that it accords with their self-identification. To validate the transgender experience and legitimize medical forms of transitioning, some invoke intersex conditions to say that biological sex itself shows up in any number of forms other than male and female. At the very least, most trans proponents argue that biological sex can be separate from one's own sense of selfhood, and that sexuality, or "gender," is whatever one deems it to be.

Intersex Conditions

Regarding the first challenge, I will here offer a brief, general observation; chapter 2 will address DSDs in greater biological detail. The crucial point is that intersex conditions involve some loss or deficiency in the reproductive or sexual capacities. Like colorblindness or partial deafness, a disorder of sexual development involves a lack of what ought to be present, relative to the fully functioning human organism. In no way do intersex conditions present other positive alternatives to male and female, since they are only intelligible as abnormalities within the male and female systems. DSDs introduce no unique organ, capacity, or function into the human organism. And this is why DSDs, like other medical conditions, are very much the exception to the norm.

Still, thanks to modern medicine, many DSDs can now be treated. In most cases medical research is able to determine whether the person is in fact male or female, despite some ambiguity or disability at the biological level. In many instances, reproductive and sexual function can be strengthened or restored, as medical practice assists in healing the biological sex that has been recognized as belonging to the person.

On a more personal level, these biological difficulties can be humanly minimized through healthy cultural forms.

It's crucial for people with intersex conditions, and for those around them, to know that sexuality is not the fullness of personhood, that human beings can live excellent lives without sexual relationships, and that reproduction includes much beyond biological parenthood, like teaching, mentoring, affirming, and challenging.

Transgender Identity

Concerning the transgender phenomenon, proper consideration of sexual development is crucial. Typically, biological males and females mature into adults who recognize themselves as such and live out their manhood or womanhood within a range of cultural forms surrounding them. Part of one's maturity as man or woman depends on appropriating one's sexuality and communicating as much through individual discernment and choice amid the realm of cultural form. Each woman will communicate herself differently from other women. Much of her development into a woman involves figuring out, with the help of others, who she is—not just woman but this particular woman— and expressing herself in that light. Particular choices in style, gesture, and interaction all factor into this personal equation. But that she naturally needs to express herself as woman is usually unavoidable. Biological sex naturally leads into its possessor's self-identification and self-expression within a cultural context. Biological sex and self-identity/ expression can't be considered simply independent realities. Recall the strangeness of a physically-developed male or female who is unaware of his or her sexuality.

Conversely, what could it mean to identify as a woman,

for example, without in fact being a female organism? And yet that is the claim made by the person identifying as transgender. All sorts of factors may contribute to a person experiencing their own sex as foreign or problematic. More will be said on such factors in the psychological account offered in chapter 3. For the purposes of this chapter, the important point is that transgender identification lacks a clear basis in reality. How is being a "trans woman" one way of being a woman? For, while history has shown us countless ways of expressing oneself as a woman in the cultural sense, all those ways have femaleness in common. If being a woman can be separated from being female, then what does *woman* mean?

The answer often given is that "femaleness" refers to biological sex, while "woman" refers to *gender*. It's worth briefly considering the various meanings of this controversial term.[13] As early as the fifteenth century and still today, the word "gender" has been used synonymously with "sex" to refer to one's being male or female. "Do you know the baby's gender?" is still a common question. In the mid-twentieth century, though, not long after "sex" began increasingly to refer to intercourse, "gender" acquired another meaning—namely, the various behavioral and sociocultural expressions associated with being male or female. Think of gender roles in society or gender-specific clothing. Notably, it became popular to maintain that sex (biology) and gender (cultural practice and expression)

---

[13] See the entry for "gender" in Merriam-Webster online: https://www.merriam-webster.com/dictionary/gender. The first meaning of the word, we should not forget, refers to grammar.

were so distinct as to be entirely separable. Quite recently, gender has acquired a third meaning: the individual perception and expression of oneself as man, woman, both, neither, or an alternative gender, all regardless of biological sex.[14]

---

[14] See, for example, the definition of "gender identity" at Medscape: https://emedicine.medscape.com/article/917990-overview. Also the resource provided by the American Psychological Association (APA) titled "Transgender People, Gender Identity and Gender Expression": https://www.apa.org/topics/lgbtq/transgender. Or the slightly different glossary from the Transgender Care Website at the University of California, San Francisco (UCSF): https://transcare.ucsf.edu/guidelines/terminology. Strikingly, "gender" itself is nowhere defined.

The APA speaks of "gender identity" as "a person's internal sense of being male, female or something else." What the "something else" refers to is not evident. In describing the various "categories or types of transgender people," the APA says this:

> *Genderqueer* is a term that some people use who identify their gender as falling outside the binary constructs of "male" and "female." They may define their gender as falling somewhere on a continuum between male and female, or they may define it as wholly different from these terms. They may also request that pronouns be used to refer to them that are neither masculine nor feminine, such as "zie" instead of "he" or "she," or "hir" instead of "his" or "her." Some genderqueer people do not identify as transgender.

Other categories of transgender people include *androgynous, multigendered, gender nonconforming, third gender*, and *two-spirit people*. Exact definitions of these terms vary from person to person and may change over time, but often include a sense of blending or alternating genders. Some people who use these terms to describe themselves see traditional, binary concepts of gender as restrictive.

The UCSF webpage defines "gender identity" as "a person's internal

On the one hand, you can see the logic between the second and third meanings of gender. *If* biology and culture are seen as truly independent of each other, then being a man or a woman in the cultural sense does not depend on one's organism. And thus we have the possibility that a biological male can identify as a "woman" in the realm of gender. On the other hand, this possibility should raise a fundamental question: What can *gender* really mean if it includes not only "women" who are biologically male, and vice versa, but also such options as "both," "neither," and most cryptically "an alternative gender"? *Gender* here cannot refer to biology, which shows only the binary organisms (male or female). The remaining possibilities are that *gender* refers to cultural forms or to one's own perceptions and feelings.

Let's consider the first possibility: when a biological male identifies as a woman, he is saying that he does not identify with the various cultural forms surrounding males but with those surrounding females instead. Therefore, despite his male organism, he is really a female. The problem is that some cultural forms are intrinsically *connected* with one or the other biological sex: accommodation of pregnant women, for example, or expectations of male service

sense of self and how they fit into the world, from the perspective of gender." Based on this definition, the webpage goes on to define "transgender," "gender nonconforming," "nonbinary," and other terms. Yet "gender" itself receives no definition. By including the word "gender" within the proposed definition of "gender identity," the statement ultimately defines "gender" as—gender. One suspects that "gender" is undefined or defined circularly because explicitly defining it would have to involve some recourse to the meanings of male and female. Alternative "gender identities" thus would be revealed as meaningless apart from the very realities they attempt to minimize: man and woman.

and sacrifice for the sake of women and children (and negatively: attitudes toward male rapists). As we have seen, sexuality itself bridges the biological and cultural realms. Intercourse, pregnancy, and parenthood are biological *and* social realities, differently experienced by men and women. Consequently, certain cultural forms are deeply integral to these realities and can't be divorced from the biological. Other cultural forms like clothing color, hairstyle, or job preference aren't intrinsically related to biology and so can apply to men or women. A person might well decide that some such forms typically associated with the opposite sex actually apply to himself or herself. But surely such forms don't constitute what we *are*. There is a reason they tend to be associated with stereotypes! Fashions and work possibilities are relatively external to us; they can come and go over the course of one and the same human life.

The second possibility is that when a biological male identifies as female, he is simply saying that no matter what his body and other people indicate, he does not perceive himself to be male; instead, he perceives himself to be female. The difficulty with this claim is that subjective perceptions or feelings are no guarantee of truth. How can a biological male know what it means to experience himself as female? Every cell in his body speaks against it. He can certainly experience himself as not comfortable with his maleness, but this experience does not mean he isn't a man. Instead, we might consider how his gender dysphoria could be helped.

One way in which gender dysphoria should *not* be alleviated is through the notion that a person can actually transition from one biological sex to another. More on this in chapters 2 and 4, but let's simply note for now that a genuine sex change is impossible. It would involve, among other things, changing every cell in the body. Attempting the impossible can easily end in brokenness and despair.

If *gender* finally amounts to one's feelings concerning oneself in the realm of sex, reproduction, and romantic love, fine. This could be a fourth possible meaning of an already ambiguous word. But let's not accept that what people *are* are their feelings. If I feel generous, this does not make me a generous person in fact. Rachel Dolezal's self-identification as a black woman understandably drew criticism from those who knew she was white.[15] We experience all sorts of feelings all the time, ones that we often know do not reflect the truth of ourselves and of others. If gender means simply the realm of feelings related to sexual identity, then, as with all other feelings, we need to discern which should be endorsed and which should not.

IX. Why Are Sexual Issues So Significant?

You might think it obvious that merely feeling oneself to be one thing or another does not make oneself so. In most areas of human life, we do think it obvious. My feeling that I should be in charge at work does not make me the best candidate. In this light, the deeper question is why the realm of sex, reproduction, and romantic love constitutes an exception. Why is it that we face massive controversies

---

[15] See, for example, https://www.nbcnews.com/news/us-news/former-naacp-leader-rachel-dolezal-agrees-plea-deal-welfare-fraud-n991566.

over these particular feelings, asking ourselves as a society whether we shouldn't endorse them to the point that medical practice, surgery, language, public policy, and rights of privacy are altered to accommodate them?

Certainly a host of intellectual and societal factors could be analyzed, as Carl Trueman shows in his excellent book *The Rise and Triumph of the Modern Self.* Chapter 3 will address gender identity from a more immediate, psychological standpoint. For now, let me suggest a few general reasons why feelings related to sexual identity are so important on the personal and social levels. As we've seen, not only does sexuality involve deep biological elements constituting organ systems and running through every cell in the body; it is also the realm of our biology that most clearly signals ourselves as persons oriented toward others and dependent upon them for self-fulfillment and even for the continuance of ourselves in children. Sexuality shows us as profoundly structured for giving and receiving love on the level of the whole person. One's sense of being man or woman, therefore, is not just one among the hundreds of ways we can identify ourselves, alongside being of a certain height, body type, or personality. It's a realm of self-identity both deeper than these biologically but also more distinctly relational. This is a place of unique vulnerability and consequently warrants freedom from violation. Even more, the decision to enter into a sexual relationship demands a thoughtfulness and choice that only the partners themselves can make and that resists complete rational articulation. Who can account for why one person loves another and vice versa? Often the couple cannot easily articulate why they love each other! Cultural forms, too, exercise influence on our sexual identities: sometimes less than they should, sometimes more, sometimes in good ways, sometimes in bad.

For these reasons, the realm of sexual self-identity can be very complex and merits appropriate attention. For example, if a person lacks certain hormones naturally associated with biological sex, that person may question his or her sexuality and will likely depend even more than usual on the support, guidance, and assistance of others. Conversely, if culture, parents, and peers fail to provide acknowledgement and guidance on a human level—or worse, if they are sexually abusive—all the normal biological structures in the world may not necessarily guarantee a healthy sense of sexual identity.

Today's culture has promoted the disintegration of the human being as naturally familial: Consider the prominence of no-fault divorce. It has diminished the importance of sexual difference by legalizing gay marriage and endorsing all sorts of genital activity as "sex." With artificial contraceptives and assisted reproductive technologies, it has undermined sexuality itself by sundering the intrinsic relation between love and reproduction. In abortion it destroys the human being who most vividly shows the gratuity, self-transcendence, and enduringness of man-woman love. The deliberate death of the child retroactively explodes human civilization as founded on love seeking completion through affirmation of the other. The effects of this disintegration on women in particular and on society as a whole are profound.[16] Is it any wonder that

---

[16] See Theresa Burke, *Forbidden Grief: The Unspoken Pain of Abortion*

such a culture is on the brink of losing the fundamental realities themselves—man and woman? In this light, the transgender movement should almost be expected. It follows a chain of cultural logic, each link of which corrupts human identities.

Alongside these phenomena that void the meaningfulness of man and woman, we are presented with hypersexualized or otherwise superficial media representations, as well as with massive consumption of pornography. It is entirely possible that our society has greatly devalued the more timeless cultural forms concerning men and women and has substituted merely superficial ones, like pink versus blue, as touchstones for recognizing ourselves. We shouldn't be surprised that many people do not wish to identify with these presentations of human sexuality. Perhaps people are reacting to the empty shells that our society has endorsed in place of the realities. Tragically, the realities themselves are being rejected too, since we have lost sight of them.

CONCLUSION

Aristotle said that what happens "naturally" is what happens in all, or at least most, cases. In this light, our human existence as men and women is natural. It may be so natural that we struggle to step back from ourselves and appreciate

(New Harbor, ME: Acorn Books, 2002). Also Mark Regnerus, *Cheap Sex: The Transformation of Men, Marriage, and Monogamy* (Oxford: Oxford University Press, 2017), which analyzes the social impact of separating sex from reproduction.

our own significance. How do you make sure that something so everyday is not taken for granted? One way is to imagine ourselves without it. Our organisms would all be the same: androgynous. No male or female body types, no reproductive or sexual organs. There would be no sexual desire, nothing about another's person that would show up as irreducibly different yet compelling, attractive, and suited to our own fulfillment. No eros. Nothing of motherhood, fatherhood, or family in general would be known. Who knows what our own self-awareness would look like, none of it founded on the intimacy between mother and child. Would culture and civilization exist? We might work together to meet the needs of survival, but perhaps more like an intelligent ant colony than a human community. No *Mona Lisa*, no *David*, no *A Midsummer Night's Dream*. No Brother Sun, Sister Moon, or God our Father.

Thankfully, this dystopian description is hypothetical, even though the logic of our culture points in such a direction. We have every reason to be grateful for what we are and, with some urgency, to share its goodness through words and actions. Because our existence as man and woman carries deep import, problems in this sphere of life can radically affect individuals and societies. Still, being human is more than being sexual, and so living out the truth of human nature remains possible for anyone. Also, we have the wisdom of the ages at our disposal. Our science is marvelously developed; our theology incorporates two thousand years of contemplating God's revelation. What I've said in this chapter calls for scientific detail and theological context. To these sources of illumination we now turn.

REVIEW

1. Being male or female is a primary element of our human experience in three ways: biologically, it is our most significant individual feature; personally, we tend to seek it first in getting to know another person; historically, we depend on it for our existence.

2. Human sexuality is the mysterious unity of love and reproduction.

3. Sexual difference is an irreducible otherness in man and woman. It cannot be erased or assimilated, yet it completes the other. The love founded on sexual difference (romantic, sexual, erotic) indicates that we are fulfilled not through self-absorption or self-expansion but through self-transcendence.

4. Sexual difference is also for the sake of reproduction. Reproduction continues and completes the meaning of romantic love since a couple together transcends themselves in giving rise to a new human being.

5. The familial structure (father, mother, child) exhibits all the natural capacities of human nature brought to fulfillment. The family is thus a natural social unit, not an arbitrary one.

6. In reproduction a man's contribution is more initiatory and external, while a woman's is more receptive and interior. This fundamental difference enables woman

to be the nexus of family relations and man to be called to realize his capacities on behalf of the family. In this way, man and woman can distinctly contribute to civilization, though such roles remain flexible.

7. Like the person itself, sexuality is present at conception but develops over time. In its mature state, sexuality is a whole-person reality: biological, psychological, social, and moral.

8. In particular, sexual identity is essential to the male or female self. Culture is the natural arena in which such identification occurs. Some cultural forms speak to something essential about men and women and are thereby nearly universal, while others are extremely particular and transitory.

9. Sexual activity involves deliberation and free choice on one's own part and on the part of another. It concerns not one's own survival but rather the flourishing of the species. For these reasons, people can be fulfilled precisely in refraining from intercourse and reproduction.

10. As a reality that is deeply biological, but also interpersonal and not fully subject to our control, sexuality calls for privacy and respect.

11. Intersex conditions do not present alternative sexes, since they are partial or deficient manifestations of male or female sexuality to begin with.

12. The notion of "gender" as truly separate from biological sex is incoherent since it refers either to cultural forms, some of which are essentially connected to biological sex, or to subjective perceptions and feelings, which do not necessarily correspond with reality.

13. Because sexuality naturally involves biological, emotional, and social dimensions, it can be fragile. In our society especially, a myriad of cultural forms threatens to subvert romantic love, sexual intercourse, reproduction, marriage, family, and men and women themselves.

FURTHER READING

Budziszewski, Jay. *On the Meaning of Sex*. Wilmington, DE: ISI, 2014.

Girgis, Sherif, Ryan T. Anderson, and Robert P. George. *What Is Marriage? Man and Woman: A Defense*. New York: Encounter Books, 2012.

Hadjadj, Fabrice. "Sexuality as Transcendence: An Interview with Fabrice Hadjadj." By Artur Rosman. *Ethika Politika*, April 14, 2015. https://ethikapolitika.org/2015/04/14/sexuality-as-transcendence-an-interview-with-fabrice-hadjadj/.

Howard, Thomas. *Chance or the Dance?* 2nd ed. San Francisco: Ignatius Press, 2018. (See especially chap. 7.)

Kass, Amy A., and Leon R. Kass, eds. *Wing to Wing, Oar to Oar: Readings on Courting and Marrying*. Notre Dame, IN: University of Notre Dame Press, 2000.

Lewis, C. S. *The Four Loves*. San Francisco: HarperOne, 2017.

McCarthy, Margaret H. "Gender Ideology and the *Humanum*." *Communio* 43, no. 2 (2016): 274–98.

Ong, Walter. *Fighting for Life: Contest, Sexuality, and Consciousness.* Ithaca, NY: Cornell University Press, 2012. (See especially chaps. 2, 3, 5.)

Regnerus, Mark. *Cheap Sex: The Transformation of Men, Marriage, and Monogamy.* Oxford: Oxford University Press, 2017.

Stern, Karl. *Flight from Woman.* St. Paul, MN: Paragon House, 1985. (See especially chaps. 1–3, 12.)

Trueman, Carl. *The Rise and Triumph of the Modern Self.* Wheaton, IL: Crossway, 2020.

Wojtyla, Karol. *Love and Responsibility.* Translated by Grzegorz Ignatik. Boston: Pauline Books and Media, 2013.

.

CHAPTER 2

A Biological Understanding of Man and Woman

Cara Buskmiller, MD
Paul Hruz, MD, PhD

"Humility is the proper attitude towards all true greatness, including one's own greatness as a human being, but above all towards the greatness which is not oneself, which is beyond one's self."

—Karol Wojtyla, *Love and Responsibility*

A BIOLOGICAL ACCOUNT of man and woman has the advantage of looking to an aspect we all have great familiarity with: our bodies. But because our bodies are prone to physical failures that sometimes have bearing on sexuality, we need to approach biology with humility. We seek to build our understanding while realizing that we won't come away with a perfect picture.

This chapter will offer a step-by-step account of the biology of male and female. At first, we understand who is a man and who is a woman by their external presentation: presence or absence of facial hair, breasts, and so on. But this first approach is not sufficient. The next level involves understanding the male and female reproductive organs. After this, we can go deeper to study the tiny cells used in reproduction (sperm and egg). Finally, we will return to the whole-organism view and find molecular differences between males and females throughout their entire bodies. Throughout these four steps (superficial, anatomic, genetic, and molecular), we find variation but we also see patterns that echo across the whole population.

After reviewing biological sex at these four levels, the reader will be equipped for two final sections. The first will review disorders in sexual development, because as our study grows more sophisticated, our ability to say something about the maleness or femaleness of a particular person also grows more complete. The last part of this chapter will discuss some contemporary errors that arise when biological reality is misunderstood.

By beginning with what can be observed and established empirically, this chapter will serve as a foundation for our subsequent explorations of the psychological, medical, and theological dimensions of manhood and womanhood.

I. A Superficial Glance and Secondary Sex Characteristics

Although it is unpopular to do so, it is legitimate to admit that there are patterns in the physical characteristics of males and females—their actions, preferences, height, and voice pitches. Evidence of this is that facial recognition programs have some measure of success at predicting whether a user is male or female. Another piece of evidence is that persons can succeed at "passing" or "presenting" as the opposite gender by employing that gender's patterns. While these patterns can lead us astray, they can also teach us something about maleness and femaleness. This section establishes that humans have distinct binary differences in physical appearance (i.e., dimorphism) that directly relate to specific roles in reproduction.

Perhaps the most glaringly obvious difference between men and women is their specific role in the reproductive process. Only females can become pregnant. The conception and embryonic development (i.e., gestation) of new human life occurs within the human female, while the male is left physically outside of gestation. This asymmetrical involvement between male and female parents has far-reaching consequences for the roles of men and women in society at large, and significant literature exists in multiple disciplines on the difference between male and female parents, differences that originate from their roles in gestation.

If jumping right to reproductive and parenting roles seems premature, it might be helpful to consider the next few differences in terms of evolution. Division of a species into males and females is not limited to humans but exists in other animals and in plants because it is evolutionarily advantageous. Every species balances the costs of reproduction as it aims to generate the maximum number of successful biological descendants (i.e., progeny). Lower life-forms like bacteria reproduce in an asexual manner, cloning themselves. This is low-cost and works when genetic diversity can be introduced by random mutations over generations (e.g., stable environment, rapid generation turnover). But mixing genetic information from two individuals in sexual reproduction increases genetic diversity when development is more time- and energy-intense, such as in complex organisms. While male and female physical features can look quite different among various species, the realm of the sexual is ultimately about reproduction, the evolutionarily essential process of rearing mature offspring.

In humans, another well-known superficial difference is the pattern of greater muscle mass and strength in males.[1] Even if an individual male does not have significant muscle mass, his capacity to build muscle exceeds most females' capacity. This strength certainly confers an advantage on the individual organism in obtaining food and fending off aggressors. But it also has costs: male muscle mass is associated with increased energy consumption, increased infection risk, and decreased longevity.

---

[1] It is well established that men have approximately 60% more muscle mass than women and nearly 90% more overall strength. See, for example, T. Ryushi, K. Hakkinen, H. Kauhanen, and P. Komi, "Muscle Fiber Characteristics, Muscle Cross-Sectional Area and Force Production in Strength Athletes, Physically Active Males and Females," *Scandinavian Journal of Sports Science* 10 (1988): 7–15; A. E. J. Miller, J. MacDougall, M. Tarnopolsky, and D. Sale, "Gender Differences in Strength and Muscle Fiber Characteristics," *European Journal of Applied Physiology* 66 (1993): 254–62, doi: 10.1007/BF00235103; R. S. Lindle, E. J. Metter, N. A. Lynch, J. L. Fleg, J. L. Fozard, J. Tobin, T. A. Roy, and B. F. Hurley, "Age and Gender Comparisons of Muscle Strength in 654 Women and Men Aged 20–93 Years," *Journal of Applied Physiology* 83 (1997): 1581–87; H. Kanehisa, S. Ikegawa, and T. Fukunaga, "Comparison of Muscle Cross-Sectional Area and Strength between Untrained Women and Men," *European Journal of Applied Physiology* 68 (1994): 148–54, doi: 10.1007/BF00244028; G. A. Thomas, W. J. Kraemer, B. A. Spiering, J. S. Volek, J. M. Anderson, and C. M. Maresh, "Maximal Power at Different Percentages of One Repetition Maximum: Influence of Resistance and Gender," *Journal of Strength Conditioning Research* 21 (2007): 336–42, doi: 10.1519/00124278-200705000-00008; and J. Garhammer, "A Comparison of Maximal Power Outputs between Elite Male and Female Weightlifters in Competition," *International Journal of Sport Biomechanics* 7 (1991): 3–11.

What tips the scale so that evolution allows male muscularity? Increased testosterone and muscle mass brings greater success in passing on the male's genes to his progeny when competing with other potential mating partners for the female. Longevity becomes less important once a man has successfully impregnated a woman and supported the offspring to reproductive maturity.[2] As expected, the lifespan of human males is about four years less than that of females. In short, there is a pattern of increased muscle mass in males, with costs balanced by reproductive advantage.

Another superficial difference is the presence of breasts in females.[3] The primary biological purpose of breasts is to produce and deliver milk to an infant, which was vital (prior to a few hundred years ago) for the propagation of the species. Breastfeeding generates a high nutritional cost for females, but this cost is balanced by reproductive preference from males based on the attractiveness of breasts.

The previous three examples of superficial patterns show that dimorphism is truly reproductive: our apparent differences are related to the biological role of men and women in the generational survival of the human species.

[2] Through controlled research, scientists have found that women usually prefer muscular men as sexual partners. This preference for the male physical form creates a reproductive advantage. See A. Sell, A. W. Lukazsweski, and M. Townsley, "Cues of Upper Body Strength Account for Most of the Variance in Men's Bodily Attractiveness," *Proceedings of the Royal Society B: Biological Sciences* 284, no. 1869 (2017): 2017.1819, doi: 10.1098/rspb.2017.1819.

[3] While males have vestigial nipples, they do not normally have glandular (milk-producing) tissue and are thus generally incapable of performing the function of breastfeeding.

For this reason, many of these patterns are called "secondary sex characteristics." While there can be a negative connotation to distinct male and female "roles," there is an alternative perspective: men and women are optimized for a team approach to building families and societies, and success as a species requires both males and females. It would be much more difficult to assign both the roles of physical protection and nursing to the same member of any species that undergoes sexual reproduction, and examples of this in biology are rare.

We can also find patterns in men's and women's behavior. While these differences have led to erroneous and potentially harmful stereotypes, our ability to meaningfully assign attributes as masculine and feminine show that the patterns are real. Examples include the increased tendency of men to prefer rough physical play and competition. Women have an increased affinity for communication and more readily establish emotional bonding. The effect of these differences can be readily observed in how men and women often relate to each other. For example, men are famously able to better compartmentalize and sequentially orient tasks in problem-solving, while women more often see interconnections and integrate. These are representative but brief observations, and it is beyond the scope of this short chapter to catalogue all of the differences between men and women's outward presentations. (See chapter 3, on the psychology of man and woman, for more detailed descriptions of cognitive, behavioral, and relational differences.)

Even as we acknowledge patterns, we see considerable heterogeneity among members of the same sex, as well as overlap between the sexes. This is why is not possible to determine the sex of a person with certainty by looking at them or witnessing some behaviors. Women are fully capable of task-oriented problem-solving, and many excel at it. Likewise, men can and do engage in integrative communication. What is remarkable, however, is to begin to notice that the patterns that we see in each sex correspond to reproductive capabilities: form follows function. On our first superficial glance at men and women, their respective roles in the biological process of reproduction are seen to be integrated with their whole bodies and their behavior. But if we stopped here and tried to define what is male and female, we would come away with very imperfect stereotypes of males being task-oriented and aggressive, and females being intuitive and distracted by offspring. We need to continue our inquiry.

II. Genitalia and the Anatomical Understanding of Sex

As we advance our biological study of what it is to be male and female, we join anatomists of the past who described how vertebrate reproductive systems work. The first lesson learned is that there are two parts of the reproductive system, broadly speaking: the genitalia (external and internal reproductive tracts involved in the anatomical act of sexual intercourse) and the gonads (testes producing sperm in males, ovaries producing eggs in females). An understanding, beyond a realization of the effects of male castration, of the gonads had to wait for the invention of the microscope. The present section will discuss genitalia and how these structures lead us to better define "male" and "female," leaving the inner workings of the gonads for the next step.

The development of male or female genitalia begins at the onset of human life, but dimorphism is not apparent for twelve to fourteen weeks after fertilization. At the earliest stages of embryonic development, male and female both have two sets of reproductive ducts. One is capable of becoming female internal genitalia, and the other, male. Without any external influence, the default developmental pathway leads to the formation of female internal and external genitalia. But male embryos secrete testosterone, which directs formation of a penis instead of a vagina. Male embryos also develop testes (see section 3 in this chapter), which produce anti-Müllerian hormone (AMH), a protein that causes the default female internal structures to regress. There are additional chemical signals, such as androgens produced in the adrenal glands and estrogens produced in the adipose tissue of embryos of both sexes. But the testosterone and AMH produced by the male testis is a dominant signal; only in the absence of this signal do we find evidence of others.

Despite the complexity of these signals, for greater than 99.9% of men and women, these developmental processes occur without difficulty. This is what allows the expectant mother to inquire about the sex of her baby by the time of the prenatal ultrasound obtained during the third or fourth month of pregnancy. By that point in time, a penis is clearly visible for male infants.

Childhood is a quiescent time for physical sexual development, and the secondary sexual characteristics that differ between males and females are not apparent. Nevertheless, it is important to recognize that all of the necessary instructions for physical sexual maturation are already present. In fact, active signals from the brain are necessary to suppress this maturation.[4] As will be discussed in chapter 3, during this period of life, leaps and bounds are made in psychological development. It is sometimes hard to untangle biology from psychology, especially regarding the early years of nurturing.

Later in life, the pituitary gland, a small hormone-secreting portion of the brain found at the base of the skull just behind the eyes, produces and secretes exquisitely regulated signals that control the gradual and often arduous transition to sexual maturity. The resulting physical changes in genitalia and secondary sex characteristics are known as puberty. Puberty is a complex physical process that is intricately interwoven with psychological and social changes of adolescence.[5] While the exact signals that start this process are poorly understood, the emergence of the ability to generate new human life roughly

[4] At the time of birth and for a brief period in the first year of life, the hormonal signals directing gonadal function are active, but for most of childhood, the gonads are quiescent. Disruption of the brain signals that normally suppress further sexual development, as can occur with traumatic brain injury, can cause precocious puberty. See A. P. Abreu and U. B. Kaiser, "Pubertal Development and Regulation," *Lancet: Diabetes & Endocrinology* 4, no. 3 (2016): 254–64, doi: 10.1016/S2213-8587(15)00418-0.

[5] Sheri A. Berenbaum, Adriene M. Beltz, and Robin Corley, "The Importance of Puberty for Adolescent Development: Conceptualization and Measurement," *Advances in Child Development and Behavior* 48 (2015): 53–92, doi: 10.1016/bs.acdb.2014.11.002.

correlates with the potential parent's physical capacity to rear a child. As one example, the nutritional requirements of pregnancy and lactation are demanding for women. As a result, puberty and fertility are delayed or impaired in undernourished women.

Following puberty, the human male or female is usually capable of engaging in the act of penile-vaginal sexual intercourse, hereafter simply called "sex." In sex, a complex orchestration of hormones, pheromones, and non-biologic events culminate in different series of effects for men and women, different because their brains and reproductive organs are different. In the part of sex that will be the most important to our discussion in this section, the male ejaculates, depositing semen (fluid including sperm) into the vagina and cervix; this action is caused by a spinal reflex, the same type of reflex that causes a hand to pull away from a hot stove. Ejaculation may sound mechanical when described this way, and in a deep sense it is. It is important to recall, however, that the event is typically contextualized by higher function, such as emotional and psychological phenomena. Anxiety or another impediment in either partner, especially in the man, can make it difficult or impossible to achieve the threshold required for ejaculation. Human reproduction, more than that of any other species, is affected by emotional and psychological states.

But that is not its greatest difference from non-human reproduction. As we will more fully discuss in later chapters, humans exist as body-soul composites. Human reproduction is not solely a series of physiologic events that fulfill biological needs. Human reproduction is an act of two persons who can expand this biological bond into a long series of personal activities, constituting a lifelong, exclusive, and rich arrangement capable of becoming a vessel of grace for them and for others, which is marriage.[6] However, even here we can see the influence of biology on human behavior. As a result of physiologic production of hormones such as oxytocin, humans, especially females, experience a significant sense of bonding as a result of sex. This occurs to some extent in many animals, but in humans, higher executive functions incorporate much more into this bonding than merely an evolutionary advantage to defending genetically related offspring.

Understanding the physical, psychological, and even spiritual aspects of the anatomical act of sex can add a lot to our biological definition of what is male and female. In a very physical way, a male provides, and a female receives. This is consonant with, but not identical to, our findings from the last section, in which we found that a male participates in family building in a more exterior way, while a

---

[6] Just as engaging in sex can create opportunities for grace, renouncing sex can as well. Abstaining from sex can serve higher purposes, such as development of virtue, support for a current or future marriage, spacing of children, and immolation in consecrated life. While sex can directly support emotional and mental health, and even aspects of physical health, it is not necessary for individual human existence or maturity. Because both its use and renunciation can involve the intellect and will, sex is dignified beyond a purely animal act, and the Catholic Church recognizes that sex is very good because it can be used to achieve human development and holiness in ways that imitate God's love particularly well. By the exercise of and abstinence from sex, men and women can become co-creators not only with their bodies but also through their higher faculties of thought and deliberate love. For this reason, consecrated men and women are said to be capable of becoming spiritual fathers and spiritual mothers.

female does so from within and in a more person-centered context. But our work is not finished.

III. Gonads and the Genetic Understanding of Sex

So far, we have begun to offer an answer to the question of what is male and what is female by looking at men's and women's observable presentations and their distinct anatomies. The next level at which we see form following function is the microscopic. This section revisits human development and reproduction, using cellular and genetic data to fill in the gaps missed by anatomists.

Male and female embryos differ from their inception because their genetic content is different. The primitive gonads appear similar from the outside, but every cell in these organs carries dimorphic instructions. In utero, a male fetus has a Y chromosome, which is necessary to direct the development of male organs and external genitalia.[7] This chromosome signals the development of testes rather than ovaries. Normal testes support the formation of male genitalia and suppress female genitalia (as

---

[7] More precisely, there is a critical piece of DNA contained in the Y chromosome, the sex-determining region of the Y chromosome (the SRY gene). This gene directs the production of the SRY protein, which serves as a signaling factor to direct the turning on and off of multiple other genes involved in sexual differentiation. Thus, it would be reductive to simply state that SRY or even the Y chromosome causes maleness. While crucial, they are by themselves not sufficient. We will see important ramifications of this in our discussion of disorders of sexual development (in section 5 of this chapter).

outlined previously) while ovaries allow the female genitalia to develop.

The ovaries and testes have roles in normal development, but everything they do (including their own development) is for the sake of human reproduction. While this assertion may seem obvious, it is nonetheless crucial.

The way that the different gonads work speaks to the complementary design of males and females. Males produce millions of sperm per day, and quality control occurs as any ejaculated sperm move toward the egg inside the female genital tract. Sperm with the most efficient shape and motility will be best able to reach a receptive egg in the Fallopian tube. Defective spermatocytes will fail to be the first to reach the egg. To produce the quantity of sperm required to have some quality sperm reach an egg, the male testis maximizes surface area for sperm production within many tiny tubes, along which sperm are produced in large amounts.

In contrast, quality control of ova happens prior to egg release: from six or seven million eggs, a woman will use only three or four hundred in her lifetime. These eggs are selected in a miniature version of natural selection every menstrual cycle[8] in response to hormonal stimulation. Each month, several follicles (fluid filled sacs in the ovary, each

---

[8] The menstrual cycle, so named for its most obvious sign of cyclic (usually monthly) bleeding, is actually a cycle of a woman's brain, ovaries, uterus, cervix, vagina, and external genitalia. Much like the spinal reflex of ejaculation, this cycle can be affected by higher cognitive and emotional states. See Julie E. Holesh, Autumn N. Bass, and Megan Lord, *Physiology, Ovulation* (Treasure Island, FL: StatPearls Publishing, 2021), https://www.ncbi.nlm.nih.gov/books/NBK441996/.

containing a maturing egg) will compete to become the dominant follicle that releases a single egg for fertilization. Given this very different process, a female ovary is almost exactly the opposite of a testis: it is a globular organ with the germinal epithelium on the outside (mathematically almost the minimum surface area for an organ of its size), the core of which is full of eggs. After the ovum is released from the ovary, the tissue that previously surrounded it begins to produce progesterone, which helps the uterine lining become richer and prepare to receive the embryo. Progesterone also activates certain glands in the cervix, which produce a different type of gel that is not hospitable to sperm (or anything else), again all for the sake of reproduction.

The interaction between an ovum and spermatocyte after sexual intercourse is the deepest level of our exploration so far. Interestingly, it is here that we find manifested one of the most simple definitions of what it means to be a male and what it means to be a female. Ever since humans noted that pregnancy and lactation separate woman from the more external defender who is man, procreation has been primary to the consideration, from a biological perspective, of what man and woman are. At the genetic level, a single spermatocyte provides paternal DNA to the waiting ovum in an event colloquially known as "conception."[9] This is offhandedly taught in high school biology classes, but it adds to our growing answer to the

---

[9] The union of an ovum and spermatocyte, commonly called "conception," is the moment when a new human life begins. For most of human history, this moment has been difficult to pin down. Modern biology has made the work slightly easier, but the word "fertilization"

fundamental question about what men and women are. The male of our species contributes to reproduction by delivering his DNA to another individual: the generation of new human life will occur outside of his body. Conversely, the female of our species is a recipient of DNA from the male: new human life will be generated within her body.

This difference in where male and female genetic contributions are united at conception is perhaps the most fundamental difference between male and female. This difference affects how each sex constructs the cells used in procreation. Spermatocytes and ova are specially fitted with physical characteristics that allow them to succeed at their different missions. An egg becomes very large with nutritious cytoplasm and many sets of organelles (specialized machinery of every cell), ready to be host to two sets of DNA. In contrast, a spermatocyte becomes almost the opposite: its cytoplasm is pared down around a tight packet of DNA, it carries only a few organelles, and it develops a long tail to propel its DNA package toward the egg. These forms fit the cells' functions: spermatocytes are efficient

---

is still not a good enough answer, as fertilization indicates a series of several events, rather than a single moment.

Modern biology's best answer to "When does human life begin?" is the conclusion of sperm-egg fusion, a very rapid process (it takes less than one second) that joins the outer membrane of the ovum with the outer membrane of the spermatocyte. This marks a physical unity and a change in behavior: no longer is there identifiable behavior of two gametes desperately attempting to reach each other, but rather there is behavior of a single-celled organism acting for its own nourishment and development. (Philosophers and theologians recognize at this point the presence of a new human soul, actualizing, organizing, and vivifying the organism.)

delivery vehicles for genetic information, and ova are prepared to absorb that DNA and prepare a future embryo to use it effectively, because the embryo rapidly divides without increasing in size or making more organelles during its first few days.

This develops our understanding even further, adding that men are in a literal way providers of genetic information and women are receivers. In addition, this continues to confirm that the answer to our central question about men and women is one that fundamentally relates to reproduction. Of course, there is more to the genetics of sexuality and gender than is covered in this brief excursus, which provides only as much as we need to see how men and women differ.[10] But as we will see in the next section, the differences between men and women extend much further than obvious traits or biological machinery.

IV. Molecular Differences and the Whole Organism

Now that we have completed a cursory look, an anatomical survey, and a cellular and genetic investigation, we are

---

[10] One important area of genetic research touching sexuality is the literature on genetics and non-heterosexual orientation. While there may be a possible genetic linkage on chromosome X related to homosexuality in males, this is not sufficient to produce homosexuality, nor does it explain non-heterosexual orientation in females; see A. R. Sanders, E. R. Martin, G. W. Beecham, S. Guo, K. Dawood, G. Rieger, J. A. Badner, et al., "Genome-Wide Scan Demonstrates Significant Linkage for Male Sexual Orientation," *Psychological Medicine* 45, no. 7 (2015): 1379–88, doi: 10.1017/S0033291714002451.

ready to look at our smallest scale yet and examine other molecular differences between men and women. Modifications of macromolecules besides DNA, and some molecules that are even tinier, differ between the sexes. This section reviews a currently evolving discipline in biology that allows us to return to the whole organism we glanced at earlier, but in a much more intricate way.

While sexual differences are most apparent in the primary sexual organs (genitalia and gonads), the signals generated by SRY (the sex-determining region of the Y chromosome) are manifested in every cell of the body by specific modifications of the genes present on each of the 46 chromosomes. These modifications are referred to as "epigenetic changes" since they do not change the actual information present in the genes but rather influence whether the genes contributed from the mother's DNA or those from the father's are used to make the proteins that carry out the functional work of cells, organs, and organ systems. This effect, which persists throughout life, is known as "genetic imprinting."

Furthermore, while each parent contributes half of a child's total DNA, many genes use only one set of instructions. Whether the functional gene comes from the mother or father can markedly influence the behavior of cells. In many ways, this reflects the relative roles of mothers and fathers throughout life. For example, paternal genes (those expressed from the father's DNA) often tend toward increased body size, whereas maternal genes (those expressed from the mother's DNA) tend toward smaller size. One theory is that this reflects the role of the male as "protector" of the mother and offspring. According to this hypothesis, larger offspring provide an evolutionary advantage in being easier to protect. Conversely, for the female, smaller offspring will have an evolutionary advantage in being easier to deliver through the vaginal canal. Whether or not this is the reason for differences in maternally or paternally imprinted genes, the phenomenon clearly reflects that males and females make unique contributions at the cellular level that affect the whole organism. This understanding will be important as we later consider conditions in which normal sexual function is disrupted or distorted.

Another way that molecular science has contributed to the understanding of differences between men and women is in personalized medicine. There are enough physiological differences between the sexes (from glial development in the central nervous system to immunoglobulin glycosylation, which regulates antibody function) to fill a textbook on sex-specific medical practices.[11] It suffices to reference that here, and to conclude our survey of normal male and female bodies. We can identify patterns in form and function through an external glance, an anatomic analysis, a cellular and genetic examination, and a consideration of hundreds of molecular changes.

Our overview of male and female bodies prepares us to propose a working biological answer to the question of what it is to be male and what it is to be female. The male's form and function is ordered toward genetic donation to a

---

[11] See the recent, comprehensive textbook *Principles of Gender-Specific Medicine: Gender in the Genomic Era*, 3rd ed., ed. Marianne J. Legato, MD (Amsterdam: Academic Press, 2017).

complementary recipient and toward serving a family in a protective role. The female's form and function is ordered toward genetic reception from a complementary donor and toward serving offspring in a nourishing role.

Importantly, in this definition there is an intrinsic and necessary relationship between the two sexes. Biological maleness can be understood only in relation to the female, and biological femaleness can be understood only in relation to the male. Each ovum and spermatocyte contains only half of the genetic complement necessary to direct human life, and one of each type of gamete is required. An ovum cannot fertilize another ovum, and a spermatocyte cannot be fertilized by another spermatocyte. Analogously to the way ova and spermatocytes are incomplete without each other, the reproductive organs make no sense independent of their orientation toward the opposite sex. At every level, male and female biology needs a complementary contribution to carry out its purpose.

V. Disorders of Sexual Development

Sexual development normally progresses uneventfully from the time of conception through the completion of puberty, allowing men and women to contribute unique and complementary functions to the reproductive process. However, there are times when something goes wrong in this intricately coordinated process. Sometimes this results from defects in the genetic information within the DNA contributed by either the father or mother. In other cases, abnormal sorting of the sex chromosomes occurs in sperm, egg, or zygote, leading the embryo to lack the necessary signals to form a fully functional testis or ovary. In still other situations, the developing child may be exposed to abnormal levels of hormones that alter the appearance of the external genitalia or structure of the internal sexual organs.[12] In considering these unique, and fortunately rare, circumstances, it is important to recognize that in each case something went wrong with the normal process of sexual development.

The ability to recognize the sex of these individuals may be challenging, particularly when the external genitalia are ambiguous in appearance, having characteristics that are seen in both male and female infants. Our earlier discussion of sexual development—the embryo's reproductive organs start from an undifferentiated state and progress to full maturation of male and female forms from the same precursor tissues—makes it easier to see how this can happen. Indeed, the physical appearance can fall anywhere along a spectrum: from the child's having the normally appearing male and female forms to a child's having both a small phallus and gonadal tissue that appears as both a testis and an ovary. In these rare circumstances, the appropriate response to the question typically posed by the new parents ("Is it a boy or a girl?") may be "I don't know yet." Doctors charged with caring for such an infant often need to perform extensive and intricate tests to understand what went wrong with the process of sexual development. Tests that are often ordered include imaging of the internal sexual organs with ultrasound, analysis

---

[12] S. F. Witchel, "Disorders of Sex Development," *Best Practice & Research Clinical Obstetrics & Gynaecology* 48 (2018): 90–102.

of the baby's chromosomes and specific sex-determining genes, and measurement of hormone levels. Through this process, the doctors are better able to determine whether the baby has the potential ability to eventually participate in reproduction as a man or woman. In many circumstances, the child born with genital ambiguity will remain infertile throughout life.

It may be helpful to consider a few specific examples of children born with disorders of sexual development (DSDs) in order to understand the challenges such anomalies present to our broader goal of understanding what it means to be a man and woman in all aspects of life. In doing so, it will be helpful to consider each of these disorders in relation to the fundamental purpose of sexuality and the unique ways that men and women contribute to the reproductive process. While the sex of individuals with normally formed and functioning sexual organs can be ascertained with relative certainty, when there are differences in the formation of the gonads, internal reproductive structures, or external genitalia, varying levels of uncertainty develop in recognizing innate sex as male or female.

Congenital adrenal hyperplasia (CAH) is perhaps one of the most commonly observed DSDs, affecting approximately one in every twelve thousand infants. This disorder is caused by a defect in the function of the enzymes that make steroid hormones in the adrenal gland. When the pathway that leads to the production of the "stress steroid" cortisol is disrupted, the body will respond by trying harder to make this hormone. The precursor molecules in the pathway will increase and be diverted to a parallel pathway, which leads to the elevated production of typical male hormones (i.e., androgens, which include the sex steroid testosterone). To better understand how this happens, consider how a dam in a river causes water behind the dam to rise and eventually flow over the river banks, flooding the surrounding land. Affected male infants will be born with normal appearing male genitalia. For female infants, the excess testosterone and other androgens will cause virilization during the pregnancy and, if the condition is left untreated, after birth. Depending on the degree of the enzyme defect, the genitalia can appear along a continuum from mild enlargement of the clitoris to genital structures approximating that of a small penis, with many individuals exhibiting an ambiguous appearance in between typical male and female forms. For such individuals, the treatment is to give back the missing cortisol, leading to a reduction in the brain signals that cause excess androgen production. Since the gonads and internal sexual anatomy are normal, the ability to conceive and bear children is preserved. Therefore, once the diagnosis has been made, it is relatively easy to determine sex. In this condition, the sex chromosomes are consistent with the individual's sexual identity as male or female. While girls with CAH often exhibit more typical male-type preferences and behaviors, most recognize and accept their identity as females.[13]

In contrast to CAH, where there is abnormal androgen

[13] K. J. Zucker, S. J. Bradley, G. Oliver, J. Blake, S. Fleming, and J. Hood, "Psychosexual Development of Women with Congenital Adrenal Hyperplasia," *Hormones and Behavior* 30, no. 4 (1996): 300–318.

production, some DSDs can result from defects in the ability of the body to respond to androgens. Strikingly, this condition of androgen insensitivity (AI) can result in people's possessing chromosomes typical of men, but genitalia typical of women.[14] AI can be either complete or partial and results from mutations in the androgen receptor. In complete androgen insensitivity, a person with a 46XY karyotype (i.e., the 46 XY chromosomes usually found in males) will be born with normal female-appearing external genitalia. Yet rather than ovaries, the person will have testes, located in the abdomen, that are capable of making testosterone and AMH, which, as we have already considered, prevents a uterus from forming. When the androgen receptor defect is partial, genital ambiguity can be present along a continuum, as seen in CAH. Since testosterone can be converted to estrogen in fat tissue, many people with AI will develop breasts at the time of normal puberty.[15] However, they will not experience menses, and sexual body hair will be diminished or absent. Some will only be recognized when they present to doctors for treatment of infertility. People with complete AI are generally recognized, both by the affected individual and by society, as female. Even

---

[14] In complete AI, external physical appearance will be fully female (including stature, muscle mass, and body proportions).

[15] L. R. Nelson and S. E. Bulun, "Estrogen Production and Action,"-supplement, *Journal of the American Academy of Dermatology* 45, no. S3 (2001): S116–S124. Estrogen production in fat tissue also occurs in males without androgen insensitivity. Effects of this higher estrogen production include faster growth in childhood and often the development of gynecomastia, particularly during pubertal development. Breast development is greater in AI due to higher levels of circulating testosterone in this condition.

though they are not able to conceive and bear children, they are able to participate in sex as recipients of sperm from a male partner.

There also exists a rare condition known as Swyer syndrome in which individuals do not have developed gonads, as a result of any of a number of problems with the signals that direct the formation of either a testis or an ovary. Often this is due to a genetic abnormality in the SRY gene, which typically originates development of the male organs. Since, as mentioned earlier, the default developmental pathway for sexual differentiation is female, infants with this condition will not be recognized at birth. Rather, they will be seen to have normal-appearing female external genitalia. However, in place of a normal ovary, all that will be present is a streak of undifferentiated tissue known as a "streak gonad." The infant will consequently be infertile. Yet if one were to examine the complement of genes present (i.e., the child's karyotype), it would be discovered that the child has a Y chromosome. From a medical standpoint, the importance of the "streak gonad" is twofold. First, lacking an ovary to produce estrogen, this child will not undergo normal puberty without treatment with exogenous estrogen. Second, the abnormal tissue that is present has a higher chance of becoming cancerous if not removed. More importantly from the perspective of our question about what makes a man or woman, how can sex be understood when the chromosomes are male and the external physical appearance is female?

Before we can fully address this fundamental question, one additional DSD should be considered. Specifically, there are rare individuals who are found to have gonadal tissue that resembles both a testis and ovary. This form of DSD is referred to as "mixed gonadal dysgenesis." It is the same condition that was previously called "hermaphroditism." There are several causes of this type of DSD. Often the problem arises early in development when two embryos, one male and one female, fuse together to form what is known as a chimera. When examining the DNA of these people, a mosaic mixture of cells with an XX and XY karyotype is observed. Since the relative amounts of XX and XY containing cells and the relative amounts of testicular and ovarian tissue present can vary, affected individuals can have a spectrum of abnormalities in both external and internal sexual organs. Most often people with this type of DSD are infertile. Depending on genital structure, they may be able to assume male or female roles in copulation. Doctors caring for these patients had previously believed that it was necessary to make an unambiguous "sex assignment" shortly after birth and to surgically modify the external genitalia to conform to this designation. However, given the many challenges in assessing both how such an individual will understand and be able to function in a specific sexual role, the current practice is to make a tentative sex assignment but to defer surgery until later in life when the patient can participate in this decision.

This select consideration of DSDs sheds light on several aspects of what does and does not define sex. First, while the composition of the sex chromosomes (XX or XY) normally determines sex, this is not a definitive factor. Indeed, AIS patients have a Y chromosome and have been treated as females probably as long as the condition has existed; conversely, there exist some individuals with XX chromosomes who appear and function as males due to the translocation (transfer) of the SRY gene from the Y chromosome to an X chromosome. Second, while sex is inherently oriented toward reproduction, the actual ability to perform this task is not an absolute requirement for the recognition of persons as man or woman. This is perhaps best understood when considering people who are either born with or develop infertility during life, including people with Turner syndrome and Swyer syndrome.[16] In an example outside DSDs, a woman who has her ovaries removed as part of cancer treatment does not cease to be a woman, nor does a man who has his testicles removed for a similar reason cease to be a man. What is most important for the understanding of sexual identity is how an individual develops with respect to the innate roles of male and female members of a species in the reproductive process. Third, although genital appearance is usually indicative of sex, this is not always the case, as in CAH and other conditions, such as 5-alpha reductase deficiency.[17] Biologically, DSDs reveal an organism's inability to achieve full maturity as male or female, whether in the reproductive or copulative dimensions, or both. In this light, DSDs can

---

[16] On Turner syndrome, see Tracy Milbrandt and Ellen Thomas, "Turner Syndrome," *Pediatrics in Review* 34, no. 9 (2013): 420–21, doi: 10.1542/pir.34-9-420.

[17] Ijeoma Okeigwe and Wendy Kuohung, "5-Alpha Reductase Deficiency: A 40-Year Retrospective Review," *Current Opinion in Endocrinology, Diabetes, and Obesity* 21, no. 6 (2014): 483–87, doi: 10.1097/MED.0000000000000116.

hardly be taken to indicate the existence of more than the two complementary sexes.

When all of the physical features necessary for an individual's participation in the reproductive process are present and functioning, recognition of a person as male or female can be made with certainty. Where any component is missing or formed in an atypical way, this task becomes progressively more difficult in relation to the degree of the abnormality. Physicians who participate in the care of children with DSDs must work within the framework of how an affected child will be able to carry out the biological role of a man or woman. Since this is often far from certain, many times the best approach is to defer any medical intervention until later in life, allowing both subjective experience and objective biological development to influence functional outcomes. In acknowledging the very real presence of children with abnormal sexual development, the basic complementary orientation of humans as male and female remains. People with ambiguous genitalia do not represent a third (or infinite spectrum) of additional sexes. There are two, and only two, gonads that contribute to human reproduction.

VI. Errors in Understanding

Many errors can occur as we try to understand the formation and function of the gonads, sexual activity, the beginning of new life, and pregnancy. Often mistakes about sexuality stem from a single, simple error: forgetting that the primary purpose of the reproductive system is reproduction. As was noted previously, the male and female components of the human reproductive system are unique among systems of the human body in that they are integral halves of a whole, meaning that the halves can achieve their purpose only when joined with a complementary half. Humans with normal lungs do not need input from another set of lungs to breathe, but humans with normal gonads always need input from another set of gonads to reproduce. Another way of seeing the uniqueness of the reproductive system is that gonads are organs for others: their presence and function are intrinsically oriented to completion as a male and female couple and for the children that can come from sexual union. When this is forgotten, the sexual organs are more likely to be used exclusively or primarily for the sake of their owner. This can take the shape of masturbation and non-reproductive sexual acts (e.g., oral "sex" or homosexual "sex"), non-sexual reproductive acts (e.g., gamete harvest for in vitro fertilization, and third-party reproduction), and mutilation (e.g., tubal ligation or gender transition).

Dipping slightly deeper into these errors shows that although they share a common mistake, they each involve additional errors about human biology, and elements of these errors actually reveal parts of the truth about men and women. This can be understood more deeply by considering non-reproductive sexual acts and non-sexual reproductive acts, especially third party reproduction, as well as transgender ideology.

Acts can be called sexual if they relate to a person's sexual organs, but not all sexual acts are reproductive. Even in couples using natural family planning (which avoids a complete dissociation between sex and reproduction), acts in foreplay are by association called sexual, since they're associated with a right use of the reproductive system. At the same time, these acts are not in themselves reproductive. Because we are physical beings embedded in time, the reproductive and sexual aspects of actions employing the reproductive systems can be separated. When performed according to biological design, sexual acts allow for reproduction, which includes the flourishing of the non-biological elements of marriage. When otherwise performed, sexual but non-reproductive acts are not associated with any reproductive end. Examples are penile-anal and penile-oral penetration (called "sex," although these represent a falling away from what sexual intercourse really is). Performance of these acts represents a severing of the intrinsic relationship between the form and function of the human person as a sexual being. Because they intentionally bypass the actual purpose of the organ systems employed, such acts cannot be directed toward a reproductive end. A special category of these acts is homosexual—that is, between persons of the same phenotypic sex. Such acts represent an additional departure from the intended use of the reproductive systems, which are biologically designed for the complementary sex.

Acts can also be reproductive without being sexual: for instance, in vitro fertilization (IVF) and other assisted reproductive technologies (ARTs). The steps of IVF include medically stimulating more eggs to mature than naturally would, then harvesting these eggs in a minimally invasive procedure; sperm are obtained usually through masturbation, and the collected gametes are combined in a laboratory. Apart from masturbation, none of these steps are sexual acts, although reproduction does occur. These reproductive but non-sexual acts can take place in the setting of mutual love between spouses but still represent a departure from what human reproduction—and therefore human sexuality—is.

Third party reproduction refers to any conception and pregnancy involving donor gametes or gestational carriers ("surrogates"). In sperm donation, candidates with desired attributes, such as higher than average academic or athletic characteristics, are selected from out of the general population. The men who are selected masturbate in order to produce semen, which is then tested for diseases, purified, and sold to patients. Semen can be used in IVF or in a slightly less dramatic procedure called intrauterine insemination (IUI). Donation of eggs also involves donor selection, but it is more regulated and involves ovarian stimulation with a series of injections over the course of a menstrual cycle. Egg donors freeze smaller numbers of gametes and are more highly compensated due to the significant physiologic stress they undergo. Eggs are sold to patients to be employed in IVF exclusively. A more extreme type of third party reproduction is undertaken by gestational carriers (incorrectly called "surrogates"). An embryo created during IVF is implanted in a gestational carrier (a traditional surrogate uses her own egg, and this practice is discouraged by medical professionals). Gestational carriers enter into legal agreements with the intended parents of the child they carry, to prevent difficult social situations. Despite these, medical decision-making can still be complex when carriers decline procedures that the intended parents desire. Gestational carriers illustrate a departure from the biological events of gestation and parturition, which are meant to be the first acts of parenthood.[18] The self-gift inherent in motherhood is extended to the unborn person by a contracted employee of his parents, not by a mother. This strange departure is deepened when the child is carried for homosexual male partners or transgender partners who are incapable of carrying a child. All third party reproduction (and, more widely, many assisted reproductive techniques) employs bodies as if they were machines.

Errors in Understanding Gender

A culture that accepts the aforementioned separations between sexuality and procreation can succumb to greater errors about what it means to be a man or a woman. Perhaps the most prevalent distortion comes from efforts to dissociate sex (a biological trait) from the social behaviors of male and female persons. To distinguish cultural expressions of masculinity and femininity (treated as psychological traits) from physical sexual traits, the term "gender" has been employed. More has been said about this distinction in the first chapter, but for our current discussion, we will remain focused on the integral connection between sex and gender as it relates to biological telos (i.e., generative purpose).

---

[18] For a discussion of facets of adoptive parenthood, which cannot include gestation and parturition, see Leslie D. Leve, Jenae M. Neiderhiser, Jody M. Ganiban, Misaki N. Natsuaki, Daniel S. Shaw, and David Reiss, "The Early Growth and Development Study: A Dual-Family Adoption Study from Birth through Adolescence," *Twin Research and Human Genetics* 22, no. 6 (2019): 716–27, doi: 10.1017/thg.2019.66.

Our ability to distinguish the concept of sex from that of gender does not mean that the two are separable within persons. As was reviewed earlier in this chapter in discussions of evolution, the outward expressions of masculinity and femininity are related to reproduction and rearing children. The specific social expressions and activities of men and women have varied in different cultures and over the millennia. Nevertheless, until very recently, the essential and exclusive roles of men and women in human reproduction were unchallenged. Many have recognized that the dissociation of the act of sexual intercourse from reproductive purpose through acceptance of contraception has contributed to a clouding of this fundamental understanding of what is male and what is female. If sexual union is merely for physical pleasure, then there is no need to limit this to activities between a man and woman. Similarly, when reproduction and intercourse are disjoined, even biological reproductive roles are no longer seen as necessarily tied to their respective sexual owners.

In the most recent manifestation of errors concerning the human person as a unified whole, modern culture has embraced the concept that there exist individuals who are "born into the wrong body." Disregard of the reproductive aspects of sexual acts allows for the claim that self-perception, independent of biological structure, is sufficient to define sex. This transgender ideology asserts that some people who have a normal male body are actually women because of their gender identity, and vice-versa.

Differences in the physical structure of the human brain provide insights into how reproductive biology, including male and female roles in raising children, is connected to behavior. For example, male brains appear structured to facilitate connectivity between perception and coordinated action, whereas female brains are designed to facilitate communication between analytical and intuitive processing.[19] However, these differences are not sufficient to explain why some individuals experience a gender identity that is discordant with biological sex. Unlike differences in the appearance of the external genitalia, the degree of structural heterogeneity found in brain anatomy and functional neural networks makes it impossible to determine from these data whether one is male or female.[20] Neuronal plasticity, the remarkable ability of the brain to adapt to environmental stimuli, leads to even greater difficulties in linking brain structure to sexual identity.[21]

Claims about being "born in the wrong body" cannot be made when one is grounded in a biological understanding of sex. If a "female" is "she whose form and function is ordered toward conceiving and developing new life within her body and toward serving offspring in a nourishing role," then regardless of a male's perception of himself,

[19] Madhura Ingalhalikar, Alex Smith, Drew Parker, Theodore D. Satterthwaite, Mark A. Elliott, Kosha Ruparel, Hakon Hakonarson, Raquel E. Gur, Ruben C. Gur, and Ragini Verma, "Sex Differences in the Structural Connectome of the Human Brain," *PNAS* 111, no. 2 (2014): 823–88.

[20] Daphna Joel, Zohar Berman, Ido Tavor, Nadav Wexler, Olga Gaber, Yaniv Stein, Nisan Shefi, et al., "Sex beyond the Genitalia: The Human Brain Mosaic," *PNAS* 112, no. 50 (2015): 15468–73, doi: 10.1073/pnas.1509654112.

[21] Nai-Wen Tien and Daniel Kerschensteiner, "Homeostatic Plasticity in Neural Development," *Neural Development* 13, no. 1 (2018): 9, doi: 10.1186/s13064-018-0105-x.

he does not possess the most basic physical features that define a female. Human males by definition do not have ovaries or other primary sexual organs that are required to produce a viable ovum, accept sperm, allow conception, or gestate and deliver a human baby. Conversely, human females by definition do not have testes or other primary sexual organs that allow for the production of sperm cells, or the typical physical attributes that support defense of a family. This is borne out by the fact that hormonal and surgical interventions that aim to give the body the physical appearance of the opposite sex do not change the actual sex of an individual.[22] From a merely biological perspective, it is not possible to change one's sex, regardless of whether medical techniques are developed that allow gonadal transplantation to occur. As already discussed, the conditions necessary for development of male or female sex

---

[22] There is evidence that not even a surgical transition helps people who identify as the opposite gender; composite outcome scores in those who have surgery and those who don't are similar, in one older study; see J. K. Meyer and D. J. Reter, "Sex Reassignment. Follow-up," *Archives of General Psychiatry* 36, no. 9 (1979): 1010–15, doi: 10.1001/archpsyc.1979.01780090096010. Moreover, surgical outcomes of sex-reassignment surgery are poorer than those of similar pelvic surgery; see Annette Kuhn, Christine Bodmer, Werner Stadlmayr, Peter Kuhn, Michael D. Mueller, and Martin Birkhäuser, "Quality of Life 15 Years After Sex Reassignment Surgery for Transsexualism," *Fertility and Sterility* 92, no. 5 (2009): 1685–89.e3, doi: 10.1016/j.fertnstert.2008.08.126.

Very problematic is the use of these treatments in children when almost no long-term data are available, apart from studies that show impairment in spatial memory for puberty-blocking medications and in preserved desistance rates; see D. Hough, M. Bellingham, I. R. Haraldsen, M. McLaughlin, J. E. Robinson, A. K. Solbakk, and

are present at the time of conception and lead to permanent changes in the programming of every cell within the body.

In presenting the biological reality of being male and female, it is important not to dismiss the real suffering experienced by many individuals with discordant sex and gender identity. There remains much that is unknown about how gender identity develops throughout life, whether and to what extent this can be influenced by internal and environmental influences, and what interventions are most effective in aiding affected individuals to live healthy and productive lives. As we began this chapter, it is helpful to acknowledge with humility that despite the incredible advances that have been made in understanding the biological aspects of human sexuality, including genetic programming, embryogenesis, hormonal signaling, and the many factors that affect fertility, there is still much more to learn.

N. P. Evans, "A Reduction in Long-Term Spatial Memory Persists after Discontinuation of Peripubertal GnRH Agonist Treatment in Sheep," *Psychoneuroendocrinology* 77 (2017): 1–8, doi: 10.1016/j. psyneuen.2016.11.029. Desistance and surgical treatment will be discussed in greater detail in chapter 4.

Like persons with same-sex attraction, persons who identify as transgender have triple the general population's risk of psychiatric hospitalization, have triple the risk of all-cause mortality (death from any cause), are almost five times as likely to attempt suicide, and are nineteen times more likely to succeed in killing themselves; see Cecilia Dhejne, Paul Lichtenstein, Marcus Boman, Anna L. V. Johansson, Niklas Långström, and Mikael Landén, "Long-Term Follow-Up of Transsexual Persons Undergoing Sex Reassignment Surgery: Cohort Study in Sweden," *PLoS One* 6, no. 2 (2011): e16885, doi: 10.1371/journal.pone.0016885.

CONCLUSION

In conclusion, we can see the biological reality emerge from the evidence visible in human bodies, including their development and normal function. The male's form and function is ordered toward genetic donation to a complementary recipient and to serve a family as a provident defender; the female's form and function is ordered toward genetic reception from a complementary donor and to serve a family in a nourishing role. As a corollary, there are only two sexes, and they are biologically complementary. Rare missteps occur in development of the reproductive system, as in any series of physical events, but these do not establish a spectrum of human sexualities. Finally, sexual intercourse is aimed at reproduction; to separate the reproductive aspect from sexual acts is to invite errors about the biological nature of males and females. With this foundation, we are now ready to consider the psychological dimensions of what it means to be a man and what it means to be a woman.

REVIEW

1. Normal reproductive development happens correctly in human fetuses 99.9% of the time, and our inborn biology unfolds as two complementary sexes: male and female.

2. Division of our species into male and female provides evolutionary advantage and can be seen throughout the eukaryotic domain.

3. Problems with development of one of the two sexes does not establish a spectrum of sex.

4. Form follows function. Males and females differ in physical and psychological traits in order to accomplish the goal of reproduction successfully. Reproduction includes not only sexual intercourse but also gestation, family life, and even the building and maintenance of society.

5. Males and females differ on multiple levels. First, they differ visibly by secondary sex characteristics; second, by external and internal reproductive anatomy; third, by hormonal milieu and genetic makeup; and fourth, by subtle modifications of non-sex-related DNA that affects men and women's health outside of relationships or reproduction.

6. Sex is determined at the moment of conception and cannot be changed by surgical or hormonal interventions designed to alter physical appearance of primary and secondary sexual traits.

7. Cultural expressions of masculinity and femininity (one meaning of the word "gender") may shift between places, times, and even people within a culture.

8. One biological definition of a male is "an organism whose form and function is ordered toward genetic donation to a complementary recipient, and toward serving a family in the role of a provident defender."

9. One biological definition of a female is "an organism whose form and function is ordered toward conceiving and developing new life within her body, and toward serving a family in a nourishing role."

10. Sexual acts (those associated with sexual arousal) between persons of the same sex fall short of what sexual intercourse (penile-vaginal intercourse) really is: the physiological and emotional bond that can spontaneously lead to new human life and can be knit into a lifelong vessel of grace for a man and a woman, which is marriage.

11. Sexual intercourse is a sexual act and a reproductive act. When the reproductive aspect of sex is not considered or is rejected, problems arise on personal and societal levels. Similarly, acts that are solely reproductive (e.g., in vitro fertilization) or solely sexual (e.g., masturbation) fail to achieve the underlying purpose of human sexuality.

Further Reading

Austin Institute for the Study of Family and Culture. *Sexuality and Gender: A Companion to* The New Atlantis *Special Report.* Lexington, KY: Author, 2019.

Condic, Maureen L. "When Does Human Life Begin?" *The National Catholic Bioethics Quarterly* 9, no. 1 (2009): 129–49. doi: 10.5840/ncbq20099184. http://bdfund.org/wp-content/uploads/2016/05/wi_whitepaper_life_print.pdf.

Congregation for the Doctrine of the Faith (CDF). "*Dignitatis Personae*: On Certain Bioethical Questions." September 8, 2008. https://www.vatican.va/roman_curia/congregations/cfaith/documents/rc_con_cfaith_doc_20081208_dignitas-personae_en.html.

Jones, Richard E., and Kristin H. Lopez. *Human Reproductive Biology*. 4th ed. Amsterdam: Academic Press, 2013.

Legato, Marianne, ed. *Principles of Gender-Specific Medicine: Gender in the Genomic Era*. 3rd ed. Amsterdam: Academic Press, 2017.

May, W. E. *Catholic Bioethics and the Gift of Human Life*. Huntington, IN: Our Sunday Visitor, 2008.

Mayer, Lawrence S., and Paul R. McHugh. "Sexuality and Gender: Findings from the Biological, Psychological, and Social Sciences." *The New Atlantis*, no. 50 (Fall 2016): esp. the executive summary, pp. 10–12. https://www.thenewatlantis.com/docLib/20160819_TNA50ExecutiveSummary.pdf.

Murray, Charles. *Human Diversity: The Biology of Gender, Race, and Class*. New York: Twelve, 2020.

Paul VI. *Humanae Vitae*. San Francisco: Ignatius Press, 1983.

Sadler, T. W. *Langman's Medical Embryology*. 14th ed. Philadelphia: Wolters Kluwer, 2019.

Tsiaris, Alexander, and Barry Werth. *The Architecture and Design of Man and Woman*. New York: Doubleday, 2004.

CHAPTER 3

The Psychology of the Sexual Difference

Andrew J. Sodergren, MTS, PsyD

Discussions of how the sexes differ are perennially popular among romantic couples, parents, self-help authors, and entertainers. In such contexts, sex differences are often stereotyped, exaggerated, and even lampooned. Conversely, the more serious discourse among social scientists has largely emphasized how much the sexes are the same, how any apparent differences are largely due to social influences, and how society could benefit from more gender-neutral programs of parenting and education. When we add into this mix the recent trend to see "sex" and "gender" as separate realities that may be disassociated from each other, it is easy to see how enormous confusion about the nature and purpose of being created male and female can result. Such confusion is all too common today.

This chapter's aim is to provide an overview of the psychology and neuroscience of the sexual difference. I will review findings from the biological and social sciences relevant to this topic and strive to present the scientific findings in a fair and accurate manner, in the most non-technical manner possible. My reflection on this topic is situated within a Catholic vision of the human person and sexuality. In particular, I take as a starting point the basic truth that male and female constitute two ways of being human. That is, there is one human nature, created by God, and male and female are two ways of having and expressing that one nature. (See chapter 6 for a theological reflection on human sexuality, and the philosophical articulation offered in chapter 1.)

This starting point has a number of implications for this chapter. To begin with, man and woman are united at the level of nature and so will share many similarities. Indeed, myriad internal and external forces (nature and nurture, to oversimplify) move the sexes toward greater similarity over the course of a lifetime. We are, after all, brothers and sisters in the same human family.

Unity in human nature is an important starting point when we consider scientific findings on differences between the sexes. However, it is equally true that the sexual difference (i.e., male and female) will affect the person at every level. To be sure, we discover our maleness or femaleness in our bodies. However, maleness and femaleness are not merely physical characteristics but affect the person all the way to his or her core (see chapters 1 and 2). John Paul II speaks of sexuality (that is, being male or female) as "constitutive for the person" and not merely "an attribute of the person."[1] In other words, male and female somehow define us in our very being. Building on his teaching, the Congregation for the Doctrine of the Faith later clarified,

---

[1] John Paul II, *Man and Woman He Created Them: A Theology of the Body*, trans. M. Waldstein (Boston, MA: Pauline Books and Media, 2006), 10:1.

The importance and the meaning of the sexual difference, as a reality deeply inscribed in man and woman, needs to be noted. "Sexuality characterizes man and woman not only on the physical level, but also on the psychological and spiritual, making its mark on each of their expressions." It cannot be reduced to a pure and insignificant biological fact, but rather "is a fundamental component of personality, one of its modes of being, of expressing and of living human love."[2]

Maleness and femaleness affect every level of the person, but this does not mean that men and women are somehow opposites or totally different. Rather, differences between them may be quite subtle and difficult or impossible to quantify. Indeed, in modern society men and women frequently fill similar roles, but their fulfillment of those roles will be affected—flavored, if you will—by their maleness or femaleness. This distinctness, while rich with meaning, may evade the quantitative methods of social scientists. We can anticipate, however, that differences between men and women will be more pronounced the more such differences pertain to spousal love and procreation, as these touch the most essential meaning of the sexual difference. Given this, I find very reasonable, from a scientific point of view, the position of psychologist Richard Lippa, which he termed

---

[2] Congregation for the Doctrine of the Faith, "Letter on the Collaboration of Men and Women in the Church and in the World" (May 31, 2004), no. 8, https://www.vatican.va/roman_curia/congregations/cfaith/documents/rc_con_cfaith_doc_20040731_collaboration_en.html.

the "gender reality hypothesis." This view holds that "many psychological gender differences are small-to-nonexistent, some are moderate, and some are large."[3]

Another important principle framing my account is well summarized by Margaret H. McCarthy of the John Paul II Institute in Washington, DC, who writes,

> The human being is not the only one who has a nature but is the one to whom this nature has been entrusted as a task, so that it might be fulfilled through freedom (not merely instinct). One does indeed have to become what one is, and so must become a woman or a man.[4]

---

[3] Richard A. Lippa, "The Gender Reality Hypothesis," *American Psychologist* 61, no. 6 (2006): 639, doi: 10.1037/0003-066X.61.6.639. Prof. Lippa is referring here to the results of quantitative research that compared males and females on various psychological measures. Researchers who conduct these kinds of studies examine not only *whether* males and females differ on a particular quality or behavior (i.e., is there a statistically significant difference?) but also the *magnitude* of any difference. This helps clarify the conclusions. The size of the statistical difference (known as an "effect size") refers to the extent to which the average male and average female differ on that variable. When I use terms such as small, moderate, or large in discussing research on sex differences, I am referring to these "effect sizes." I direct readers wanting to learn more about this kind of research to Lippa's book *Gender, Nature, and Nurture*, 2nd ed. (New York: Taylor and Francis, 2005), which, though a bit dated, remains a very helpful, balanced guide to the science of sex differences in psychology.

[4] Margaret H. McCarthy, "Gender Ideology and the *Humanum*," *Communio: International Catholic Review* 43, no. 2 (2016): 275–98, at 290.

Maleness and femaleness are both something that we *are* and something that we have to *become*. This highlights the importance of development (see chapter 1, section 5, and chapter 2, sections 1–4). Since maleness and femaleness affect the whole person, we anticipate that processes of sexual differentiation will be at work as physical and psychological development unfolds. Some of this development—especially early in life—may occur with little direct cooperation from the individual, as unwilled forces flowing from within the person and external forces such as family and culture interact to affect sexual development. However, over time the person becomes an active agent in this process as his or her values, desires, and self-understanding increasingly influence behavior, preferences, and social environment. When we become active agents, we have the opportunity to engage our freedom in cooperation with God's design and the guidance and support of others to grow into our identities and vocations as men and women.

Indeed, it is helpful to reflect for a moment on the sheer complexity of sexual identity development before going on to specific findings about how this unfolds. Lippa again is a useful guide. He attempts to capture the complexity of sexual identity development through the notion of "causal cascades."[5] The idea here is that one set of factors spills over and affects another set of factors, which affects another and so on, like a cascading waterfall. However, some of these factors feed back again and affect prior ones, adding even greater complexity over time. Lippa identifies seven different sets of factors in sexual identity

[5] Lippa, *Gender, Nature, and Nurture*, 219–26.

development that interact in this cascading and looping manner such that they are likely impossible to disentangle. These dimensions include biological or genetic factors, family influences, peer influences, sociocultural influences, one's own cognitive development and thinking about gender, related emotions and attitudes, and, last, one's own behavior. Each of these areas affects others in a cascading fashion as the person and his or her sexual identity develop over time. As we explore various scientific findings about sex differences and sexual identity, sometimes more emphasis will be given to one or another set of causes that research has suggested may explain a particular finding. However, we must always bear in mind the complexity of development and the interconnectedness of these various factors. (Lippa's analysis maps onto the description, in chapter 1, of sexuality as holistically present in the human person, involving biological structures, familial relations, sociocultural forms, and self-awareness and self-expression.)

One final principle stemming from the Catholic vision of the person needs to be emphasized. Scientists study fallen human beings in a historical context marked by sin. The picture of humanity that appears in their findings is a mixture of God's original design for men and women, and the effects of sin. Thus, we cannot infer directly that a given finding is necessarily the way things *ought* to be or is a pure manifestation of God's original design for male and female. Rather, the image we see in the scientific findings is that of a wounded but redeemed humanity, which evinces various distortions of sexual difference alongside aspects of truth, goodness, and beauty. We do well to remember this as we contemplate the psychology of the sexual difference.

I. Body and Brain at the Beginning of Life

As discussed in the previous chapter on the biology of man and woman, sexual differentiation begins with genetic donation and reception, which we refer to as "conception." Because of the presence of the Y chromosome, the male's gonads become testes and begin producing large amounts of testosterone during the fetal period.[6] As a result, male and female fetuses are exposed to vastly different amounts of this masculinizing hormone, which affects not only the reproductive organs but also various aspects of the brain. Indeed, the hormonal milieu of the developing baby in the womb has been shown in animal research to affect nervous system development in several ways: the growth of new neurons (nerve cells), the specific type of neuron these cells become, the physical characteristics of neurons, the number of connections they form with other neurons, rates of neuron death, and so forth. These cellular changes accumulate to create differences in the size of various brain

---

[6] There is another surge of sex hormones shortly after birth, but then levels remain low until puberty; see Margaret M. McCarthy, *Sex and the Developing Brain*, 2nd ed. (San Rafael, CA: Morgan & Claypool, 2017). I want to clarify for the reader that I am citing a different McCarthy here than the one I quoted earlier. The prior quotation came from Margaret H. McCarthy, Associate Professor of Theological Anthropology at the Pontifical John Paul II Institute in Washington, DC. The second McCarthy being cited here is Margaret M. McCarthy, Professor and Chair of the Dept. of Pharmacology at the University of Maryland School of Medicine.

regions and the networks of connections being formed between different brain regions.[7]

This pathway of sexual differentiation (chromosomes affect gonads, which affect hormones, which affect masculinization or feminization) is robust and well established in the scientific literature (see also chapter 2). However, recent research has shown that some aspects of sexual differentiation in the brain occur independent of sex hormones and are directed by the chromosomes themselves. That is, the very presence of XX or XY chromosomal pairs within the developing baby's brain cells appears to be responsible for some degree of sexual differentiation. According to two leading researchers in this area, "XX and XY cells function differently, before or after they are influenced by gonadal steroids, by virtue of the direct sex-specific effects of X and Y gene expression within the cells themselves."[8] In other words, "every cell in a male brain is to some degree fundamentally different than every cell in a female brain."[9]

This direct impact of the sex chromosomes themselves on the developing brain has also recently gained emphasis

---

[7] See, for review, Melissa Hines, "Sex-Related Variation in Human Behavior and the Brain," *Trends in Cognitive Science* 14, no. 10 (2010): 448–56, doi: 10.1016/j.tics.2010.07.005; Melissa Hines, "Gender Development and the Human Brain," *Annual Review of Neuroscience* 34 (2011): 69–88, doi: 10.1146/annurev-neuro-061010-113654; and Margaret M. McCarthy, *Sex and the Developing Brain*.

[8] Margaret M. McCarthy and Arthur P. Arnold, "Sex Differences in the Brain: What's Old and What's New?," in *Sex Differences in the Brain: From Genes to Behavior*, ed. Jill B. Becker, Karen J. Berkley, Nori Geary, Elizabeth Hampson, James P. Herman, and Elizabeth Young (Oxford: Oxford University Press, 2008), 17.

[9] Margaret M. McCarthy, *Sex and the Developing Brain*, 83.

through the study of "epigenetics." Epigenetics refers to various processes in an organism that affect which genes get activated, which ones remain dormant, and how genetic material gets translated into physical structures, thus influencing the development and functioning of the organism and even what gets passed on to offspring. Research is beginning to accumulate showing that sex chromosomes (either X or Y) may play a key role in influencing various epigenetic processes.[10] For example, researchers recently studied a sample of 544 adults and found over six thousand genes, common to both sexes, that showed different expression in males and females.[11] Among other things, this means that even if two people both have a given gene, whether and how that gene manifests in them may differ based on their sex chromosomes. Needless to say, this is a new, rapidly developing area of science that will continue to shed light on the vast and mysterious ways our maleness or femaleness manifests itself through the brain and body.

As we have seen so far, genes, epigenetics, and sex hormones all work together in various ways to promote sexual differentiation in utero and beyond. As a result, males and

---

[10] See, for review, Elena Jazin and Larry Cahill, "Sex Differences in Molecular Neuroscience: From Fruit Flies to Humans," *Nature Reviews: Neuroscience* 11, no. 1 (2010): 9–17; and Vikram S. Ratnu, Michael R. Emami, and Timothy W. Bredy, "Genetic and Epigenetic Factors Underlying Sex Differences in the Regulation of Gene Expression in the Brain," *Journal of Neuroscience Research* 95, nos. 1–2 (2017): 301–10, doi: 10.1002/jnr.23886.

[11] Moran Gershoni and Shmuel Pietrokovski, "The Landscape of Sex-Differential Transcriptome and Its Consequent Selection in Human Adults," *BMC Biology* 15, no. 7 (2017), doi 10.1186/s12915-017-0352-z.

females follow distinct developmental paths from the earliest moments of life. Though our understanding about how genes and epigenetics contribute to these distinct developmental paths has grown, the traditional view—that most of the sex differences we tend to observe in the body and in behavior primarily result from the different hormonal milieux of developing boys and girls—is still valid. Indeed, sex hormones in the womb have been shown to have what researchers refer to as "organizational" effects, for they affect the very way the child's developing nervous system gets set up, or "organized," and these effects remain stable long after hormone levels drop off.[12] The organizational effects of sex hormones in early life create lasting—perhaps even permanent—changes in the nervous systems of males and females. These effects are distinct from the "activational" effects of hormones that appear only when these hormones are currently circulating in the body.

Regardless of their origin (genes, epigenetics, hormones), these various biological factors clearly influence the development of male and female babies in many ways. Such differences interact with the developing child's environment to produce differing experiences even in the womb. Male babies, for example, show greater vulnerability to a wide range of developmental problems early in life and unfortunately also experience greater adversity in coming into the world.[13] One can say that at a biochemical

---

[12] See Hines, "Gender Development and the Human Brain," 71; and Margaret M. McCarthy, *Sex and the Developing Brain*, 19–23.

[13] For review of the following findings, see Janet A. Dipietro and Kristin M. Voegtline, "The Gestational Foundation of Sex Differences in Development and Vulnerability," *Neuroscience* 342 (2017): 4–20,

level, the womb is a less hospitable environment for a male, possibly due to the fact that his cells have XY sex chromosomes, which differ from his mother's, who is always XX. Indeed, research shows that more males are conceived than females, but they die at higher rates during the first part of pregnancy and from mid-gestation onward. Pregnancies with male fetuses are also associated with higher rates of various complications (such as gestational diabetes, placenta previa, preeclampsia). Male babies in the womb are more vulnerable to the negative impact of exposure to chemical agents or toxins (like lead, certain pharmaceuticals, etc.) and maternal stress. It is not surprising, then, that male babies experience greater rates of pre-term birth and low birthweight than do females. Birth also appears to be more stressful for male babies, and birth complications and injuries tend to occur with male babies more frequently than with females as well. One of the unfortunate results of all this vulnerability and adversity is that males have higher rates of prenatal or neonatal death, and this increased risk continues through the first year of life after birth (e.g., due to increased risk of SIDS).

Neuroscientists have also begun to examine the ways male and female babies' brains develop differently in the womb. There is evidence of different trajectories of growth in the brain, such that females' brains appear to develop more quickly than males'. Dipietro and Voegtline refer to this as girls' "accelerated neuromaturation."[14] They cite

doi: 10.1016/j.neuroscience.2015.07.068.

[14] Dipietro and Voegtline, "The Gestational Foundation of Sex Differences in Development and Vulnerability," 13–14.

research showing that in the fetal period, female babies are more responsive to external stimuli and show more advanced learning ability compared to boys. In a recent, related study, researchers conducted brain scans of children in utero and examined patterns of "functional connectivity," which refers to the development of interconnected networks of neurons, a sign of maturation. The researchers found that girls and boys tended to show quite different patterns of functional connectivity, with girls showing more developed networks across distant regions of the brain, linking higher brain centers with lower structures.[15] It is possible that this greater connectivity in the developing female brain underlies their greater ability to learn from external stimuli while still in the womb. The only area where the males in this study showed advantage over the females was in local connectivity within the cerebellum, a structure that rests above the spinal cord at the base of the brain and is believed primarily to be involved in coordinating body movements.[16] Interestingly, there is some evidence that male babies show more individual bouts of physical movement in the womb as they near the end of gestation, perhaps reflecting this difference in brain development, though this interpretation needs further study.[17]

[15] M. D. Wheelock, J. L. Hect, E. Hernandez-Andrade, S. S. Hassan, R. Romero, A. T. Eggebrecht, and M. E. Thomason, "Sex Differences in Functional Connectivity during Fetal Brain Development," *Developmental Cognitive Neuroscience* 36 (2019): 100632, doi: 10.1016/j.dcn.2019.100632.

[16] Wheelock et al., "Sex Differences in Functional Connectivity during Fetal Brain Development," 100632.

[17] Dipietro and Voegtline, "The Gestational Foundation of Sex Differences in Development and Vulnerability," 10.

This brief summary shows that from conception to birth, powerful biological forces are in play that translate into different developmental paths for boys and girls. These various forces affect not only the structure of their reproductive organs but also the organization of the developing brain and nervous system, bringing about different strengths and liabilities. Boys and girls are also subject to different experiences in the womb and during birth. All of this contributes to our understanding of the sexual difference that continues to unfold in childhood and adulthood.

II. Sex Differences Emerging in Childhood

Given the different developmental processes at work before birth, it is not surprising to see subtle differences appear in the behavior of infant boys and girls. A series of studies described by Simon Baron-Cohen gave newborn babies the opportunity to look at a human face or a mechanical object. Researchers measured how much time the newborns spent looking at the different stimuli to assess their level of interest in either faces or mechanical objects. Across studies, newborn girls have shown a preference for looking at human faces, whereas newborn boys have shown a preference for looking at mechanical objects.[18] This finding is especially striking because of how early it appears—the first few days of life after birth.

A similar line of research has repeatedly shown that when toddlers are given a variety of toys to play with, boys

---

[18] Simon Baron-Cohen, *The Essential Difference* (New York: Basic Books, 2003), 54–56.

show a strong preference for playing with toys that are mechanical in nature (e.g., a toy truck), whereas girls will spend slightly more time playing with dolls and domestic toys rather than mechanical toys. There is strong evidence from a variety of sources that shows that this difference is largely due to the organizational effects of sex hormones in the womb and is not primarily learned. For instance, these differences in toy preferences have been found to occur with *non-human primates* as well.[19] In addition, researchers have observed that girls as well as female primates of non-human species show more interest in infants and caring for the young than their male counterparts.[20] In both cases, we see males showing more interest in things and females showing more interest in other people (or primates). Again, various lines of research—including the findings regarding non-humans—converge to suggest that these early differences in interests and play preferences are largely the result of early biological factors (such as hormones) rather than external pressures (such as modeling and social norms). This conclusion is reinforced by research that shows that girls who have been abnormally exposed to elevated levels of male sex hormones in the womb (e.g., those with congenital adrenal hyperplasia) show more boy-typical toy preferences.

One explanation that has been offered for these differences in the visual interests and toy preferences of infants

[19] See Hines, "Gender Development and the Human Brain," 74, 79; Hines, "Sex-Related Variation in Human Behavior and the Brain," 451; and Margaret M. McCarthy, *Sex and the Developing Brain*, 99–103.

[20] Margaret M. McCarthy, *Sex and the Developing Brain*, 99–100.

has to do with sex differences in vision. Leonard Sax argues for this in his book *Why Gender Matters*, as does brain researcher Melissa Hines.[21] They both cite research showing sex differences in the human visual system; this research highlights the masculinizing effects of testosterone early in life, which appears to result in enhancements in the ability to perceive *location* and *motion*, such that males tend to perform better at visual-spatial tasks that emphasize these qualities.[22] It is possible that this bias in the male visual system makes cars, trucks, and things than can move more interesting for boys to look at and to handle. Sax further argues that females' visual systems are more developed in their ability to perceive color and texture, inclining them to prefer to look at and play with objects that maximize those qualities (for example, dolls, human faces). The research seems to be somewhat mixed on whether females perceive color *better*, but it does support the notion, at the least, that males and females tend to perceive color *differently*, as a result of differences in the way their visual systems have developed.[23]

---

[21] Leonard Sax, *Why Gender Matters*, 2nd ed. (New York: Harmony Books, 2017); Hines, "Gender Development and the Human Brain." Diane F. Halpern, in her book *Sex Differences in Cognitive Abilities*, 4th ed. (New York: Psychology Press, 2013), argues for a more limited interpretation of some of Sax's findings. Her research corroborates much of this chapter's discussion of brain differences and is a good comprehensive resource regarding cognitive and brain differences between the sexes.

[22] See, for example, Israel Abramov, James Gordon, Olga Feldman, and Alla Chavarga, "Sex & Vision I: Spatio-Temporal Resolution," *Biology of Sex Differences* 3, no. 20 (2012), doi: 10.1186/2042-6410-3-20.

[23] See, for example, Israel Abramov, James Gordon, Olga

While it is not entirely clear yet exactly when the following differences fully emerge, there is strong evidence that the human auditory (i.e., hearing) and olfactory (i.e., smelling) systems also show notable sex differences. In regard to hearing, research shows that newborn girls produce louder and more frequent otoacoustic emissions (OAEs).[24] OAEs are small clicking sounds produced by the inner ear and are believed to reflect how well the cochlea is working in amplifying sound. This sex difference is one of several that may contribute to girls having slightly more sensitive hearing than boys. Indeed, as Sax summarizes, research suggests that females, as compared to males, have a greater sensitivity to differences in volume and may experience a somewhat lower threshold for when sounds become uncomfortably loud.[25] Girls and women tend to also show greater hearing acuity, especially for high-pitched sounds. This difference appears to be rather small in early childhood and increases over the course of development. The only area of hearing in which boys tend to outperform girls pertains to the localization of

Feldman, and Alla Chavarga, "Sex & Vision II: Color Appearance of Monochromatic Lights," *Biology of Sex Differences* 3, no. 21 (2012), doi: 10.1186/2042-6410-3-21. For review, see John E. Vanston and Lars Strother, "Sex Differences in the Human Visual System," *Journal of Neuroscience Research* 95, nos. 1–2 (2017): 617–25, doi: 10.1002/jnr.23895.

[24] See Dennis McFadden, "Masculinization Effects in the Auditory System," *Archives of Sexual Behavior* 31, no. 1 (2002): 99–111, doi: 10.1023/a:1014087319682.

[25] Leonard Sax, "Sex Differences in Hearing: Implications for Best Practice in the Classroom," *Advances in Gender and Education* 2 (2010): 13–21.

sounds (i.e., the ability to locate the source of a sound in three-dimensional space).[26]

In regard to the sense of smell, a recent analysis combined the results of many prior studies, cumulatively involving around eight thousand individuals. The researchers note that smells "can have numerous effects on the human nervous system" and are known to affect various aspects of psychological functioning, including mood, stress response, vigilance, evoked memories, and interpersonal perception.[27] They found that females perform slightly better than males on every aspect of olfaction they tested: smell sensitivity, discriminating between smells, and identifying smells. While the magnitude of these differences is relatively small, the researchers remarked on how consistent they were across all aspects of olfaction. They further note that some of these differences in smell begin to emerge in early childhood.

These studies of vision, hearing, and smell show that the distinct developmental paths of males and females from conception onward affect the way these senses work and therefore how boys and girls, men and women, perceive the world. These are manifestations of the distinct ways in which their nervous systems are being organized early in life. As noted earlier, research supports the notion that, starting in the womb, girls' brains develop more quickly

[26] Sax, "Sex Differences in Hearing," 13–21.

[27] Piotr Sorokowski, Maciej Karwowski, Michał Misiak, Michalina Konstancja Marczak, Martyna Dziekan, Thomas Hummel, and Agnieszka Sorokowska, "Sex Differences in Human Olfaction: A Meta-Analysis," *Frontiers in Psychology* 10 (2019): article 242, p. 1, doi: 10.3389/fpsyg.2019.00242.

than boys' and tend to have more robust connections among distant parts of the brain. Research pertaining to children and adolescents shows similar results. For example, a brain scan study of nearly four hundred young people (ages three to twenty-seven) found "robust sex difference in developmental trajectories."[28] The results showed that across many different indices, the girls' brains developed more quickly, reaching full maturity one to four years earlier than boys', depending on what aspect of the brain is being measured. Similarly, another brain scan study of nearly one thousand young people (ages eight to twenty-two) showed that the girls' brains had significantly more connections across the two hemispheres (right and left) of the brain, whereas the boys' brains were more connected within the hemispheres.[29] The researchers remark that their findings give strong support for the notion that the brains of girls and women are optimized to be more interconnected, sharing information across the right and left hemispheres of the brain. The brains of boys and men appear to be more lateralized,

[28] Rhoshel K. Lenroot, Nitin Gogtay, Deanna K. Greenstein, Elizabeth Molloy Wells, Gregory L. Wallace, Liv S. Clasen, Jonathan D. Blumenthal, et al., "Sexual Dimorphism of Brain Developmental Trajectories during Childhood and Adolescence," *Neuroimage* 36, no. 4 (2007): 1067, doi: 10.1016/j.neuroimage.2007.03.053.

[29] Madhura Ingalhalikar, Alex Smith, Drew Parker, Theodore D. Satterthwaite, Mark A. Elliott, Kosha Ruparel, Hakon Hakonarson, Raquel E. Gur, Ruben C. Gur, and Ragini Verma, "Sex Differences in the Structural Connectome of the Human Brain," *PNAS* 111, no. 2 (2014): 823–28, doi: 10.1073/pnas.1316909110. For a discussion of the landmark significance of this study, see Larry Cahill, "Fundamental Sex Difference in Human Brain Architecture," *PNAS* 111, no. 2 (2014): 577–78, doi: 10.1073/pnas.1320954111.

or asymmetrical, optimized for processing information within a particular region of the brain. The only place this tendency was reversed was in the cerebellum, where males showed greater connections across the center line of this brain structure than females. The implications of this are not fully understood, but recall, from earlier, that the cerebellum is believed to be essential for coordinated movement. The researchers conclude, "Overall, the results suggest that male brains are structured to facilitate connectivity between perception and coordinated action, whereas female brains are designed to facilitate communication between analytical and intuitive processing modes."[30]

As mentioned earlier in this chapter, there is some evidence that, near the end of pregnancy, male babies in utero engage in more individual bouts of movement than female babies. Research reviewed by Lippa suggests that boys continue to be more physically active in early childhood, and this difference appears to grow larger as children age.[31] Indeed, there are well-known sex differences in overall style of play that emerge early in life and have been documented in non-human primates as well. Namely, boys tend to engage in much more rough-and-tumble play than girls do, and the research again appears to point back to hormonal

---

[30] Ingalhalikar et al., "Sex Differences in the Structural Connectome of the Human Brain," 823. Here and in the following paragraph we might recall the second chapter's consideration of evolutionary biology, which noted the male as especially adapted for more exterior sorts of protection and provision, and the female as suited for contribution by way of more intimate nourishment.

[31] Lippa, *Gender, Nature, and Nurture*, 26, 34, 43.

effects in the womb.[32] Lippa further cites research showing that boys' play tends to involve larger groups of playmates, within which struggles for social dominance are prominent.[33] Boys tend to break more of adults' rules and engage in more unprovoked aggression. Indeed, ample research on aggression shows that males, in general, tend to engage in more acts of aggression from toddlerhood onward.[34] They also, on average, engage in more risk-taking than girls, especially in the presence of others, and tend to score higher on measures of impulsivity.[35]

These findings are closely related to a large body of research on temperament, which shows similar sex differences. Developmental psychologists understand temperament as largely biologically based tendencies that emerge early in life and form one of the foundations for later personality. Researchers examine dimensions of temperament, such as emotional reactivity, ability to self-regulate, physical activity levels, and the like. A recent, large analysis of over two hundred studies on childhood temperament showed that girls demonstrate significantly higher levels of "effortful control," a temperament factor pertaining to one's ability to control impulses and engage in focused attention. Boys,

---

[32] See Hines, "Gender Development and the Human Brain," 71–72; and Margaret M. McCarthy, *Sex and the Developing Brain*, 113.

[33] Lippa, *Gender, Nature, and Nurture*, 42–43.

[34] John Archer, "Sex Differences in Aggression in Real-World Settings: A Meta-Analytic Review," *Review of General Psychology* 8, no. 4 (2004): 291–322, doi: 10.1037/1089-2680.8.4.291.

[35] See Sax, *Why Gender Matters*, 27–36; Catharine P. Cross, Lee T. Copping, and Anne Campbell, "Sex Differences in Impulsivity: A Meta-Analysis," *Psychological Bulletin* 137, no. 1 (2011): 97–130.

on the other hand, scored moderately higher than girls on "surgency," which encompasses such things as activity-level, impulsivity, and high-intensity pleasure.[36] Given these findings, it is not surprising that girls—on average—tend to perform slightly better on measures of moral development in childhood, such as resisting temptation, delay of gratification, and displays of empathy or sympathy.[37] It seems that a variety of factors converge to give girls an advantage in this domain, whereas boys may need more time for the self-regulatory circuits in their brains to mature and more help from others to develop these moral qualities to the same degree as their female contemporaries.

Boys also come into the world carrying higher risk of experiencing a number of early psychological difficulties encompassing learning and behavioral control. Indeed, boys show higher rates of intellectual disability, learning disorders, elimination disorders (e.g., encopresis and enuresis), autism, ADHD, oppositional defiant disorder, conduct disorder, Tourette's disorder, and early-onset schizophrenia.[38] According to Martel, boys are approxi-

---

[36] Nicole M. Else-Quest, Janet Shibley Hyde, H. Hill Goldsmith, and Carol A. Van Hulle, "Gender Differences in Temperament: A Meta-Analysis," *Psychological Bulletin* 132, no. 1 (2006): 33–72, doi: 10.1037/0033-2909.132.1.33.

[37] Lippa, *Gender, Nature, and Nurture*, 20–22.

[38] See American Psychiatric Association, *Diagnostic and Statistical Manual of Mental Disorders*, 5th ed. (Washington, DC: American Psychiatric Publishing, 2013) [hereafter, *DSM-5*]; Cynthia M. Hartung and Elizabeth K. Lefler, "Sex and Gender in Psychopathology: *DSM-5* and Beyond," *Psychological Bulletin* 145, no. 4 (2019): 390–409; and Margaret M. McCarthy, *Sex and the Developing Brain*, 118–20.

mately three times more likely to be diagnosed with these early-onset disorders than are girls.[39] Girls are at risk for certain psychological problems too, but the ones in which the prevalence is tipped in their direction tend to show up later in development, and so will be discussed in the following section.

III. Family Influences

Children do not come into the world in a vacuum but are conceived and born into the world already immersed in a web of relationships. The characteristics of their parents and family members and the relationships co-created with the new child have powerful effects on the child's psychological development. This begins even before a child is born, as the expectant parents form expectations about what this child will be. They envision their child, choose a name, and begin making decisions regarding decorating, clothing, toys, books, and education, decisions that will affect the child's sexual identity development in myriad ways.

While many parents try to refrain from imposing sexual stereotypes on their children, and some even go to great lengths to engage in gender-neutral parenting, research shows that despite these efforts, parents and other adults do tend to treat children differently based on the perceived sex of the child. For example, a well-known series of past experiments referred to as the "Baby X" studies involved

---

[39] Michelle M. Martel, "Sexual Selection and Sex Differences in the Prevalence of Childhood Externalizing and Adolescent Internalizing Disorders," *Psychological Bulletin* 139, no. 6 (2013): 1221–59, doi: 10.1037/a0032247.

passing an unfamiliar infant to an adult and observing how the adult interacted with the child. Some of the adults in these studies were told the infant was a boy and others were told it was a girl, even though all along it was one and the same baby with whom all of the adults interacted. Researchers frequently observed how the adults acted differently toward the infant depending on this one piece of information: whether they believed the child was a boy or a girl. Quite often, there were measurable differences in the adults' reactions to the child. Bornstein nicely summarized the findings of these and related studies on how knowledge of a child's sex elicits different reactions from adults:

> Boys are described as "big" and "strong" and are bounced and handled more physically than girls who are described as "pretty" and "sweet" and are handled more gently. Even before birth, after finding out their child's gender via ultrasound, parents describe girls as "finer" and "quieter" than boys who are described as "more coordinated" than girls.[40]

As Palkovitz describes, "Differential expectations lead to differential interpretations of child behavior and to differential treatment of boys and girls."[41] Indeed, across

[40] Marc H. Bornstein, "Parenting x Gender x Culture x Time," in *Gender and Parenthood: Biological and Social Scientific Perspectives*, ed. W. Bradford Wilcox and Kathleen Kovner Kline (New York: Columbia University Press, 2013), 92.

[41] Rob Palkovitz, "Gendered Parenting's Implications for Children's Well-Being: Theory and Research in Applied Perspective," in *Gender and Parenthood*, 220.

many research studies, parents are frequently observed to treat their sons and daughters differently in regard to how much they talk to them, the topics they address, what or if any emotion-related words are used, how they interact in regard to problem-solving and emotion regulation, the way they play with their children, what types of behavior they encourage or discourage, and the like.[42] For example, researchers have observed that parents are more tolerant of anger in boys and fear in girls, talk with boys more about anger and with girls more about sadness, and also tend to emphasize emotional suppression with boys more than girls.[43] Similarly, in regard to touch and play, boys tend to be handled more roughly than girls, and fathers tend to roughhouse with their sons more than with their daughters.

Bornstein summarizes a number of ways parents teach their children about maleness and femaleness and guide their sexual identity development.[44] First, through *modeling*, children observe their parents' differences in dress, behavior, and responsibilities and begin to mentally associate these differences with their developing understanding of male and female. Parents—whether intentionally or not—also act differently around sons and daughters, thus modelling different behaviors for each of them to imitate. Second, through *scaffolding*, parents informally teach their sons and daughters about the types of behaviors that they

---

[42] Palkovitz, Gendered Parenting's Implications for Children's Well-Being," 219–21.

[43] Lippa, *Gender, Nature, and Nurture*, 159–63.

[44] Bornstein, "Parenting x Gender x Culture x Time," 93–96.

regard as appropriate for them by engaging them in different activities. Take for example, the father who involves his five-year-old son in a series of home repair projects while his wife involves their eight-year-old daughter in helping her cook dinner. In this situation, each child is being subtly taught about the kinds of activities that their parents may want them to engage in, and this will inform their yet-immature understanding of male and female. Third, parents sometimes take a more direct approach through *reinforcement or punishment* of behavior, depending on whether they regard it as appropriate for a child of a given sex. Studies do show that, in general, parents "encourage girl-typical play (e.g., play with dolls) more in girls and boy-typical play (e.g., play with trucks) more in boys."[45] "In short, parents engage in *gender policing* when their children engage in cross-sex activities. Fathers tend to police more than mothers, and everyone polices boys more than girls."[46] Fourth, Bornstein describes how boys' and

---

[45] Lippa, *Gender, Nature, and Nurture*, 159.

[46] Lippa, *Gender, Nature, and Nurture*, 163. Given the current cultural climate regarding gender identity, it is likely that the amount of "gender policing" that parents engage in is currently decreasing. However, it is not likely to disappear altogether, for powerful biological, psychological, and social forces affect the ways in which fathers and mothers differentially engage with their sons and daughters, and these are not likely to be entirely overcome by shifting cultural trends. It is also important to note, in light of the current cultural climate, that *we should not assume that all gender policing is bad or harmful.* In fact, parents have a duty to teach their children about the meaning of male and female and to help their sons and daughters become men and women. What is probably more important than minimizing "gender policing" is to become more aware and deliberate of what we as parents want to teach our children about maleness

girls' psychological development differs through the distinct *opportunity structures* their parents and others offer them. Adults will present girls and boys with different toys, activities, and experiences, which serve to provide them different opportunities to learn skills. These different opportunities and the skills and experiences that flow from them nudge boys' and girls' development in different directions and further inform the developing child's understanding of maleness and femaleness and what sort of behavior is appropriate or expected of him. Finally, the presence of *siblings* in the home further provides many opportunities for modeling, scaffolding, reinforcement or punishment, and differential learning opportunities.

These valuable insights into the myriad and profound ways parents and family influence the development of children's sexual identity largely come from a social learning perspective. We gain greater depth of understanding by reflecting on the fact that children come into the world with a basic drive or instinct to form an emotional bond— what psychologists refer to as an "attachment"—with their parents. These attachment bonds are designed to aid the children's survival by enabling them to maintain the accessibility and responsiveness of their parents, who provide protection from danger, comfort in distress, and support for exploring the world. John Bowlby, the father of attachment theory, rightly emphasized that attachment is essential for survival, and so a child's instinctive drive to form and maintain these emotional bonds with his parents

and femaleness and the best way to do so given the concrete needs and circumstances of each family and child.

has incredible psychological weight and life-and-death urgency.[47] All of the various types of social learning regarding sexual identity, as described earlier, occur within the context of these emotionally powerful attachment relationships.

Because forming and maintaining these attachment bonds is so significant and essential for the developing child, he comes into the world equipped to adapt to the social environment of the family. This entails a keen ability to perceive his parents' body language, facial expressions, tone of voice, and behavior. Indeed, beginning in the first year of life, young children are constantly learning what to expect from the people around them, especially their parents, and observing how the relationships in the family work so as to best adapt to them to ensure that their physical and emotional needs are met. Most significant for this learning is how each parent behaves toward and with the child, which gradually shapes the child's expectations and habitual behavioral responses as well as their implicit view of self. For example, if I cry when I am sad and mother comforts me so that I feel better, I learn that expressing distress directly is valued in this relationship and helps me to feel safe, secure, and loved. I will gradually develop an expectation that when expressed directly, my emotional pain will be responded to supportively by my mother (and possibly others), such that I can generally expect her to be there for me. This leads to a state called "secure attachment," in which the child feels confident that others will

[47] J. Bowlby, *Attachment and Loss*, vol. 1, *Attachment* (New York: Basic Books, 1982; first published in 1969).

be there to protect, comfort, and support him. However, such learning experiences do not always go so ideally, and children develop varying degrees of attachment "security" with 40–50% of children in the general population showing one of several kinds of "insecure" attachment (e.g., avoidant, ambivalent, disorganized), in which the child is unable to develop confidence that others will be reliably responsive to his needs for protection, comfort, or support.[48] These patterns of attachment, whether secure or insecure, are learned adaptations to the actual experiences the child has had interacting with his parents and family. Hundreds of studies have shown that the best developmental outcomes are associated with secure attachment in childhood, whereas insecure attachment is associated with increased risk for a wide range of psychological, social, and even physical problems.[49]

A child's ability to attain secure attachment is also affected by the broader family context. Especially influential is the relationship between the child's parents.[50] In cases where the parents are happily married (i.e., securely attached to each other), the child is more likely to show secure attachment to both parents. Children can literally

---

[48] Marinus H. Van Ijzendoorn and Pieter M. Kroonenberg, "Cross-Cultural Patterns of Attachment: A Meta-Analysis of the Strange Situation," *Child Development* 59, no. 1 (1988): 147–56, doi: 10.2307/1130396.

[49] Ross A. Thompson, "Early Attachment and Later Development," in *Handbook of Attachment: Theory, Research, and Clinical Applications*, 3rd ed., ed. Jude Cassidy and Phillip R. Shaver (New York: Guilford Press, 2016), 330–48.

[50] R. M. Fearon and J. Belsky, "Precursors of Attachment Security," in *Handbook of Attachment*, 3rd ed., 291–313.

feel when their parents are happy and in love with each other. This helps them to feel safe and secure in the family. Not only do children witness the marital relationship directly but they are also indirectly affected by its effects on each parent. A strong marriage empowers parents to provide more responsive, emotionally attuned care to the children. If the marriage is strained or nonexistent, it is much more difficult for the child to form a secure attachment to either parent. For example, research has shown that mothers who are happily married tend to provide the most sensitive, responsive care, and their children are thereby more likely to be securely attached to them. Conversely, an unmarried woman or one in a strained relationship does not have the benefits of having her own needs for safety and security met through a permanent, stable, and loving bond with her husband. This negatively affects her ability to be a safe haven and secure base for her children, and thereby impairs her children's attachment to her. However, the impact of the marital relationship is even stronger on the child's relationship with the father, who in some cases may be absent or seen as an unwelcome outsider to the mother-child bond.[51] Indeed, as Solomon and George stated, "The early infant-father relationship is subject in many respects to the mother-father relationship,

---

[51] See, for instance, J. Belsky, "Parent, Infant, and Social-Contextual Antecedents of Attachment Security," *Developmental Psychology* 32 (1996): 905–13, doi: 10.1037/0033-295X.103.2.320; and C. A. Frosch, S. C. Mangelsdorf, and J. L. McHale, "Marital Behavior and the Security of Preschooler-Parent Attachment Relationships," *Journal of Family Psychology* 14, no. 1 (2000): 144–61, doi: 10.1037/0893-3200.14.1.144.

which influences whether the father chooses and/or is permitted to enter the 'circle' of the infant-mother bond."[52] As a result, the lack of a strong bond between a mother and father is extremely detrimental to a child's chances of forming a secure attachment with the father. This lack of a secure attachment to the father may detrimentally affect the child's development, including the development of sexual identity.[53]

Through these various experiences in relationship with his parents and in observing his parents, the child is essentially trying to figure out what strategies will help him secure his place in this family such that he can at least minimally get his physical and emotional needs met. This process happens in an unreflective, largely pre-verbal way in the early years of life and is surely intertwined with the

---

[52] Judith Solomon and Carol George, "The Measurement of Attachment Security in Infancy and Childhood," in *Handbook of Attachment: Theory, Research, and Clinical Applications*, 1st ed., ed. Jude Cassidy and Phillip R. Shaver (New York: Guilford Press, 1999), 287–316, at 294.

[53] While the lack of secure attachment with father likely has a negative impact on the sexual identity development of all children, this is especially true for boys. An important aspect of developing a healthy masculine identity for a boy is forming a bond with a father-figure, with whom the boy can begin to identify. Indeed, boys need to feel akin to their fathers and other males in order to find a home in the world of men. This process can be short-circuited if the father is absent, if his relationship with the mother is strained, if the mother discourages the father-son bond, if the father behaves badly toward the son, or if the father and son have difficulty bonding for whatever reason. While girls have a slightly easier time, in the sense that they can more readily identify with their mother's femaleness, they, too, benefit from a secure bond with a father-figure who helps them discover the "otherness" of maleness in light of their femaleness.

child's early learning about the sexual difference as well. The child's ongoing experiences with his parents help him gradually answer a host of questions such as the following: What happens when I show vulnerable emotions like sadness or fear? What happens when I show stronger emotions like anger or exuberance? Are my parents more responsive to me when I play with these kinds of toys or those kinds of toys? Do I feel more safe and secure in my family when I act tender and affectionate or tough and independent? How do I need to act to increase my mother's or father's interest in bonding with me? What are the advantages of being male or female in this family? What sorts of activities, responsibilities, and privileges go with each sex? How does my family react to me when I act more like Dad (or big brother) or more like Mom (or big sister)? What gains me the most love and affection? In summary, what behaviors and interests best help me secure my place in this family? As the child seeks answers to these questions through his day-to-day interactions with and observations of parents and siblings, he is implicitly developing attitudes and behavior patterns as well as his own self-image and understanding of the expectations of others. All of this is occurring in tandem with the child's ongoing sexual maturation and growing understanding of the sexual difference. Thus, it is reasonable to conclude that the unfolding of a child's attachment relationships with mother and father in the family will influence the core self-image he develops, including his self-understanding as male or female. To understand further how these experiences in the family might affect that sexual self-understanding, let us take a brief look at the notion of "gender identity."

IV. The Development of Gender Identity

The notion of "gender identity" pertains to one's perceptions of and attitudes about oneself in regard to maleness and femaleness. In most cases, this subjective sense of self accords with the objective reality revealed by the body. However, in some cases, there is a disconnect between the two, such that a person's subjective view, which may be referred to as "gender identity," differs from the bodily reality. Researchers have referred to gender identity as "a set of cognitions encompassing a person's appraisals of compatibility with, and motivation to fit in with, a gender collective."[54] In their thorough review of the scientific literature, Perry and colleagues note that gender identity is a highly complex aspect of one's self-image, and they go on to discuss no fewer than eight dimensions of it. I will highlight a few of the aspects most pertinent for the present discussion.

First, it is important to note that nearly all children can correctly label themselves as boys or girls by around age three and understand by the time they reach kindergarten that this is a permanent attribute.[55] Alongside these important cognitive achievements, the child is also beginning to associate certain qualities and behaviors

[54] David G. Perry, Rachel E. Pauletti, and Patrick J. Cooper, "Gender Identity in Childhood: A Review of the Literature," *International Journal of Behavioral Development* 43, no. 4 (2019): 289, doi: 10.1177/0165025418811129. By "gender collective" they mean the broad community of males or females.

[55] Perry et al., "Gender Identity in Childhood"; David R. Shaffer, *Developmental Psychology: Childhood and Adolescence*, 6th ed. (Belmont, CA: Wadsworth/Thomson Learning, 2002), 464–65.

with each sex in a this-goes-with-this and that-goes-with-that fashion, based on thousands of interactions with and observations of others. Gradually, children develop a sense of how similar or dissimilar they are to others of the same sex and to the behavior, attitudes, values, and expectations associated with their sex. Researchers such as Perry and colleagues refer to this as the child's "felt same-gender typicality."[56] Children who score higher on this dimension tend to also exhibit higher self-esteem, less depression, better peer relations, and more pro-social behavior, while also experiencing less peer victimization. Conversely, children who score low on measures of "felt same-gender typicality" tend to show more emotional and behavioral problems, but this is typically only the case when they also experience a high degree of pressure to conform to gender-related expectations. Important for these reflections is the finding that "secure attachment to parents and peers promotes felt same-gender typicality whereas avoidant or anxious attachment . . . undermines it."[57] In other words, feeling secure in one's relationships with parents and peers promotes a sense of kinship with members of the same sex that then promotes greater identification with one's biological sex, along with other positive outcomes. Lack of this sense of security contributes to a weaker identification with one's sex.

Another key variable that contributes to children's sexual identity development is referred to by researchers as "felt *other*-gender typicality."[58] As the name indicates, this

---

[56] Perry et al., "Gender Identity in Childhood," 289.
[57] Perry, et al., "Gender Identity in Childhood," 294.
[58] Perry, et al., "Gender Identity in Childhood," 290.

measures the extent to which the child perceives himself as similar to members of the other sex. These self-perceptions may spur the child to spend more time with peers of the other sex and develop more cross-gender behaviors, which in turn intensify self-perceptions of being more similar to the other sex. Children who score high on this dimension tend not to see "gender" as biologically fixed and tend to experience more frustration with their maleness or femaleness. If children high on this dimension are also low on "felt *same*-gender typicality," they are especially at risk for adverse outcomes such as low self-esteem, depression, and body dissatisfaction.[59]

A third important dimension of a child's sense of himself as male or female identified by researchers is "gender contentedness."[60] This refers to the extent the child feels emotionally satisfied or at ease with his physical sex. If "felt *same*-gender typicality" is like perceiving oneself to be part of a team (i.e., the male team or the female team), then gender contentedness is the equivalent of liking and taking pride in one's team. It is a sort of team spirit regarding one's sex. Research suggests that higher gender contentedness is associated with a number of positive outcomes for children, including self-esteem, peer acceptance, fewer emotional problems, and less peer victimization. However, too much of a good thing can be a problem, as some studies indicate that certain people who score very high on measures of gender contentedness can fall into a kind of narcissistic superiority regarding their sex, which can be problematic. Barring that

[59] Perry et al., "Gender Identity in Childhood," 298–99.
[60] Perry, et al., "Gender Identity in Childhood," 290.

extreme, however, some amount of gender contentedness is good for children. Interestingly, here, too, a child's attachment security seems to play an important role. Perry and colleagues cite four recent studies supporting a link between insecure attachment and low gender contentedness. They write, "Insecure attachment . . . is associated with gender discontent, especially if the attachment is gender-atypical in nature (avoidant for girls, anxious for boys)."[61]

Thus, research is increasingly showing that children who are fortunate enough to experience secure attachment with their parents are more likely to perceive themselves as similar to members of the same sex and are more likely to feel content about their sex. Children who develop insecure forms of attachment (especially avoidant girls and anxious-ambivalent boys) are more likely to perceive themselves as different from members of the same sex and feel less content about their sex.

This comes as no surprise to those who have treated children with gender dysphoria (formerly known as gender identity disorder) or spent time reading professional literature on this subject. Problems with attachment to mother, father, or both abound in studies of early-onset cases of gender dysphoria. In their seminal work summarizing their research and clinical experience, Zucker and Bradley provide an integrative model for gender dysphoria in children that brings together temperament, parental issues and expectations, marital problems, insecure attachment, emotion regulation, and family dynamics to explain this

---

[61] Perry, et al., "Gender Identity in Childhood," 292.

clinical phenomenon.[62] This model harmonizes well with the more recent research cited by Perry and colleagues, who speculate, "Possibly, attachment insecurity encourages children who perceive salient cross-gender attributes in themselves to conclude that an other-gender identity would suit them better than a same-gender one."[63] In short, for some children in some families, identifying with the other sex may be a desperate, unconscious attempt to meet important developmental needs such as attachment.[64]

---

[62] Kenneth J. Zucker and Susan J. Bradley, *Gender Identity Disorder and Psychosexual Problems in Children and Adolescents* (New York: Guilford Press, 1995).

[63] Perry et al., "Gender Identity in Childhood," 292.

[64] This does not mean that such cross-sex identification is unproblematic. Indeed, the scientific literature is replete with evidence for heightened psychological distress, mental health problems, and suicidality co-occurring with cross-sex identification. For a survey of this literature, see Kenneth J. Zucker, "Gender Identity Disorder in Children and Adolescents," *Annual Review of Clinical Psychology* 1 (2005): 467–92, doi: 10.1146/annurev.clinpsy.1.102803.144050; Riittakerttu Kaltiala-Heino, Maria Sumia, Marja Työläjärvi, and Nina Lindberg, "Two Years of Gender Identity Service for Minors: Overrepresentation of Natal Girls with Severe Problems in Adolescent Development," *Child and Adolescent Psychiatry and Mental Health* 9, no. 9 (2015), doi: 10.1186/s13034-015-0042-y; Kenneth J. Zucker, "Adolescents with Gender Dysphoria: Reflections on Some Contemporary Clinical and Research Issues," *Archives of Sexual Behavior* 48, no. 7 (2019): 1983–92, doi: 10.1007/s10508-019-01518-8; Kenneth J. Zucker, Anne A. Lawrence, and Baudewijntje P. C. Kreukels, "Gender Dysphoria in Adults," *Annual Review of Clinical Psychology* 12 (2016): 217–47, doi: 10.1146/annurev-clinpsy-021815-093034; and Lawrence S. Mayer and Paul R. McHugh, "Sexuality and Gender: Findings from the Biological, Psychological, and Social Sciences," *The New Atlantis* 50 (Fall 2016): 1–143, https://www.thenewatlantis.com/wp-content/

This connection between attachment insecurity and later cross-gender identification was recently corroborated by an Italian study comparing 95 adults with confirmed gender dysphoria and a control group of 123 other adults.[65] Using the Adult Attachment Interview, the gold-standard for measuring attachment outcomes in adults, the researchers discovered that 73% of the gender dysphoric adults showed evidence of insecure attachment, compared to only 39% of the control group. The groups also differed markedly on a measure of complex trauma.[66] For example, they found that 56% of the gender dysphoric adults had experienced four or more developmental traumas, whereas only 7% of the control group had. All of these findings were statistically significant. While this study is correlational in nature and therefore cannot prove causality, it adds strong evidence that one's history of secure or insecure attachment and family dynamics are integrally linked with the formation of gender identity.

uploads/legacy-pdfs/20160819_TNA50SexualityandGender.pdf. See also the discussions in chapter 2, section VI, and chapter 4, especially section VI.

[65] Guido Giovanardi, Roberto Vitelli, Carola Maggiora Vergano, Alexandro Fortunato, Luca Chianura, Vittorio Lingiardi, and Anna Maria Speranza, "Attachment Patterns and Complex Trauma in a Sample of Adults Diagnosed with Gender Dysphoria," *Frontiers in Psychology* 9 (2018): 60, doi: 10.3389/fpsyg.2018.00060.

[66] The researchers defined complex trauma "as a set of experiences of cumulative, chronic, and prolonged traumatic events, most often of an interpersonal nature, involving primary caregivers and frequently arising in early childhood or adolescence" (Giovanardi et al., "Attachment Patterns and Complex Trauma in a Sample of Adults Diagnosed with Gender Dysphoria," 2).

V. Teachers and Peers

Parents and family members are not the only ones with whom children form relationships and who have the power to influence sexual identity development. Indeed, most children spend many hours per day under the supervision of various teachers who—intentionally or not—may influence a growing child's understanding of the sexual difference and his sexual self-understanding: namely, modeling, scaffolding, reinforcement or punishment, and differential opportunities. As noted by Hines, teachers also have been observed to "encourage children to engage in gender-typed play."[67] Indeed, Lippa reviews research on how teachers sometimes react to boys and girls differently even when the students are engaging in similar behavior.[68] Some have been observed to discipline or redirect girls more gently and with greater reliance on verbal communication while responding to boys in a more decisive and stern manner. Some evidence suggests that this form of differential treatment further affects the strategies these children then adopt when trying to influence the behavior of others.[69]

[67] Hines, "Gender Development and the Human Brain," 81.

[68] Lippa, *Gender, Nature, and Nurture*, 164–65.

[69] Data shows that in the current educational climate in the United States and many other industrialized nations, girls have a distinct advantage. An analysis of over three hundred previous studies and many thousand students, researchers found that girls tended to outperform boys academically as measured by grades; see Daniel Voyer and Susan D. Voyer, "Gender Differences in Scholastic Achievement: A Meta-Analysis," *Psychological Bulletin* 140, no. 4 (2014): 1174–1204. This female advantage was small in magnitude but statistically significant. This difference in academic performance was especially consistent across

Peers also are an important source of influence in the development of sexual identity. Beginning in the grade-school years, children tend to spend large amounts of time associating with peers. During this time, the phenomenon of spontaneous sex segregation emerges and intensifies. That is, boys tend to congregate with other boys and girls tend to congregate with other girls. Children begin to do this spontaneously in the preschool years, and it has been observed across cultures.[70] This segregation tends to intensify until around the time of puberty, when boys and girls begin to show more interest in each other. Thus, fitting in with the same-sex peer group is psychologically important for young children through the grade-school and middle-school years.

samples of US children but was also found in many (but not all) international samples. It encompassed all subject areas, but the female advantage was especially noticeable in language, whereas it was much smaller in mathematics. In the face of this female advantage, many educators and researchers have puzzled and even lamented over the lack of female representation in college majors and careers encompassing the physical sciences, technology, and engineering. Most often, the low number of women in these fields is attributed to messages young people receive from parents, teachers, peers, and so forth about which sex tends to be better at particular subjects and associated stereotypes regarding what subjects are appropriate for each sex (for a review and discussion of sex disparities in STEM fields, see Sapna Cheryan, Sianna A. Ziegler, Amanda K. Montoya, and Lily Jiang, "Why Are Some STEM Fields More Gender Balanced Than Others?," *Psychological Bulletin* 143, no. 1 [2017]: 1–35, doi: 10.1037/bul0000052). Boys and girls seem to be learning from their teachers and the educational system various notions about male and female and experiencing pressures in one way or another to conform to such expectations.

[70] Shaffer, *Developmental Psychology*, 467–68; also Lippa, *Gender, Nature, and Nurture*, 44, 165–66.

It is not entirely known why this spontaneous sex segregation occurs. One probable reason pertains to the different styles of play that boys and girls employ. As noted earlier, boys tend to engage in more rough-and-tumble play than girls do. This results in boys' tending to seek out other boys to engage in activities that appeal to their mutual interests. Similarly, many girls find boys' play behavior off-putting and thus prefer other girls to share in activities that are mutually enjoyable for them. These differing social groups tend to take on different qualities that reflect these play preferences as well as other temperamental and emerging personality features. Boys' social groups tend to be larger, more boisterous, and more focused on dominance and hierarchy. Girls' social groups tend to be smaller and more focused on inclusion.[71]

---

[71] See Lippa, *Gender, Nature, and Nurture*, 42–43. In Harvard researcher Joyce Benenson's book *Warriors and Worriers* (Oxford: Oxford University Press, 2014), she engages these questions and provides a rather nuanced view. While defending innate differences between the sexes, she argues that both males and females engage in collaboration and cooperation within their same-sex peer groups but for different purposes and in different ways. She shows evidence that males seek out peer groups partly as a surer means of accomplishing the tasks of protecting and providing for their families. Such groups need hierarchy in order to be efficient, which helps explain why men typically engage in more ritualistic types of competition that—despite their physicality—do not necessarily involve enmity with other males in the group. Benenson goes on to argue that females typically seek out more intimate one-on-one relationships in order to secure sources of support and help (with childrearing) while subtly competing with other, excluded—and even persecuted—females for potential mates and resources. Benenson shows that females, unlike males, are particularly motivated to conceal this competitiveness, which can be quite brutal despite its subtlety. See also Walter Ong,

Another reason for this self-imposed segregation pertains to the growing cognitive development of boys and girls. As they come to understand themselves as male or female and acquire conceptual and experiential knowledge of what it means to be male and female, they develop a tendency to see other members of the same sex as part of their in-group and members of the other sex as part of the out-group. This in-group versus out-group manner of thinking lends added motivation to associate with same-sex peers and to avoid outsiders.[72]

These experiences of navigating same-sex peer groups surely contribute not only to overall psychological development but also to boys' and girls' sexual identity development in particular. As they attempt to negotiate these relationships and find their place socially, some boys and some girls find it easy to relate with members of the same sex. These experiences will likely aid these children's development of high "felt same-gender typicality." Conversely, some children—perhaps due to differences in appearance, temperament, or interests—experience difficulty fitting in with same-sex peers. These experiences may contribute to developing lower "felt same-gender typicality." Similarly, differing experiences interacting with the other sex may contribute to developing differing levels of "felt other-gender typicality." All of these various experiences with

Fighting for Life: Context, Sexuality, and Consciousness (Ithaca, NY: Cornell University Press, 1981), who discusses a man's tendency toward ritualized competition as one facet of his need to differentiate himself from the feminine (maternal) environment of infancy.

[72] See Shaffer, *Developmental Psychology*, 467–68; and Lippa, *Gender, Nature, and Nurture*, 165–66.

peers likely contribute to a child's degree of "gender contentedness" and their views of the other sex as well.

In addition, peers take on some of the roles previously filled by adults in enforcing values pertaining to maleness and femaleness. Children who fit their peers' expectations of how girls or boys should look and behave tend to be more well-liked and accepted. Conversely, those who do not quite fit those expectations are more likely to experience some degree of rejection or ostracization. Boys tend to police each other the most, often enforcing fairly rigid sex stereotypes around what is appropriate for boys and denigrating those who do not measure up to these expectations. Girls may experience this too, but research suggests that they do so less often, which is due in large part to their receiving somewhat more latitude from peers and adults in regard to their dress and behavior in the grade-school years.

Nonetheless, as we have seen, both boys and girls who have more difficulty feeling secure in their relationships with their parents—and now with their peers as well—tend to also experience more difficulties in their sexual identity development. These children are more likely to perceive themselves as different from other members of the same sex, experience distress over their sexual identity, and may explore cross-gender identification. Indeed, as Perry and colleagues state,

> Insecurity of multiple origins—insecure relationships with parents and friends, victimization or rejection by peers—fosters between-gender forms of gender identity (and erodes felt same-gender typicality). This suggests that insecure children

latch onto gender roles and rules to make their world feel safer and more predictable.[73]

VI. Puberty

As noted in the previous section, spontaneous sex segregation begins to decrease as children approach puberty, which is a time of rapid growth and development for both boys and girls. Shifting from the realm of social influences on sexual identity back to the biological, puberty is kicked off when structures within the brain initiate a cascade of hormones that result in a sharp increase in the release of sex hormones from the gonads (i.e., the ovaries or testes). In females, the ovaries release estrogen and progesterone. These hormones contribute to the feminization of the brain and body as well as the onset of menstrual cycles. In males, the testes begin releasing large quantities of testosterone, which contributes to the masculinization of the brain and body, contributing to muscle and hair growth as well as increases in sexual and aggressive urges.

The physical maturation brought about by puberty is often welcomed by boys, and research suggests that boys who mature early experience social and psychological advantages. Early-developing boys tend to be more popular and experience more social success. Naturally, they tend to exude more confidence. The picture for girls is often more complicated. While some girls may eagerly anticipate certain aspects of physical maturation, those who develop early tend to experience more distress and social problems

---

[73] Perry et al., "Gender Identity in Childhood," 301.

as a result. The changes to their bodies make them stand out more from their peers in ways that are not comfortable for them and sometimes result in teasing. Early maturing girls may also begin to garner attention from older boys, which—whether experienced as distressing or welcomed—can sometimes lead to other problematic behavior, such as experimenting with smoking, drinking, drug use, and sexual activity.[74]

In general, puberty tends to be harder on girls than on boys. The onset of menstrual cycles is experienced negatively by some, especially if they are not well prepared and supported by female role models. In addition, many girls tend to feel self-conscious about the changes happening to their bodies. As a result, concerns about body image can emerge as girls-becoming-young-women compare themselves to others and to perceived ideals of how an attractive woman "should" look. Some will go to great lengths to change or conceal perceived flaws in their physical appearance to avoid teasing or to try to match perceived ideals. Not surprisingly, beginning in this time period, women exhibit higher rates of eating disorders as well as most anxiety disorders and depressive disorders.[75] Indeed, according to Martel, from adolescence onward, these difficulties "are more common in females than in males at a ratio of at least two to one."[76]

---

[74] Shaffer, *Developmental Psychology*, 164–66.

[75] Hartung and Lefler, "Sex and Gender in Psychopathology"; Margaret M. McCarthy, *Sex and the Developing Brain*, 118–19.

[76] Martel, "Sexual Selection and Sex Differences," 1221. Women from adolescence onward also show higher rates of nightmare disorder, somatic symptom disorder (formerly somatization disorder and pain

With puberty also comes the emergence of sexual desire. This mysterious aspect of human life is surely influenced by biological, psychological, and social factors. Unfortunately, there are few scientifically grounded, coherent theories in the field of psychology to explain the type of sexual attractions a person will begin to experience in adolescence. One exception is Daryl Bem's "exotic becomes erotic" theory.[77] According to Bem's model, biological factors such as genes and prenatal hormones do not directly influence the sort of person (male or female) to which an individual will be attracted as an adolescent and adult. Rather, these biological factors influence the young child's temperament, including such factors as activity level and aggressiveness. These factors in turn influence the kinds of activities to which a given child will be drawn (for example, rough-and-tumble play and

disorder), and conversion disorder, as well as personality disorders that are hyper-relational in nature (namely, borderline personality disorder and histrionic personality disorder). Men show higher rates of disorders involving impulse-control problems or other disruptive, maladaptive conduct. Examples include conduct disorder, pyromania, kleptomania, most substance use disorders, and antisocial personality disorder. Males also have higher rates of all the paraphilias (e.g., masochism, sadism, pedophilia, etc.), gender dysphoria, and certain personality disorders that are less relational in nature (obsessive-compulsive personality disorder, paranoid personality disorder, and schizoid personality disorder); see *DSM-5*; and Hartung and Lefler, "Sex and Gender in Psychopathology."

[77] D. J. Bem, "Exotic Becomes Erotic: A Developmental Theory of Sexual Orientation," *Psychological Review* 103, no. 2 (1996): 320–35; D. J. Bem, "Exotic Becomes Erotic: Interpreting the Biological Correlates of Sexual Orientation," *Archives of Sexual Behavior* 29, no. 6 (2000): 531–48, doi: 10.1023/a:1002050303320.

competitive sports, or artistic-and-creative play and sub-
dued socializing). Children who are drawn toward activities
that are typically associated with their sex will find it easier
to bond with members of the same sex. They will tend to feel
comfortable with members of the same sex and form same-
sex friendships more easily. Those whose temperament does
not naturally incline them toward such sex-typical activities will have a harder time fitting in with same-sex peers.
As a result of these various experiences, the child inclined
toward sex-typical activities will perceive himself as different from children of the opposite sex, most of whom tend to
prefer activities that are different from his own. Conversely,
the child who is more inclined toward sex-*atypical* activities will perceive himself as different from *same*-sex peers
and more similar to other-sex peers. Such a child will also
likely have an easier time relating to other-sex peers and,
as a result, will spend more time playing and socializing
with them.

Bem points out that when we are around people we
perceive to be different from ourselves, we tend to experience heightened physiological arousal. This is not sexual
arousal per se but activation of the autonomic nervous
system akin to being in a slightly stressful situation. Our
hearts beat a little faster, our blood pressure increases a bit,
we may sweat more, and so on. Many children may not be
aware of these reactions, so the reactions remain unconscious. Others may feel and express these reactions as a
dislike for these peers perceived to be different (e.g., "girls
are icky," "boys are rude," etc.). Regardless, when a child
reaches puberty and experiences sexual maturation, these
perceptions of being different and the resultant feelings

of autonomic activation can get reinterpreted—transformed—into erotic interest. Being around those people who are different from me creates a buzz of physiological activity in my body. All of those markers of autonomic arousal now become understood as indications of sexual interest. Now, I tell myself that my heart beats faster, I feel flush, and my palms sweat because I am attracted to this other person. After all, they have always seemed kind of mysterious to me. In this way, according to Bem, the exotic becomes erotic.

Bem argues that this theory explains both attraction to the other sex as well as attraction to the same-sex (for those so inclined). Most people perceive themselves as different from members of the other sex, and it is to members of that sex they eventually become attracted. However, some children grow up perceiving greater difference with members of the same sex. Indeed, Bem cites ample data showing that those who experience same-sex attraction in adolescence and adulthood tend to score much higher than other-sex attracted individuals on measures of childhood gender nonconformity. In other words, the research data supports Bem's view that it is childhood gender nonconformity—engaging in sex-*a*typical behavior—and the associated psychological and social experiences (e.g., feeling different than same-sex peers) that accounts for much of the later experience of same-sex attraction. In this way, Bem's theory shows one pathway for how certain combinations of predispositions *and* experiences can contribute to patterns of sexual attraction that are not in accord with the nature and purpose of our maleness and femaleness. Indeed, in my clinical experience, this model resonates with many of the men who seek therapy for help with unwanted same-sex attractions.

While Bem's theory is useful as far as it goes, it omits the importance of the family of origin in the development of one's patterns of sexual interest. As discussed earlier in this chapter, the family is the place where we form emotional bonds, or "attachments," to our primary caregivers. Our experiences in these attachment relationships surely have a role to play in shaping our emerging sexuality as we grow. This is especially likely since, in adulthood, sexual interest and sexual behavior become intertwined with our primary attachment relationships such that an adult's primary attachment figure is typically his spouse (or other long-term sexual partner). From adolescence onward, sexuality becomes a new language for expressing one's attachment-related feelings and needs as well as a new strategy for attaining the safety and security in the arms of another that our attachment instinct impels us to pursue. In this way, an adult romantic partnership mimics in many ways the bond between an infant and parent. Indeed, in a classic paper, Hazan and Shaver noted several similarities between infant-caregiver and adult romantic attachments: both feel safe when the other is nearby and responsive; both engage in close, intimate, bodily contact; both feel insecure when the other is inaccessible; both share discoveries with one another; both play with one another's facial features and exhibit a mutual fascination and preoccupation with one another; both engage in "baby talk."[78]

[78] Cindy Hazan and Phillip Shaver, "Romantic Love Conceptualized as an Attachment Process," *Journal of Personality and Social Psychology*

Thus, attachment and sexuality are intimately related from adolescence onward. Indeed, an increasingly large body of psychological research supports this view.[79] On the basis of this research, we can confidently say that for adults, sexual behavior is an important means of regulating attachment-related feelings and a way to get attachment-related needs met, ideally within the context of life-long marriage. However, it is also likely the case that, beginning in adolescence, sexuality presents an opportunity to revisit unmet attachment needs or unresolved attachment wounds from the past in the context of a sexual relationship. Thus, the sort of people to whom we are sexually drawn and the kind of relationship we wish to co-create with them are connected in various ways with the internal legacy of our childhood attachment experiences with our mothers, fathers, and families.

Regardless of whom an adolescent finds attractive and what has contributed to that tendency, the sexual maturation of the body and subsequent experience of erotic desire are key markers in the passage to adulthood. So far, we have traced the psychological development of sexual identity from conception through puberty. Bearing in mind the myriad of cascading and looping forces influencing sexual identity development, it is now time to turn our attention to sex differences in adulthood.

52, no. 3 (1987): 511–24, doi: 10.1037/0022-3514.52.3.511.

[79] For a review of the literature, see Mario Mikulincer and Phillip R. Shaver, *Attachment in Adulthood*, 2nd ed. (New York: Guilford, 2016), chap. 12.

VII. Sex Differences in Adulthood

When contemplating the sexual difference in adulthood, it is helpful to begin with what is perhaps most obvious though often overlooked: the body. As described in the previous chapter on the biology of man and woman, the male's longer growth spurt and exposure to high levels of testosterone—in utero and again from puberty onward—contribute to the naturally larger, more muscular physique of the typical man compared to that of the typical woman. Indeed, a recent meta-analysis involving 113 studies and tens of thousands of adults revealed that, on average, men exhibit significantly greater upper body strength, lower body strength, total body strength, muscular tension, muscular power, muscular endurance, and cardiovascular endurance than women.[80] All of these differences were quite large in magnitude. Men also scored higher on measures of core strength, though this difference was more modest in size. The only areas in which women have tended to outperform men in these tests of raw physical abilities include measures of flexibility and some measures of fine motor control.[81] Last, as is the case in childhood, men tend to be more physically active than women.

These differences in stature, strength, and physical

---

[80] Stephen H. Courtright, Brian W. McCormick, Bennett E. Postlethwaite, Cody J. Reeves, and Michael K. Mount, "A Meta-Analysis of Sex Differences in Physical Ability: Revised Estimates and Strategies for Reducing Differences in Selection Contexts," *Journal of Applied Psychology* 98, no. 4 (2013): 623–41, doi: 10.1037/a0033144.

[81] Courtright et al., "A Meta-Analysis of Sex Differences in Physical Ability"; Lippa, *Gender, Nature, and Nurture*, 16–17, 34–35.

abilities are often dismissed as essentially meaningless, but in reality, they have enormous impact—even if we fail to notice it in everyday life—on how the sexes perceive and relate to each other and how families and societies structure themselves in regard to sex roles. This is only scratching the surface, however, for the most essential differences between a man's body and a woman's body pertain to reproduction. We will return to that topic shortly. For now, let's go a bit deeper than physical strength and ponder sex differences in the adult human brain.

As described earlier, research has shown that girls' brains tend to develop more rapidly than that of their male peers, with girl brain volumes peaking around age ten and a half and boy brain volumes reaching their peak around fourteen and a half.[82] Nonetheless, adult male brains are larger (even after controlling for their larger bodies), while women's brains appear more densely packed in many areas, as evidenced by findings indicating that women show greater cortical thickness in certain regions and more gyrification (i.e., folding) in the frontal and parietal lobes.[83] The hippocampus (a brain structure necessary for the encoding of new memory) shows several differences between the sexes, including structure, neurochemical make-up, and reactivity to stressful

---

[82] Hines, "Gender Development and the Human Brain," 80.

[83] Hines "Gender Development and the Human Brain," 80; and Amber N. V. Ruigrok, Gholamreza Salimi-Khorshidi, Meng-Chuan Lai, Simon Baron-Cohen, Michael V. Lombardo, Roger J. Tait, and John Suckling, "A Meta-Analysis of Sex Differences in Human Brain Structure," *Neuroscience and Biobehavioral Reviews* 39, no. 100 (2014): 34–50, doi: 10.1016/j.neubiorev.2013.12.004.

situations.[84] The amygdala, a structure involved in processing emotional information, also has been seen to demonstrate several notable sex differences in structure and function. Adjusting for overall brain size, the amygdala is notably larger in males than females. Research has also consistently shown different patterns of activation between men and women when viewing emotional stimuli. Early studies reviewed by Cahill showed "a preferential involvement of the left amygdala in memory for emotional material (generally visual images) in women, but a preferential involvement of the right amygdala in memory for the same material in men."[85] A more recent meta-analysis added the nuance that these sex differences depend on whether the person is responding to stimuli involving positive or negative emotions.[86] This is an example of a frequent finding in neuroscience: even when performing the same task, men's and women's brains often function differently (i.e., enlist different regions, structures, or circuits even if overall performance on that task is equivalent[87]).

Other brain structures that show sex differences are portions of the hypothalamus and surrounding structures deep in the brain, which are involved in regulating the

---

[84] Larry Cahill, "Why Sex Matters for Neuroscience," *Nature Reviews Neuroscience* 7 (2006): 477–84.

[85] Cahill, "Why Sex Matters for Neuroscience,"480.

[86] Jennifer S. Stevens and Stephan Hamann, "Sex Differences in Brain Activation to Emotional Stimuli: A Meta-Analysis of Neuroimaging Studies," *Neuropsychologia* 50, no. 7 (2012): 1578–93, doi: 10.1016/j.neuropsychologia.2012.03.011.

[87] See Cahill, "Why Sex Matters for Neuroscience," for several examples.

autonomic nervous system. Some clusters of cells in this region of the brain, cells believed to be involved in sex drive and aggression, are larger in males than in females. In addition, there are some differences in the structure and function of brain regions in the occipital and parietal lobes of the cerebral cortex, areas that are involved in perception of motion and spatial reasoning.[88] Cahill also notes that the prefrontal cortex is rich in sex hormone receptors, making it a likely candidate to demonstrate sex differences, and it is implicated in some research demonstrating sex differences in various abilities, such as working memory and stress response.[89]

As with girls', adult women's brains tend to demonstrate greater connectivity between the two hemispheres of the brain. This is supported by research on sex differences in the corpus callosum, the thick brain structure that connects the left and right hemispheres. Research has shown differences in the structure and functioning of the corpus callosum that favor the interpretation of greater cross-hemispheric processing in women. Indeed, functional imaging studies have shown that women tend to engage both sides of their brain more readily in language-based tasks, whereas men's language processing tends to be more lateralized to the left side of the brain only.[90] In general, it appears that women's brains are more organized for processing across the center line of

[88] Hines, "Sex-Related Variation in Human Behavior and the Brain," 452–53.

[89] Cahill, "Why Sex Matters for Neuroscience," 481.

[90] Hines, "Sex-Related Variation in Human Behavior and the Brain," 453; and "Gender Development and the Human Brain," 78.

the brain as well as in complex networks spanning remote areas of the brain, whereas men's brains are optimized to process information better within the same hemisphere and in circuits in proximate brain areas.[91]

In a brain scan study of over five thousand adults, Ritchie and colleagues also found greater functional connections in women's brains in what is known as the "default mode network."[92] This is a network of brain regions that is active when a person is engaging in more interior, contemplative types of thought—what researchers have called "internal mentation" (e.g., remembering something about one's past, imagining and planning for the future, pondering the thoughts and feelings of others, etc.).[93] While Ritchie and colleagues' data support the notion that, on average, women's brains are more primed for this kind of reflective activity, they also found that men's brains showed stronger connections between areas involved in processing information from the external senses and planning motor behavior.[94] In other words, men's brains, on average, appear more outward focused and action-oriented.

---

[91] Cahill, "Fundamental Sex Difference in Human Brain Architecture"; Margaret M. McCarthy, *Sex and the Developing Brain*; Stuart J. Ritchie, Simon R. Cox, Xueyi Shen, Michael V. Lombardo, Lianne M. Reus, Clara Alloza, Mathew A. Harris, et al., "Sex Differences in the Adult Human Brain: Evidence from 5216 UK Biobank Participants," *Cerebral Cortex* 28, no. 8 (2018): 2959–75, doi: 10.1093/cercor/bhy109.

[92] Ritchie et al., "Sex Differences in the Adult Human Brain."

[93] Jessica R. Andrews-Hanna, "The Brain's Default Network and Its Adaptive Role in Internal Mentation," *Neuroscientist* 18, no. 3 (2012): 251–70, doi: 10.1177/1073858411403316.

[94] Ritchie et al., "Sex Differences in the Adult Human Brain," 2970.

Moving to the area of cognitive abilities, we see that men and women do not systematically differ on overall IQ. However, there are some differences that tend to emerge in specific areas of cognitive performance.[95] Men tend to score moderately higher on measures of spatial reasoning (in other words, the ability to mentally rotate objects or make other mental estimates involving three dimensional objects).[96] Conversely, women tend to score slightly higher than men on some tests of verbal ability, such as fluency. As described earlier, a large body of research shows that female students tend to outperform male students academically by a small but consistent margin. This female advantage extends from elementary school through graduate school and is largest in language courses.[97] A recently published meta-analysis that reviewed 617 studies spanning forty years of research on episodic memory showed a modest overall female advantage in episodic memory, but this effect depended on the type of material being remembered.[98] The female advan-

---

[95] See, for review, Lippa, *Gender, Nature, and Nurture*, 33–34; and Janet Shibley Hyde, "Gender Similarities and Differences," *Annual Review of Psychology* 65 (2014): 373–98, doi: 10.1146/annurev-psych-010213-115057.

[96] Daniel Voyer, Susan D. Voyer, and Jean Saint-Aubin, "Sex Differences in Visual-Spatial Working Memory: A Meta-Analysis," *Psychonomic Bulletin & Review* 24, no. 2 (2017): 307–34, doi: 10.3758/s13423-016-1085-7; Jillian E. Lauer, Eukyung Yhang, and Stella F. Lourenco, "The Development of Gender Differences in Spatial Reasoning: A Meta-Analytic Review," *Psychological Bulletin* 145, no. 6 (2019): 537–65, doi: 10.1037/bul0000191.

[97] Voyer and Voyer, "Gender Differences in Scholastic Achievement," 1189–91.

[98] Martin Asperholm, Nadja Högman, Jonas Rafi, and Agneta Herlitz, "What Did You Do Yesterday? A Meta-Analysis of Sex Differences

tage emerged most prominently in tasks that were verbal in nature (remembering words or sentences), remembering images that could be named, and remembering locations. Conversely, a male advantage was observed for tasks that drew upon more nonverbal, spatial reasoning abilities, such as remembering abstract images and routes. Women also demonstrated an advantage in remembering people's faces as well as remembering sensory information connected with odor, taste, and color.

In regard to emotionality, research cited by Lippa showed that women tend to be more emotionally expressive and more self-disclosing of emotion than men, especially when it comes to the more vulnerable feelings of sadness and fear, whereas men are more likely to express anger.[99] A recent meta-analysis by Else-Quest and colleagues additionally showed that women tend to experience somewhat more self-conscious emotions, such as guilt and shame, than men do.[100] Women tend to perform somewhat better on tests of emotion recognition (i.e., accurately naming what emotion *another person* is experiencing),[101] whereas men tend to show greater diffi-

in Episodic Memory," *Psychological Bulletin* 145, no. 8 (2019): 785–821, doi: 10.1037/bul0000197.

[99] Lippa, *Gender, Nature, and Nurture*, 39–41.

[100] Nicole M. Else-Quest, Ashley Higgins, Carlie Allison, and Lindsay C. Morton, "Gender Differences in Self-Conscious Emotional Experience: A Meta-Analysis," *Psychological Bulletin* 138, no. 5 (2012): 947–81, doi: 10.1037/a0027930.

[101] Ashley E. Thompson and Daniel Voyer, "Sex Differences in the Ability to Recognise Non-Verbal Displays of Emotion: A Meta-Analysis," *Cognition and Emotion* 28, no. 7 (2014): 1164–95, doi: 10.1080/02699931.2013.875889.

culties in being able to identify and name their *own* feelings (i.e., higher scores of "alexithymia").[102]

When experiencing emotional distress, women tend to engage in a much wider array of coping behavior than men do, and women are especially more likely to seek social support.[103] Indeed, UCLA psychologist Shelley Taylor and colleagues have argued that since most of the past studies on the human stress response were conducted with men, this has led to a male-biased understanding. Indeed, in this body of literature, the notion of "fight-or-flight" has dominated the discussion of the human stress response for nearly a hundred years. However, as Taylor and colleagues have shown, humans also possess a distinct stress-response system, coined "tend-and-befriend," that promotes turning to others in the face of challenges.[104] Furthermore, they argue that women in particular are especially inclined to respond to stress in this "tend-and-befriend" manner, whereas men are more inclined to fight or flee. Both

---

[102] Ronald F. Levant, Rosalie J. Hall, Christine M. Williams, and Nadia T. Hasan, "Gender Differences in Alexithymia," *Psychology of Men & Masculinity* 10, no. 3 (2009): 190–203, doi: 10.1037/a0015652.

[103] Lippa, *Gender, Nature, and Nurture*, 39–41; Lisa K. Tamres, Denise Janicki, and Vicki S. Helgeson, "Sex Differences in Coping Behavior: A Meta-Analytic Review and an Examination of Relative Coping," *Personality and Social Psychology Review* 6, no. 1 (2002): 2–30, doi: 10.1207/S15327957PSPR0601_1.

[104] Shelley E. Taylor, Laura Cousino Klein, Brian P. Lewis, Tara L. Gruenewald, Regan A. R. Gurung, and John A. Updegraff, "Biobehavioral Responses to Stress in Females: Tend-and-Befriend, Not Fight-or-Flight," *Psychological Review* 107, no. 3 (2000): 411–29, doi: 10.1037/0033-295X.107.3.411.

men and women can and do engage in either method of responding to stress; however, on average, men and women are instinctively inclined to respond somewhat more in one of these distinct ways. There appears to be good support in the research literature for this notion. Shelley and colleagues briefly discuss the results of a meta-analysis on support-seeking during stress,[105] stating that women are much more likely than men to seek support at such times. They write,

> Specifically, of the 26 studies that tested for gender differences, 1 study found no differences, and 25 studies favored women's greater seeking and use of social support; there were no reversals. Moreover, these findings have substantial cross-cultural generalizability.[106]

Despite this evidence base, there is still ongoing debate over the notion of a basic sex difference in stress response, but there seems to be something credible to this notion, and the identification of "tend-and-befriend" has certainly enriched the discussion.

Other research in the emotional domain has shown that, on average, men tend to score higher on measures of

[105] A. Luckow, A. Reifman, and D. N. Mcintosh, "Gender Differences in Coping: A Meta-Analysis" (poster presented to the annual meetings of the American Psychological Association, San Francisco, CA, August 1998).

[106] Shelley E. Taylor, Sally S. Dickerson, and Laura Cousino Klein, "Toward a Biology of Social Support," in *Handbook of Positive Psychology*, ed. C. R. Snyder and Shane J. Lopez (Oxford: Oxford University Press, 2002), 562.

thrill-seeking, risk-taking, and general impulsivity. Conversely, women tend to score higher on measures of seeking to *avoid* harm and exhibiting more "punishment sensitivity."[107] Indeed, women tend to score higher on measures of anxiety in general as well as on various measures of self-control.[108]

In regard to self-image, males tend to score slightly higher on measures of self-esteem from childhood onward.[109] However, when asked specifically about how one feels about oneself in regard to behavioral conduct and moral or ethical considerations, women tend to score somewhat higher than males.[110] In general, though, men tend to report feeling better about themselves than women. For instance, a recent analysis of 71 published studies revealed a consistent though modest difference favoring men on self-compassion. The authors placed this result in context, saying that it "is consistent with past findings that females tend to be more critical of themselves and to use more negative self-talk than males do."[111] This tendency on

---

[107] Lippa, *Gender, Nature, and Nurture*, 12–16; Cross et al., "Sex Differences in Impulsivity."

[108] Hyde, "Gender Similarities and Differences," 388; Lippa, *Gender, Nature, and Nurture*, 12–16.

[109] Hyde, "Gender Similarities and Differences," 388–89.

[110] Brittany Gentile, Shelly Grabe, Brenda Dolan-Pascoe, Jean M. Twenge, Brooke E. Wells, and Alissa Maitino, "Gender Differences in Domain-Specific Self-Esteem: A Meta-Analysis," *Review of General Psychology* 13, no. 1 (2009): 34–45, doi: 10.1037/a0013689.

[111] Lisa M. Yarnell, Rose E. Stafford, Kristin D. Neff, Erin D. Reilly, Marissa C. Knox, and Michael Mullarkey, "Meta-Analysis of Gender Differences in Self-Compassion," *Self and Identity* 14, no. 5, (2015): 512, doi: 10.1080/15298868.2015.1029966.

the part of men to have more positive views of self is not always adaptive, however, as shown by a recent review of the research on narcissism.[112] Across a large body of literature, men have tended to score moderately higher than women on standardized measures of narcissistic personality traits, a finding that has been consistent over the last few decades and across age groups.

When it comes to our relationships with other people, psychological research reveals a number of differences between men and women.[113] On average, women tend to outperform men on their abilities to recognize faces and decode body language. The average woman also tends to engage in much more facial expressiveness, body expressiveness, social smiling, and eye contact in her interactions than does the average man. Conversely, men tend to score higher on the following in their dealings with other people: physical distance in approaching others, physical distance when being approached by others, body restlessness, expansiveness, speech errors, and filled pauses. Women tend to score slightly higher than men on gregariousness (a facet of extroversion) and much higher than men on measures of tender-mindedness. In general, women tend to score higher on the personality trait of agreeableness and on measures of conforming to social influence. On the other hand, men have tended to score higher on measures

[112] Emily Grijalva, Daniel A. Newman, Louis Tay, M. Brent Donnellan, P. D. Harms, Richard W. Robins, and Taiyi Yan, "Gender Differences in Narcissism: A Meta-Analytic Review," *Psychological Bulletin* 141, no. 2 (2015): 261–310, doi: 10.1037/a0038231.
[113] See, for review, Lippa, *Gender, Nature, and Nurture*, 18–26; Hyde, "Gender Similarities and Differences."

of assertiveness and social dominance.[114] Indeed, across a large body of data, men are also more aggressive and physically violent than women. For instance, the United Nations Office on Drugs and Crime commissioned a "Global Study on Homicide," which showed that 95% of all those convicted of homicide worldwide in the most recent year were men, as were 79% of the victims.[115]

Interestingly, research with other primates shows similar figures. For instance, a longitudinal study of chimpanzees and bonobos found that of all instances in which an ape killed another ape, 92% of the perpetrators were male, as were 73% of the victims.[116] In addition, according to data reported to the FBI, at least 78% of all violent crimes in the year 2018 were committed by men.[117] These findings harmonize with psychological research reviewed and analyzed by Archer that shows that males are more aggressive than females from early childhood onward.[118] Male aggression peaks in the late teens and extends through young adulthood, declining in mid-life onward,

---

[114] Lippa, *Gender, Nature, and Nurture*, 16; and Hyde, "Gender Similarities and Differences," 383.

[115] United Nations Office on Drugs and Crime, *Global Study on Homicide 2013*, http://www.unodc.org/documents/gsh/pdfs/2014_GLOBAL_HOMICIDE_BOOK_web.pdf.

[116] Michael L. Wilson, Christophe Boesch, Barbara Fruth, Takeshi Furuichi, Ian C. Gilby, Chie Hashimoto, Catherine L. Hobaiter, et al., "Lethal Aggression in *Pan* Is Better Explained by Adaptive Strategies than Human Impacts," *Nature* 513, no. 7518 (2014): 414–17, doi: 10.1038/nature13727.

[117] These figures were retrieved from https://crime-data-explorer.fr.cloud.gov/explorer/national/united-states/crime on January 5, 2020.

[118] Archer, "Sex Differences in Aggression in Real-World Settings."

which mirrors the rise and fall of testosterone across the male's lifespan. Regardless of the cause, on average, males are more aggressive and, at every stage of development, more likely to be violent than females.

In the area of morality, researchers have long examined how people respond when they are presented with a hypothetical moral dilemma and asked to make a determination about the right course of action and why. Carol Gilligan famously argued that men and women tend to approach such moral dilemmas differently.[119] She contrasted two moral orientations: a morality of justice and a morality of care. The former emphasizes making moral decisions based on rules of fairness and related principles. The latter emphasizes helping those who are in need and upholding responsibilities to care for others with whom one has a relationship. Psychologists Jafee and Hyde conducted a meta-analysis in which they found that across many dozens of studies, women were slightly more likely to employ a care orientation to resolving moral dilemmas, whereas men were slightly more likely to employ a justice orientation.[120] While these differences are small in magnitude, they do fall in the predicted directions across

---

[119] Carol Gilligan, *In a Different Voice: Psychological Theory and Women's Development* (Cambridge, MA: Harvard University Press, 1982), 18–64, 164–74. See also C. Gilligan and G. Wiggins, "The Origins of Morality in Early Childhood Relationships," in *The Emergence of Morality in Young Children*, ed. J. Kagan and S. Lamb (Chicago: University of Chicago Press, 1987), 280–86.

[120] S. Jaffee and J. S. Hyde, "Gender Differences in Moral Orientation: A Meta-Analysis," *Psychological Bulletin* 126, no. 5 (2000): 703–26, doi: 10.1037/0033-2909.126.5.703.

a sizable body of research, suggesting that there is some value to the notion that while men and women can and do utilize both sets of considerations when facing moral dilemmas, there appears to be, on average, a slight preference for women to use a care orientation and men to use a justice orientation.

These tendencies in cognition, emotion, self-image, and relationships likely reflect a complex mixture of biological factors, social influences, and personal choices that continually interact over the course of development. Regardless of their origin, these various tendencies also influence the sorts of academic fields and occupations toward which men and women are drawn, which may in turn further influence some of the tendencies previously discussed. Research shows that adult men tend to be drawn in higher numbers into fields focusing on "things" and "data," such as technology, engineering, and the "hard sciences," whereas women tend to be drawn to fields that are more person-oriented. Using a well-known framework for assessing occupational interests, researchers have shown that, on average, more men are drawn to careers regarded as "realistic" (for example, carpenter, engineer) or "investigative" (professor, lawyer), whereas more women are drawn to careers regarded as "social" (teacher, social worker), "artistic" (musician, artist, designer), or "enterprising" (salesperson, hospitality).[121] Analyzing the results of this body of research, Su and colleagues found that these different preferences reflect large differences between the average man and average woman on the dimension of interest in things

---

[121] Lippa, *Gender, Nature, and Nurture*, 30–33.

versus people, with men scoring much higher on interest in things, and women much higher on interest in people.[122]

This fits well with the theory developed by Simon Baron-Cohen, whose review of research on infants' preferences for looking at faces or objects was discussed earlier. He argues that nature has favored the male brain to excel at "systematizing" (e.g., analyzing data), whereas the female brain has been prepared to excel at "empathizing."[123] While both men and women can and do engage in both systematizing and empathizing, on the whole, a variety of forces beginning with biological factors in the womb encourage our development in these two distinct directions such that, in adulthood, men and women tend to show the relative strengths and interests described earlier.

A related area of research pertains to men and women's religiosity. It is commonly believed in the social sciences that women are more religious than men. For example, sociologist Rodney Stark conducted an analysis of forty-nine different nations using data from the World Value Survey, which asked participants to what extent they consider themselves "a religious person," regardless of whether they attend church. In nearly every country, the results suggested that women are more religious than men.[124] While considering the effects of socialization and

---

[122] Rong Su, James Rounds, and Patrick Ian Armstrong, "Men and Things, Women and People: A Meta-Analysis of Sex Differences in Interests," *Psychological Bulletin* 135, no. 6 (2009): 859–84, doi: 10.1037/a0017364.

[123] Baron-Cohen, *The Essential Difference*, chaps. 4 and 6.

[124] Rodney Stark, "Physiology and Faith: Addressing the 'Universal' Gender Difference in Religious Commitment," *Journal*

the interesting findings of Thompson, who found that religiosity is correlated with feminine characteristics in individuals of either sex,[125] Stark ultimately sided with a biological interpretation of this international sex difference in religiosity. He argued that the different hormones to which males and females are exposed in development and throughout adulthood affect their aptitude for entering into a relationship with God. Specifically, he argued that the copious amounts of testosterone to which men are exposed pushes them toward risk-taking and noncompliance, creating barriers to religiosity.

Sullins, however, published an important article showing that the relationship between sex and religiosity is much more nuanced than Stark's analysis indicated.[126] For instance, Sullins demonstrated that whether women are found to be more religious than men depends somewhat on how the questions are asked and what aspects of religion are investigated. He made a distinction between "affective" (more personal or interior) aspects of religion, such as personal prayer, and "active" (more external, behavioral) aspects of religion, such as belonging to a church, attending church services, and engaging in church activities. Sullins showed that when the more active aspects of religion are assessed,

for the Scientific Study of Religion 41, no. 3 (2002): 495–507, doi: 10.1111/1468-5906.00133.

[125] Edward H. Thompson, Jr., "Beneath the Status Characteristic: Gender Variations in Religiousness," *Journal for the Scientific Study of Religion* 30, no. 4 (1991): 381–94, doi: 10.2307/1387275.

[126] D. Paul Sullins, "Gender and Religion: Deconstructing Universality, Constructing Complexity," *American Journal of Sociology* 112, no. 3 (2006): 838–80, doi: 10.1086/507852.

the sex ratio between men and women begins to balance out and in some cases reverse. He also showed that the tendency for women to be more religious than men is not as universal as Stark suggested. In cultures dominated by Islam or Judaism, the sex ratio tends to be more balanced and, in the case of the "active" aspects of religion (such as attending services), often favors men. Recent data analyzed by the Pew Research Center supports this more nuanced view.[127] While cross-culturally, women were found to be more likely than men to affiliate with a religion and to report praying daily, differences in attending worship services varied across religious groups, with women being more prevalent in areas traditionally dominated by Christianity and men being more prevalent in areas dominated by Islam (Afghanistan and Pakistan) or Judaism (Israel). Thus, it seems that when researchers focus on the personal, "affective" aspects of religion, women predominate, but this difference is minimized or even reversed when focusing on the more public or exterior aspects of religion.[128]

---

[127] Pew Forum on Religion and Public Life, *U.S. Religious Landscape Survey,* June 2008, https://www.pewresearch.org/wp-content/uploads /sites/7/2008/06/report2-religious-landscape-study-full.pdf.

[128] That women's religiosity emphasizes more than men's the aspect of a personal relationship with God fits with findings reported by other research groups as well. For instance, the Pew Forum's 2008 *U.S. Religious Landscape Study*, which involved more than 35,000 American adults, found that the more a given religious denomination emphasizes a personal relationship with God, the higher the proportion of women adherents they tend to have. The religious groups that put less emphasis on such a personal relationship tend to have a higher proportion of male members. At the extreme, 70% of atheists (i.e., those who deny God altogether) in this survey were male.

I began this section by discussing the bodies of men and women and will now conclude by returning to the body and exploring how men and women differ in their sexuality. Despite cultural changes over the last fifty years, research still supports the notion that men are more interested in sex than women are, and men are more frequently the initiator of sexual behavior.[129] In surveys, men score significantly higher on sexual permissiveness, openness to casual sex, openness to premarital sex, and openness to extramarital sex.[130] Men report having more sex than

Similarly, the Baylor Institute for Studies of Religion 2006 report, "American Piety in the 21st Century," included data from over 1,700 adults who were asked questions about their views of God. The responses were categorized according to four different views of God: Benevolent (highly engaged with humanity and warm), Authoritarian (highly engaged and punitive), Critical (low engagement and punitive), and Distant (low engagement with humanity and non-punitive). Women in this study were twice as likely as men to report belief in a Benevolent God. They were also slightly more likely to report belief in an Authoritarian God. Both of these views see God as highly engaged with humanity, thus emphasizing the relational aspect. Conversely, men were more likely than women to report belief in a Critical God or a Distant God, and were almost three times as likely to be atheist as women. See Baylor Institute for Studies on Religion, "American Piety in the 21st Century: New Insights to the Depth and Complexity of Religion in the US," September 2006, https://www.baylor.edu/content/services/document.php/33304.pdf.

[129] Roy F. Baumeister, Kathleen R. Catanese. and Kathleen D. Vohs, "Is There a Gender Difference in Strength of Sex Drive? Theoretical Views, Conceptual Distinctions, and a Review of Relevant Evidence," *Personality and Social Psychology Review* 5, no. 3 (2001): 242–73, doi: 10.1207/S15327957PSPR0503_5.

[130] See Janet Shibley Hyde, "The Gender Similarities Hypothesis," *American Psychologist* 60, no. 6 (2005): 581–92, doi: 10.1037/

women, having more partners, and desiring more partners. Men also report much higher rates of masturbation and pornography use.[131] As Baumeister put it, "Men think about sex more often than women, desire sex more often, desire more partners, like more different sex acts, masturbate more often, sacrifice more resources and take more chances for sex, initiate sex more often, refuse it less often, desire it earlier in the relationship, and rate their own sexual desires as stronger than women's."[132]

Rates of homosexuality, gender dysphoria, and nearly all paraphilias are higher among men than among women as well. In choosing partners, men tend to value physical attractiveness more highly than women do, who, on the other hand, tend to value social class, ambition, intelligence, and character more than men do.[133] Men are also more likely to meet criteria for a sexual addiction.[134]

Beyond these statistical differences, men and women experience their sexuality differently. For many men, the sexual urge is experienced as a drive that needs to be sated, and the relational meaning of sexual activity can be

0003-066X.60.6.581; and Lippa, *Gender, Nature, and Nurture*, 584, table 1.

[131] Hyde, "Gender Similarities and Differences."

[132] Roy F. Baumeister, "Gender and Erotic Plasticity: Sociocultural Influences on the Sex Drive," *Sexual and Relationship Therapy* 19, no. 2 (2004): 136, doi: 10.1080/14681990410001691343.

[133] See Lippa, *Gender, Nature, and Nurture*, 26–30.

[134] Janna A. Dickenson, Neil Gleason, Eli Coleman, and Michael H. Miner, "Prevalence of Distress Associated with Difficulty Controlling Sexual Urges, Feelings, and Behaviors in the United States," *JAMA Network Open* 1, no. 7 (2018), doi: 10.1001/jamanetworkopen.2018.4468.

somewhat of an afterthought. Women, on the other hand, seem to more intuitively grasp the personal and relational significance of sexual involvement. Psychologist Sue Johnson describes these differences well in her book *Love Sense*.[135] She discusses recent research findings suggesting that when exposed to sexual cues, men and women's brains respond somewhat differently. In particular, the self-control aspects of a woman's brain, as well as areas related to attachment, become much more active than in the typical man's brain. In addition, unlike men, who experience sexual desire in a very bodily way, women may not even be conscious of sexual desire, despite showing objective physiological signs of sexual arousal.[136] For women, conscious sexual desire is more likely to come about when she feels safe and connected to her partner rather than simply being physically aroused. Johnson reflects on how women are physically smaller than men and have much more of a personal investment in sexual relations because of the possibility of pregnancy. As a result, women naturally have higher sexual inhibitions, making safety in the relationship and trust in one's partner essential prerequisites to sexual desire. Johnson further explains that the goal of a sexual encounter may be orgasm for a man, but for a woman, the sense of intimacy and closeness may be more important.[137]

---

[135] Sue Johnson, *Love Sense: The Revolutionary New Science of Romantic Relationships* (New York: Little, Brown, 2013).

[136] See also Timm B. Poeppl, Berthold Langguth, Rainer Rupprecht, Adam Safron, Danilo Bzdok, Angela R. Laird, and Simon B. Eickhoff, "The Neural Basis of Sex Differences in Sexual Behavior: A Quantitative Meta-Analysis," *Frontiers in Neuroendocrinology* 43 (2016): 28–43, doi: 10.1016/j.yfrne.2016.10.001.

[137] Johnson, *Love Sense*, 131–35.

Social psychologist Roy Baumeister has further contributed to our understanding of the distinctiveness of female and male sexuality.[138] He has argued that female sexuality is more "plastic" than male sexuality in the sense that it is more amenable to social influence and therefore is more likely to change over time. Baumeister has gathered evidence from many studies indicating that female sexuality is more influenced by education, culture, religion, and relationship status than is male sexuality. In other words, several factors—the extent to which a woman experiences sexual desire, for whom that desire is oriented, whether she engages in sexual behavior, and how she understands her sexuality—all may vary over time and be subject to at least these broad categories of social influence. This fits with Lisa Diamond's longitudinal research on women's sexuality, in which she coined the term "sexual fluidity" to describe the experience of many women in her study who changed how they labeled their sexual orientation over time, often in concert with changes in relationship status.[139] According to her observations, Diamond asserts that this fluidity comes from the fact that women are more likely

---

[138] Roy F. Baumeister, "Gender Differences in Erotic Plasticity: The Female Sex Drive as Socially Flexible and Responsive," *Psychological Bulletin* 126, no. 3 (2000): 347–74, doi: 10.1037/0033-2909.126.3.347; Baumeister, "Gender and Erotic Plasticity."

[139] Lisa M. Diamond, "Female Bisexuality from Adolescence to Adulthood: Results from a 10-Year Longitudinal Study," *Developmental Psychology* 44, no. 1 (2008): 5–14, doi: 10.1037/0012-1649.44.1.5; see also J. Michael Bailey, Paul L. Vasey, Lisa M. Diamond, S. Marc Breedlove, Eric Vilain, and Marc Epprecht, "Sexual Orientation, Controversy, and Science," *Psychological Science in the Public Interest* 17, no. 2 (2016): 45–101, doi: 10.1177/1529100616637616.

to say that they are attracted to the *person* (i.e., the person with whom they are currently in love) rather than the sex of the person (i.e., man or woman).[140]

Here again, we come upon the theme of women being more person-oriented than men, which has shown up in many of the findings described previously. It seems that nature and nurture work together to incline and equip women in a particular way for relationship. In general, women appear more attentive and sensitive to others, are more inclined to connect with and take care of others, cooperate more readily with others, and the like. Men, on the other hand, are blessed with greater physical size and strength and aptitudes for systematizing, which can help them overcome great physical challenges, make analytical discoveries, and find innovative solutions to problems. With proper guidance and support, men's tendencies toward justice, dominance, and aggression can be channeled toward steadfast protection of their values, ideals, family, friends, and nation, as well as relentless pursuit of goals in the face of challenges. This orientation to person can be seen also in religious practice: women seem more readily drawn into personal relationship with God marked by prayer and devotion, whereas men's religiosity, which may be somewhat harder for them to establish, depends on a sense of belonging and active participation. Last, men's sex drive ensures that coupling and reproduction will

---

[140] Lisa Diamond, "What Does Sexual Orientation Orient? A Biobehavioral Model Distinguishing Romantic Love and Sexual Desire," *Psychological Review* 110, no. 1 (2003): 173–92, doi: 10.1037/0033-295X.110.1.173.

happen, whereas women's greater need for safety, trust, and commitment helps increase the chances that children will be brought into the world in the context of a stable, loving family.

These statements, of course, are crude overgeneralizations and meager attempts to make sense of the vast and complex field of study that is the psychology of the sexual difference. Nonetheless, all of this research can help us begin to see how, in light of their similarities and differences, men and women—while sharing enormous similarities—possess distinct profiles of strengths and weaknesses, which can be mutually enriching. In this way, men and women are prepared by nature and nurture to work together for their own good and the good of society.

CONCLUSION: THE MEANING OF THE SEXUAL DIFFERENCE

In seeking to understand the psychology of the sexual difference, we have charted a winding course through different stages of development and a wide range of factors, including the biological, the psychological, and the social. The end result is a dizzying array of findings on how males and females are similar and yet different. What remains is to try to draw some coherent meaning from it all. In this regard, it is useful to step back and ask what the basic meaning of male and female is. Biologically, male and female are defined not strictly by chromosomes, hormones, or other attributes but by the ability to assume the respective roles in reproduction based on the differing structures of the sexual aspects of the body. Indeed, as Mayer and McHugh explain, the underlying basis of maleness and femaleness is the distinction between the reproductive roles of the sexes; in mammals such as humans, the female gestates offspring and the male impregnates the female. More universally, the male of the species fertilizes the egg cells provided by the female of the species. This conceptual basis for sex roles is binary and stable, and allows us to distinguish males from females on the grounds of their reproductive systems, even when these individuals exhibit behaviors that are not typical of males or females.[141]

Thus, in a basic biological sense, the purpose of the sexual difference is to be able to assume one of two roles in reproduction. Broadening our lens to include all of the psychological factors and experiences described in this chapter allows us to grasp a greater vision of the whole. This broadened vision helps us to see that the ultimate meaning of the sexual difference—that is, the ultimate purpose of maleness and femaleness—is *fatherhood* and *motherhood*, not merely in the act of reproduction but in the full sense of a *vocation*.

The various biological, psychological, and social forces at work from conception onward that affect sexual differentiation and maturation are meant to help boys and girls become men and women capable of assuming the roles of father and mother, such that they can draw upon their relative strengths to collaboratively bring new life into the

---

[141] Lawrence S. Mayer and Paul R. McHugh, "Sexuality and Gender: Findings from the Biological, Psychological, and Social Sciences," *The New Atlantis* 50 (Fall 2016): 90, https://www.thenewatlantis.com/wp-content/uploads/legacy-pdfs/20160819_TNA50SexualityandGender.pdf.

world, protect it, nurture it, and, in so doing, leave the world a better place. Indeed, human children need both fathers and mothers to grow up optimally, and abundant research supports this notion.[142] While fathers and mothers are both equipped to provide protection and nurture, they do so in different ways.[143] For example, both mothers and fathers can serve as a safe haven for their children to come to for comfort in times of distress as well as a secure base from which they can draw strength to go out and explore the world. However, interestingly, researchers have observed that in promoting a child's attachment security, the safe haven dimension is most important in relationship with the mother. This dimension, involving responsiveness to the child's distress, is important in promoting attachment security with the father as well. Furthermore, research suggests that with fathers, even more important is the father's ability to challenge and support the child's independence through playful interaction.[144] Thus, while both fathers and mothers can and should be both safe haven and secure base for their children, the way they do so looks somewhat

---

[142] See D. Paul Sullins, "The Case for Mom and Dad," *The Linacre Quarterly* 88, no. 2 (2021), doi: 10.1177/0024363921989491; also W. Bradford Wilcox, *Why Marriage Matters: Thirty Conclusions from the Social Sciences*, 3rd ed. (New York: Institute for American Values, 2011); and The Witherspoon Institute, *Marriage and the Public Good: Ten Principles* (Princeton, NJ: The Witherspoon Institute, 2008).

[143] Palkovitz, "Gendered Parenting's Implications for Children's Well-Being"; Ron D. Parke, "Gender Similarities and Differences in Parental Behavior," in *Gender and Parenthood*, 120–63.

[144] Karin Grossmann, Klaus E. Grossmann, Elisabeth Fremmer-Bombik, Heinz Kindler, Hermann Scheuerer-Englisch, and Peter Zimmermann, "The Uniqueness of the Child-Father Attachment Relationship:

different and has a different emphasis, and children develop most optimally when they are blessed with secure bonds with both an attuned mother and an attuned father.

In short, the similarities between men and women enable them to engage in many of the same roles in regard to protecting and nurturing the young. Yet their differences result in fulfilling those roles in somewhat different manners or with differing emphases, and children benefit from this diversity of experiences with mothers and fathers. The various sex differences observed in this chapter enable mothers and fathers to form a mosaic of complementary strengths that become rich assets for the family they form together and especially for their children. Indeed, for the sake of future generations, we would do well to rediscover the timeless purpose of child-rearing and education—to help boys and girls develop their capacity to be good fathers and mothers.

REVIEW

1. Men and women share a common human nature, show many overlapping qualities, and over time typically move toward greater similarity on a number of levels.

2. While being male or female affects the whole person, some sex differences may be very subtle or impossible

Father's Sensitive and Challenging Play as a Pivotal Variable in a 16-Year Longitudinal Study," *Social Development* 11, no. 3 (2002): 301–37, doi: 10.1111/1467-9507.00202; and Solomon and George, "The Measurement of Attachment Security in Infancy and Childhood."

to quantify, while others, especially those connected to sexual activity and reproduction, are more pronounced.

3. Sexual identity development includes biological factors; family, peer, and sociocultural influences; and one's own thoughts, attitudes, and choices.

4. Genetic, hormonal, and epigenetic factors affect the development of males and females in utero: not only their reproductive systems but also their brain, vulnerability, and behavior.

5. Studies in newborns and adults indicate that females typically show greater interest in people while males show greater interest in things.

6. Boys and girls possess slight differences in the respective strengths of their visual, auditory, and olfactory systems, as well as in the patterns of their brain activity.

7. Boys and girls tend to differ in preferences regarding play style and group setting, tendencies toward aggression and risk-taking, and ability to control impulses.

8. Males are more prone to learning disorders, autism, and conduct disorders, while females are at greater risk for depression and anxiety disorders.

9. Secure emotional attachment to and between parents is very important for child development, including development of sexual identity. Children who experience secure attachment bonds in their family are more likely to be content with their sex and identify with it. Studies of early-onset cases of gender dysphoria show many problems with parental attachment and family dynamics.

10. Older boys and girls naturally segregate into same-sex groups, typically differing in size and structure. Difficulties with such groups can affect normal development of sexual identity.

11. One explanation for same-sex attraction may be childhood patterns of perceiving oneself to be different, for some reason, from members of one's own sex, who can then become objects of erotic attraction at the time of puberty.

12. The legacy of one's attachment to parents or other caregivers in childhood likely plays a role in one's patterns of sexual interest.

13. Men's and women's brains often function differently even if performing the same task. Women's brains appear biased toward more interior, reflective modes of thought, whereas men's brains appear biased toward external perception and action.

14. Cognitively, men and women slightly differ in spatial reasoning and verbal abilities.

15. Emotional expression and recognition, as well as response to emotional distress, tend to manifest differently in men and women.

16. Socially, women and men tend to differ in facial expressiveness, body expressiveness, physical distance from or proximity to others, body restlessness, agreeableness, and assertiveness.

17. Men are more physically violent than women.

18. Women exhibit a slight preference for a "care" orientation toward moral dilemmas, while men incline toward a "justice" orientation.

19. In general, the male brain appears somewhat biased toward systematizing, and the female brain appears somewhat biased toward empathizing.

20. Men and women seem to differ in their inclinations toward various dimensions of religiosity.

21. Men and women differ in their overall interest in sexual activity as well as in their experiences of sexual arousal and attraction.

22. Women seem more inclined and equipped for personal relationship, attentiveness and sensitivity to

others, and connection and cooperation. In calling for safety, trust, and commitment, they increase the likelihood of more stable and loving social environments.

23. Men are inclined and equipped for overcoming physical challenges, for systematizing, analytical discovery, and protection of family and ideals. Their greater sex drive ensures that coupling and reproduction will occur.

24. The ultimate purpose of maleness and femaleness is fatherhood and motherhood, not merely in the act of reproduction but in the full sense of a vocation.

FURTHER READING

Benenson, Joyce F. *Warriors and Worriers: The Survival of the Sexes.* Oxford: Oxford University Press, 2014.

Lippa, Richard A. *Gender, Nature, and Nurture.* 2nd ed. New York: Taylor and Francis, 2005.

McCarthy, Margaret M. *Sex and the Developing Brain.* 2nd ed. San Rafael, CA: Morgan & Claypool, 2017.

Wilcox, W. Bradford, and Kathleen Kovner Kline, eds. *Gender and Parenthood: Biological and Social Scientific Perspectives.* New York: Columbia University Press, 2013.

CHAPTER 4

Are Men and Women Interchangeable? Transgender Surgery and Care for the Self-Identified Transgender Person

Patrick W. Lappert, MD

ONE OF THE DIFFICULTIES we encounter in examining the surgical care of the self-identified transgender person is the tendency to get lost in scientific and technical details of diagnosis and treatment. It is all too easy to forget that the real subject of our concern is a living human person suffering from a real and grievous problem. It involves a sadness so profound that it can cause persons to view their own bodies not as an indivisible part of their personhood but rather as a "thing" that they "have," a "thing" that is felt to be somehow opposed to their "real" personhood. Sometimes that feeling of self-alienation is so profound that the person will seek the help of physicians and surgeons, hoping they can physically overwhelm their own bodies and, in doing so, turn them into a means of personal fulfillment.

We may be tempted to see the transgender person as a caricature of a person, who is nothing more than a collection of disordered desires and whose suffering is of their own making. There is the added temptation to think of the proponents of these ideas of transgenderism—doctors, social activists, legislators—as diabolical, irrational fiends whose chief aim in life is to make a handsome living off the suffering of a severely wounded group of people. In opposing their efforts, we can be tempted to see them also as caricatures, as nothing more than selfish, malevolent liars. This attitude is wrong, however: they are people trying to work for what they believe to be the good of others.

Both of these mis-characterizations are commonplace in our very public discussion of transgenderism, and both of them lack charity. This lack of charity is a direct result of speaking in incomplete truths; for charity is ultimately the perfect love of God, in whom we see the complete Truth. The truth that we seek in our examination of this most profound question on the nature of the human person is more than a complex sum of scientific evidences and philosophical propositions. As Christians, we know that the Truth is actually a person, the God-Man Jesus Christ, and thus it is to him that this conversation must ultimately lead. To love the truth is to love the Lord, and the perfection of that love in us is charity.

Knowing this, we can examine human nature, delving as deeply as we wish into the science that informs the practice of medicine, and we can be confident that there isn't a single detail, no matter how obscure, that could contradict or overthrow our faith and tempt us to think that three millennia of Judeo-Christian thought should be discarded in light of "new scientific evidence." Our confidence should be a source of patience and willingness to endure whatever calumnies might be chosen from that dark and ever-shifting language used to characterize the opponents of transgenderism as "haters" and "phobics." We are not here to win arguments but to win friends to the truth about the nature of the human person, a nature with two distinct and complementary sexes, each completing the other in a union of self-giving love that is the very wellspring of human life.

As we have seen in preceding chapters, many perspectives can be taken on the subject of transgenderism, including the philosophical, biological, and psychological. In this chapter, we will examine the surgical perspective in detail. Specifically, we will address the question of whether one can, by surgically altering the physical appearance of the human body, transform a person's nature as a male or female member of our species. We will also address the underlying premises of this specific medical approach to gender dysphoria in light of the ultimate goal of true and lasting human flourishing.

I. Overview of Surgery

The surgical care of the human person is a work unlike any other. The very idea of entrusting a loved one to the hands of someone who proposes to "make them better" by carefully wounding them always deserves close examination. Even when we are trying to manage lethal conditions, it is important for us to ask, and to have answered, some key questions about the goals of care and the moral implications of surgery: Is this surgery in the best interest of the patient, or are we simply extending suffering?[1] Is this

---

[1] For further considerations regarding end-of-life care, see Jordan Potter, "The Principle of Double Effect in End-of-Life Care," *National Catholic Bioethics Quarterly* 15, no. 3 (2015): 515–29.

human experimentation, or do I have a well-founded basis for believing that the patient will benefit? Are the goals of surgery morally sound? Given that in the particular case of transgender surgery we are on such radically new ground, these questions must be more than just a simple balancing of risk against benefits. Transgender surgery demands examination in light of foundational moral principles about human dignity and our understanding of what it means to use surgery for the good of another person.

In order to fairly judge transgender surgery, we have to build on first principles of how we understand the human person, the principles that guide surgical practice, and the relationship between having the correct diagnosis and making an effective surgical plan. Finally, we must objectively examine the reported medical evidence on the success of transgender surgery in improving the lives of people who are suffering.

II. Perfecting Human Nature

It would be a statement as plain as potatoes to say that "in order to be a good surgeon, you have to begin with a thorough understanding of what a human being is." From the very first hours of medical school, we begin with an examination of the human form in the study of anatomy, and learn of the form's relationship to functioning in human physiology. As you are memorizing the wondrous details of structure, you are at the same time memorizing the wondrous elegance of their functioning. When you memorize the branches of the facial nerve and their course across the face, you simultaneously memorize the names of the muscles that they animate and the movements they produce. When you study the detailed structure of the interior of the heart, you are learning how the order in those structures produces order in the movement of blood, and how a little failure of form will produce particular failures of vital functions.

We learn early on that all of those minute details are somehow important, even if, as students, we don't yet know how or why. We know that we are preparing ourselves to recognize if something is out of place or deformed so that we will know how to restore it. Perhaps a human function isn't going right because something is deformed, or perhaps something has become deformed because some malfunction has changed it. Another early lesson in medical school is that human perfection in form and function isn't a particular number or an exact proportion. Human perfection is a kind of "almost." For example, you could say that the human heart is almost in the middle of the chest; or that the human face is bilaterally symmetrical, almost; or that the aorta runs down the middle of the abdomen, sort of. You can speak of normal blood pressure, just as soon as you realize that it is actually a range of numbers. At the same time, however, you learn that outside that normal variation, human flourishing suffers, and a good doctor must be able to see that.

When I was in the last year of my general surgery residency, I and the two other chief residents were required to write evaluations of the younger surgeons in training. The three of us were struggling to put into words why we had doubts about a particular junior resident. We were agreed that he was a very diligent, reliable medical officer, with an excellent fund of knowledge and good technical skills. One of the chiefs found the perfect words for us when he summarized the situation by saying, "Dr. Smith will make an excellent surgeon, if and when he is able to distinguish health from disease." We had a good laugh until the silence that followed showed us the unassailable wisdom in those words. It is not enough to have memorized all those details about normal structure and function if you lack judgment. Clinical judgment is the ability to separate what matters from what doesn't as you examine a dozen things about a person that are "almost" but not quite right, and to recognize that people can live quite nicely even while they are, by all objective accounts, far from perfect. Clinical judgment is a surgical virtue that stands on a knowledge of details but that doesn't get lost in the details.

Those details of form and function that we learn help us to understand why it is that a person doesn't feel well, and why he or she is unable to live a full life. Sometimes the imperfections are curious and trivial; sometimes they are startling and heartbreaking. Great or small, we see them as real, and we are able to plan for the care of the person by taking definite steps in the direction of human perfection, even while we recognize that we may not actually achieve perfection.

It has been helpful to me, in my thinking about human flourishing in the order of nature (which is the proper domain of medicine and surgery), to consider human flourishing in the order of grace. Recall that the action of God's grace in our lives does not change our nature; it perfects it. Furthermore, God's grace acts in our lives to make saints out of us, and no two saints are alike. We become a lot like each other in terms of the perfection of the virtues, but at the same time, those perfections ultimately reveal our unique and unrepeatable personhood. As the soul is unshackled from sin, it is set free to move in the unfettered response of love, the offering of ourselves freely to God and to neighbor.

So it is with human perfection in our bodily aspect. We do not seek physical perfection so that we can all look the same and move in the same way. Rather, we understand that the restoration of form and function can, in some measure, free persons from particular physical impediments and allow them to move and act with greater freedom and in a less self-conscious way. This un-self-conscious character is one of the defining features of health. Healthy persons are able to direct their energies to the people and things around them without constantly thinking about themselves. It is like the difference between a child singing at the top of his or her lungs without the slightest hint of embarrassment (and to the great delight of their parents), and the same child sitting in sullen silence because of a toothache. Illness and deformity tend to turn us in on ourselves, whereas restoration helps to make us more capable of living for others.

Of course, these are generalizations, and the exceptions are among the most startling pieces of evidence for the supernatural. You need look no further than the stories of Hermanus Contractus (Herman the Cripple) or Blessed Margaret of Costello to see persons with terrible physical disfigurements who lived their lives entirely for others. Conversely, it can be seen that our health- and beauty-crazed culture is producing specimens to rival the perfection of Greek statues, whose hearts are of apparently the same stuff, suggesting an interior deformity that is a poverty all its own.

We always need to remember that in seeking bodily perfection, we have to know when to stop. In the case of our souls, there is no need to set a limit on perfection, because the physician of our souls, the one doing the perfecting, is the infinite God, who knows perfectly their unique dimensions and proportions. However, there is a limit to bodily perfection, and for a couple of reasons. The first is that the surgeon is human and not divine. The second reason is that the quest for physical perfection is easily perverted into a kind of self-obsession that divorces persons from themselves and others, which divides the single human nature; pits reason, free choice, and appetites against the body; and treats our embodied nature as a kind of possession to be dominated. Here we see a kind of forerunner of the transgender anthropology.[2]

III. Rejecting Human Nature

What we shall see as this discussion unfolds is that today there is an apparent willingness to believe that objective

---

[2] We see in this mentality a similarity to the act of idolatry in its most traditional sense. Namely, we take something physical that is somehow under our sway, and we simultaneously exercise total control over it (fashioning it as we like) and worship it. In this case, the "it" is our very self in its bodiliness, which makes the idolatry not only more dangerous morally (since self-love, or pride, is the root of all sin) but also more disastrous humanly (because of the self-contradiction involved: we worship and hate ourselves).

details about the human body do not define a person. In our day, it is very common for people to speak of themselves as "having a body," in the same way that you might have a three-piece suit or a summer dress. In this view of themselves, people even use strongly political language to express this sense of "ownership" over their bodies. This idea is very strongly believed by many, doctors and patients alike. They see the body as being merely the personally "owned" material over which they choose to exercise a kind of therapeutic tyranny, a practice now given the name "gender affirmation surgery."

Living, as we do, in an age that values science and technology for its ability to enhance the freedoms of man, it is paradoxical to find that liberty is now being defined in a way that places it in opposition to objective truth. A particularly striking example has come from the United States Supreme Court: "At the heart of liberty is the right to define one's own concept of existence, of meaning, of the universe, and of the mystery of human life." These words, taken from Justice Anthony Kennedy's writing for the majority opinion in *Planned Parenthood of Southeastern Pennsylvania v. Casey*, show us the profoundly corrosive effect that the materialist worldview has had in this area where medical practice and public law intersect. It seems paradoxical that a materialist worldview would produce such a subjective and radically individualistic view of what it means to be a free human person, yet that is what we now have: a mandate to discard realities for the sake of ill-defined and changeable feelings. As we will see, this abandonment of the truth has severe consequences for the practice of medicine.

It will be helpful for us to begin by examining an area of surgical care that isn't colored by strong cultural biases and political language. We can use this example to establish the language and principles of good surgical decision-making. If we do this first, we will be able to more accurately see how well transgender medicine and surgery meet, or fail to meet, the moral and ethical standards that are common to all medical care.

IV. SURGERY OF THE HAND

I would like to consider the example of hand surgery as a good comparative case, because it involves surgical care of a uniquely human thing. Uniquely human, not merely because of the opposable thumb but because of the relationship that it has to human aspirations and to the sense that people have of themselves. The deep relationship that the hand has to who we think we are and what we think we are called to is important for this discussion. The very word "hand" carries precisely the meaning of the relationship between the aspirations of the soul and the accomplishments of the will: "I had a hand in making that a success." The word even speaks of the ease with which a thing may be made to serve the will in satisfying the desires of the heart: "That pocketknife sure came in handy."

Hand surgery has clear objective and subjective criteria for diagnosis, pre-operative planning, surgical decision-making, and post-operative evaluation of success. Because hand surgery is not burdened with the titanic weight of political language that encumbers any discussion of human sexuality, we can reason like good doctors whose eyes are focused only upon the suffering person who stands before us.[3]

The Hand: Form and Function Par Excellence

Historically, surgery of the hand began as a special area of plastic surgery. For most of human history, surgery has been about the restoration of those parts of a person that are visible. For this reason, most of the earliest recorded surgeries were procedures that we today would call "plastic surgery."[4] Until recently, surgery was something endured out of absolute necessity, rather than something undertaken as a personal self-improvement project. Wounds from combat, hunting, or other accidents were the initial subjects for surgery. Whatever the cause of the injury or loss, once the initial problems of bleeding and infection had been managed, the next question, and the essential question in the mind of the surgeon, became "Can we restore form and function?"

If a man's hand is mangled by a farm tool, for example, causing the loss of his thumb, the first urgency is to

---

[3] Incidentally, even though humanity has seen the hand throughout recorded history as the icon of how our wills apply themselves to the desires of our hearts, the language of gender ideology suggests that the human hand has now been supplanted as the icon of the will. Human sexual expression has now become the central and most essential quality that defines human fulfillment. It would now seem that it is the appearance and employment of one's genitals that has preeminence in that singularly human relationship between the body's physical abilities and our highest aims in life.

[4] Joseph G. McCarthy, *Plastic Surgery*, vol. 1 (Philadelphia: W. B. Saunders, 1990), chap. 1, pp. 2–7.

stop the bleeding and prevent infection. Sometime later, after the wound has healed, the patient will ask, "Will I be able to go back to work? Will I ever have use of my hand again?" We arrive at a moment of decision about whether surgery might be able, in some measure, to restore his hand. To rephrase his question in the language we established earlier, "Can surgery safely and effectively restore what is objectively wrong with his hand, so that his hand might serve him in satisfying the needs of his life and the aspirations of his heart?"

This rephrasing may seem a bit poetic and out of character for the rigorous and technical nature of surgery, but it really isn't. In fact, that balancing of objective truth about what a hand is, and the more subjective and personal aspect of what it means to our particular patient, is typical of hand surgery. We don't just ask ourselves what is objectively wrong with the hand; we have to look at what the loss means to this particular person, because it is a crucial factor in deciding to what lengths we will go to restore it. We also have to bring with us a sober understanding of the likelihood that we will succeed. Recall from our earlier discussion that surgery aims at human perfection, but we never expect to achieve some single ideal outcome, because humanity's natural state is an "almost" kind of thing to begin with. When you add in the effects of surgery, that "almost" gets even more distant. There are always technical shortcomings, problems with post-operative scarring, challenges in rehabilitation, and so on. We do not want to give false hopes, because empty optimism will lead to the most avoidable complication in surgery: disappointment.

Disappointment results when a surgeon fails to

adequately discuss with the patient the possible outcomes, including the possibility of a poor result. Disappointment can also result if the patient does not hear the discussion of the real possibilities due to his attention being occupied by fantastic expectations of the rich and fulfilling life that awaits him after surgery. If the hand surgeon's office and her webpage are covered with images of smiling patients with perfect hands playing violin concertos, the patient will be less likely to be intellectually and affectively present in the consultation room when he is being prepared to give consent for surgery. His mind will be looking forward to what he anticipates will be a success, and the unbounded joy that will surely follow.

So now, let's look at our example case of the man who lost his thumb in the farm implement, and go through the objective details of his loss, as well as the personal dimension of his wound, all of which will guide the choices and inform our expectations of surgery.

Making a Diagnosis

Our patient is a thirty-six-year-old married father of three children. He is an independent family farmer. He is right-hand dominant and has lost his left thumb, which was sharply amputated at its base by the blade of a mowing tool. He has normal sensation throughout his injured hand. His strength and range of finger movement is normal.

He has essentially lost all grip function in his "helping hand," that is, the hand that holds the work steady while his dominant right hand does the job. His left hand holds the two-by-four in place, while his right hand drives the nail; his left hand holds the ledger, while his right hand signs the payroll checks.

In choosing a method for the reconstruction of his hand, the aesthetics of his reconstruction is of comparatively minor importance. Additionally, because his livelihood would suffer greatly by a long recuperation, the method of reconstruction should avoid, if possible, creating new injuries that would prolong the time that he could not be active in the management of his farm operation.

Here is what we mean: A proven method of replacing a missing thumb is to transplant the patient's own second toe, implanting it onto the remaining stump of his thumb. The bones would be joined with small plates and screws, the tendons attached, sensory nerves joined together, and the arteries and veins connected. The result is a fully functional, although somewhat slender, thumb. The price paid would be the loss of the second toe, and the creation of a foot wound that would require a period of immobility to allow that wound to heal properly. Long-term, we would expect the foot to have no real functional deficit.

Another method of replacing the thumb would be to move the index finger of the wounded hand into the thumb position. In this case, the result would be essentially the same, and the only real deficit would be that his helper hand would only have three fingers. This method would not incur the problem of an injured leg. While the injury would be temporary and without any long-term consequences, inability to walk on the foot for ten to fourteen days is a significant price for an independent farmer. In the index-finger-becomes-thumb method, he could get on with his working life while having a bulky splint on his hand for a week, then begin his program of therapy to rehabilitate the reconstructed hand.

The most important difference between the two methods I proposed is what we call the "donor defect": the defect created by the reconstruction. In the case of our farmer, the donor defect from turning his index finger into a thumb is negligible, whereas the donor defect of turning his toe into a thumb is significant. The toe-to-thumb operation produces a donor defect that immobilizes the patient for a period of time.

Both operations will produce an aesthetic result that is imperfect. The first method produces a small, slender thumb and a foot with only four toes. The second method produces a somewhat less slender thumb and a hand with only three fingers. To a married, middle-aged farmer, both aesthetic results are essentially unimportant.

However, consider the same thumb amputation injury to the left hand of a right-hand-dominant, unmarried eighteen-year-old woman in her first year of college, who is studying to be a paralegal assistant. For this patient, a powerful grip is less important right now. The aesthetic appearance of her left hand is of vastly greater importance because that is the hand that all of her friends and family will likely be looking at when she shows them her engagement ring. In her case, we might offer her the option of delaying a definitive reconstruction and for now creating a custom prosthetic thumb that would be non-functional but aesthetically beautiful. Modern prosthetics are startling in their utterly life-like appearance. Whenever she wishes at some later time, if the functional loss becomes too burdensome, she could opt for a reconstruction like our farmer has had.

These examples teach us important lessons about plastic surgery. We began by objectively defining the defect. We were able to do this because we have studied the truth about what a hand objectively is. We learned all those beautiful details of form and function that make the hand such a wonderful instrument of the human intellect and will. Next we analyzed the effect that the defect has on human beings in general terms. We moved in closer to examine how this defect will affect this particular person, both in form and in function. Having fully and particularly characterized the defect, we were then ready to consider methods of reconstruction. We learned that no method of reconstruction is perfect in both form and function, and that surgical planning always involves a trade-off of both form and function. Having selected options for reconstruction, we asked ourselves what the "donor defect" would be, and this issue itself involved trade-offs in form and function.

The result of working our way through these questions in an orderly fashion is that we are more likely to choose methods that, to the best of our present abilities, approaches human perfection as we seek to restore what was lost.

Reconstructive surgery is really an embracing of the true, the good, and the beautiful. The truth is rooted in the functioning of the hand: its range of movement and its power of gripping, pinching, pressing, and caressing. The beauty is seen in the balance of its parts, the cascade of the fingers when the hand is at rest, the exquisite and delicate sensitivity to objects lightly touched, and the heroic calluses of a hand that has faithfully served. In the case of the hand, its goodness is seen in its service to the person who, having seen the true, the good, and the beautiful, has chosen to pursue them.

Gender "Affirmation" Surgery

The name for the surgeries performed on transgender persons has changed over the years. None of the terms have been particularly precise. Initially the term "sex change" surgery was used. This term dates to a time when the word "gender" applied only to grammar. The dimorphism of the human person was simply defined as "sex, male or female." The inaccuracy in the term "sex change" stemmed from the erroneous idea that surgery can actually change your sex, which of course it cannot, as we know from chapter 2: sex is a reality present in every cell, and nearly every tissue, of the body. When that language was in use, the test of a person's sex was as simple as examining external genitalia (a test that has an accuracy greater than 99%); thus it would make the error of calling the surgery "sex change" excusable. Even so, when diagnostic errors were made, they could be spectacular. In an important and sadly ironic sense, dropping the use of the word "sex" in the surgical language is certainly an improvement, given that sterility is the typical result of completed affirmation surgery.

The present use of the term "affirmation" surgery implies that an objective truth is being affirmed. What is actually being affirmed, though, is a collection of personally held beliefs that have no biological reality to support them. The word "affirmation" was chosen not because some new scientific discoveries have made gender measurable, apart from the evidence that has always been there. The transgender condition is entirely subjective, so what is being affirmed is a feeling.

"Transitioning" from biological-sex presentation to the cross-sex presentation is a highly variable process of change. Some persons proceed incrementally over time, while others change over a very brief time. Some persons confine themselves to a few simple changes in name, dress, and mannerisms, while others will continue on to the use of hormonal medications and the whole gamut of surgical procedures.

Historically, this variability has been ascribed to the varying degrees of gender dysphoria (distress over biological sex), and variation in the degree to which the person has been able to manage the distress. The majority of persons with cross-sex identity who suffer from internal distress about that identity do not present themselves for care. Consider the findings of multiple studies which found that a majority of young children with cross-sex self-identity will see these ideas about their sex resolve themselves spontaneously in adolescence.[5] The pro-trans-

---

[5] See, for reference, the desistance rates reported in these studies:

73–94% desistance rate in The World Professional Association for Transgender Health [WPATH], "Standards of Care for the Health of Transsexual, Transgender, and Gender-Nonconforming People, Version 7," *International Journal of Transgenderism* 13, no. 4 (2012): 165–232, doi: 10.1080/15532739. 2011.700873.

88% desistance rate in Kelley D. Drummond, Susan J. Bradley, Michele Peterson-Badali, and Kenneth J. Zucker, "A Follow-Up Study of Girls with Gender Identity Disorder," *Developmental Psychology* 44, no. 1 (2008): 34–45, doi: 10.1037/0012-1649.44.1.34.

63% desistance rate, and examines social factors associated with

gender organization World Professional Association for Transgender Health (WPATH) writes in its most updated guideline,

> In follow-up studies of prepubertal children . . . who were referred to clinics for assessment of gender dysphoria, the dysphoria persisted into adulthood for only 6–23% of children. . . . Boys in these studies were more likely to identify as gay in adulthood than as transgender. . . . Newer studies, also including girls, showed a 12–27% persistence rate of gender dysphoria into adulthood.[6]

Adolescents seem to be a different population, and one study cited by WPATH noted 100% persistence of adolescent transgender identity.[7] However, this small study is

persistence: Thomas D. Steensma, Jenifer K. McGuire, Baudewijntje P. C. Kreukels, Anneke J. Beekman, and Peggy T. Cohen-Kettenis, "Factors Associated with Desistance and Persistence of Childhood Gender Dysphoria: A Quantitative Follow-Up Study," *Journal of the American Academy of Child and Adolescent Psychiatry* 52, no. 6 (2013): 582–90, doi: 10.1016/j.jaac.2013.03.016.

88% desistance rate: Devita Singh, "A Follow-Up Study of Boys with Gender Identity Disorder" (PhD diss., University of Toronto, 2012), Tspace (1807/34926/1).

[6] WPATH, "Standards of Care for the Health of Transgender, Transsexual, and Gender-Nonconforming People."

[7] Annelou L. C. de Vries, Thomas D. Steensma, Theo A. H. Doreleijers, and Peggy T. Cohen-Kettenis, "Puberty Suppression in Adolescents with Gender Identity Disorder: A Prospective Follow-Up Study," *Journal of Sexual Medicine* 8, no. 8 (2011): 2276–83, doi: 10.1111/j.1743-6109.2010.01943.x.

insufficient to conclude that adolescents are a more stable group, as other exploratory studies and cases document adolescents who desist and detransition.[8] While detransitioning has been described since the nineties, current WPATH guidelines do not mention detransitioning.[9]

Among those who experience a persistence in cross-sex self-image, many will discover that they can keep their friends and maintain good relations in their family by acting in sex-typical ways while managing their anxiety by secretly cross-dressing and play-acting. For many, this secret, self-comforting behavior is enough to keep the obsessive cross-sex idea, and the anxiety that it provokes, under control. In a time when transsexualism was more widely considered a psychopathology, there was considerable pressure on these persons to keep "their true self" a secret, and so the content of the obsessive thoughts would be associated with a sense of shame. Such a secret sense of themselves could be carried throughout adult life, only occasionally being discovered.

Consider the many recent examples of what one might call very manly men who suddenly surprise family and friends with the public declaration that they have always

---

8   Lisa Littman, "Parent Reports of Adolescents and Young Adults Perceived to Show Signs of a Rapid Onset of Gender Dysphoria," *PLoS One* 13, no. 8 (August 16, 2018): e0202330, doi: 10.1371/journal.pone.0202330 [published correction appears in *PLoS One* 14, no. 3 (March 19, 2019): e0214157]. See also the Pique Resilience Project, at https://www.piqueresproject.com.

9   A. J. D. Kuiper and Peggy T. Cohen-Kettenis, "Gender Role Reversal among Postoperative Transsexuals," *International Journal of Transgenderism* 2, no. 3 (1998).

thought of themselves as women and now no longer want to "live a lie." Christopher Beck (who now goes by "Kristin") was a farm boy who at age five showed a preference for dressing in girls' clothing and for feminine toys.[10] He was encouraged by his parents toward more masculine pursuits. He attended the Virginia Military Institute, then enlisted in the US Navy. He completed what is considered the most grueling training anywhere in the military, was designated a Navy SEAL, was deployed thirteen times (seven of those deployments being combat deployments), was awarded the Bronze Star with the "V" device, married twice, and fathered two children.

After his separation from the Navy, and with the assistance of a psychologist from Georgetown University, Beck "came out as a woman," telling a news presenter that while he was in the Navy, "no one ever met the real me." He had lived with the secret for over forty years. Considering the exacting investigations required to grant a top security clearance to a Navy SEAL, this was quite a secret.

Stories like Beck's will be more common in the days ahead, after which they will become rare again, largely because the shame associated with cross-sex self-identification is evaporating and is now being replaced with a sense of great heroism. People who have been living a secret transsexual life are now opting to come out in public and are seeking the full support of family, friends, physicians,

---

[10] See Daniel Brown, "Meet Kristin Beck, the Transgender Navy SEAL Hero Fighting Trump's Proposed Trans Ban," *Business Insider,* July 27, 2017, https://www.businessinsider.com/meet-kristin-beck-2017-7.

government institutions (including schools), the military, and the wider culture (including religious institutions). It is now commonplace to see people with very masculine bodies wearing summer dresses, their hair thinned by a lifetime of male hormones but colored brightly and professionally coifed, and struggling to conceal their masculine voice under the affected tones of an older woman speaking as if to a grandchild. Having decided to embrace publicly the cross-sex persona, they begin the process of "transitioning."

V. Transitioning

Transitioning is the name given to the process, whether gradual or abrupt, during which persons change their appearance and their affect, seeking to present themselves as being of the opposite sex. Depending upon how complete the transition, it can be a very expensive proposition. Because the greatest financial costs are medical in nature, the question is raised, "Will my insurance pay for this?"

A tremendous amount of political coercion has been applied to both public and private insurance to make sure that these kinds of medical services will be covered. It is precisely here that the thought processes become alarmingly contradictory. On the one hand, the claim is made that transgender is just an example of the normal variation in the human person and that transitioning is a personal expression of liberty that breaks the chains of old, oppressive cultural forces that limited "gender expression." The problem is that it is hard to make health insurance providers pay for very costly and personal political expressions, particularly if the claim is being made that the patients are healthy and normal.

In order to trigger the insurance processes to pay for medications or procedures, you have to begin with a diagnosis, and the diagnosis has to be supported by "evidence." Once the diagnosis code has been satisfied, the patient is then "authorized" to receive particular care that has an assigned "procedure code." For example, to get a breast reduction paid for, the woman has to be evaluated and found to have large breasts that cause symptoms of back and shoulder pain. If the diagnosis criteria for large breasts cannot be met (with measurements, photographs, and evidence of chronic back pain), then the insurance company will not pay for the surgery.

So the question arises, how can you get an insurance company to pay for surgery on a person who does not seem sick? You invoke a category of suffering that, ostensibly, can be remedied only by medicine and surgery, and that wards off the idea that the person is fine. This suffering is called "gender dysphoria." The diagnosis is a simple one: the person is profoundly sad about his or her apparent gender (sex). How can this be understood to merit medical and surgical intervention, given that such interventions are profound, have medical risk, and are expensive? You have to have something that looks like evidence to support the diagnosis.

Testing the patient for gender dysphoria is the first step in the transition process. The tests seek to establish that there is a dissonance between the person's perception of their masculinity or femininity, and the gender that they were "assigned" at birth. Proponents of this view of sex and gender use the term "assigned" to imply an oppressive process that has no real basis in fact. It adds a political dimension to the question. Examples of these tests of gender dysphoria can be found online, on many websites that purport to help people discover if they are transgender.[11] The questions concern the person's desires regarding gender identity and preferences for cross-sex clothing, mannerisms, opposite-sex friends, and so on. The official tests are not very different.

While these tests can certainly give some idea of how much difference there is between the person's natal sex and their own sense of gender, or of what gender they would prefer to be, none of these tests have any demonstrated predictive value; the tests are unable to predict which patients will benefit from transgender services.[12]

Nonetheless, the results of these tests are used to support a diagnosis of gender dysphoria, which is then used in the billing processes that fund the various treatments. If the patient is a pre-adolescent child, these tests will be used to justify the administration of puberty-blocking drugs. These are given in order to prevent the child from developing secondary sexual characteristics, which the child fears having. In the case of boys, the puberty blockade will prevent the masculinization of the face, including facial

---

[11] See, for example, https://www.psycom.net/adult-gender-dysphoria-test/

[12] Julie Graham, "Guidelines for Psychosocial Assessments for Sexual Reassignment Surgery or Gender Affirmation Surgery: Comprehensive Assessments and Psychoeducation," November 30, 2013, San Francisco Department of Public Health website, https://www.sfdph.org/dph/files/THS/TransgenderHealthServices_MH%20Guidelines.pdf (see esp. p. 5, para. 2).

hair and masculine musculoskeletal development, and it will prevent the lower voice that is the result of growth of the laryngeal structures. Additionally, puberty blockade prevents the growth of the genital structures. In the case of girls, such blockade primarily aims at the prevention of development of the breasts. The professionals who operate gender clinics in pediatric hospitals claim that such therapy "buys time" for the children to reach sufficient personal maturity so that they can "decide for themselves" whether to continue up the ladder of transitioning, including surgeries. It should be noted that this strategy of "buying time" while awaiting intellectual maturity involves using drugs that have essentially unknown effects on brain maturation.

At some point, the clinic will begin the use of cross-sex hormones in an effort to drive physical development in the direction of the gender presentation that the child has chosen. Boys will be given large doses of estrogen hormones, and the girls will be given similarly large doses of testosterone, or "T," to use the popular slang.

While these hormonal interventions are going on, the child will be coached in the development of a cross-sex persona. The name, hairstyle, clothing, speech patterns, and mannerisms are all crafted to affirm the cross-sex identity. It is also at this point that family, friends, school staff, and others are invited into the process. This invitation is extended using an appeal for mercy. Family and friends are reminded at every turn that transgender persons have a very high incidence of self-harm, including suicide. They are told with seeming scientific certainty that the only way to prevent suicide is to help the child develop fully into this new person being crafted. The professionals will speak in very rehearsed language, repeated from one practitioner to the next, of "the journey of self-discovery," in which, through medical and surgical interventions, the child will "uncover who they really are, who they've always known themselves to be." This language is read in patient clinic notes, letters to parents, and on gender clinic websites.

Because the threat of self-harm is always hovering in the background, any effort to offer the child anything other than full support for his or her transition will be labeled as ignorant, hateful, trans-phobic, closed minded, cruel, and uncaring. The WPATH guidelines for the care of transgender children state,

> Treatment aimed at trying to change a person's gender identity and expression to become more congruent with sex assigned at birth has been attempted in the past without success. . . . Such treatment is no longer considered ethical.[13]

Later in the chapter we will show that this assertion is not supported in the scientific literature and that what is called desistance, or reversion to gender expression that is congruent with biological sex, is quite common among children (over 80%) and also very common among adults, where it is described as "transition regret."

One of the essential features of the WPATH Standards of Care is that much of it is devoted to defining who is competent to render an opinion on the direction

---

[13] WPATH, "Standards of Care for the Health of Transgender, Transsexual, and Gender-Nonconforming People."

that care should take. In essence, the document defines as competent only those persons who not only have the credentials in psychology, psychiatry, and counseling but also a priori agree with the primary informing principle of WPATH—namely, that persons who are gender nonconforming, transsexual, or transgender are not suffering from a psychological problem. Rather, such persons must be seen to be suffering from an error of *gender assignment at birth*, and interior anguish caused by a world that does not understand *their true self.* If the professional does not see the patient in that light, then by definition he has not been adequately trained and is therefore not qualified to offer an opinion.

What began as an invitation to participate through an appeal for mercy quickly becomes a compulsion to cooperate in the whole process, even to the exclusion of parental prerogatives. The clinics that provide these interventions are well versed in the language used to accuse parents and family of child abuse, and family law courts are quickly called in to compel cooperation from parents while holding the threat of loss of custody over their heads.

It should be clearly understood that puberty blockade in otherwise healthy children has long-term consequences with which no one has any experience. These drugs have long been used in the care of children suffering with precocious puberty; however, that condition is a medical pathology with well-characterized and often severe consequences. Puberty-blocking drugs suppress the effects of an over-production of sex hormones so that functionally the child will develop in a more normal internal hormonal environment. The self-identified transgender child, on the other hand, is hormonally normal. In these children, puberty blockade is shutting down a normal process in the hope of forcing physical development in the unnatural direction of the opposite sex. There is no body of evidence to support the safety of such interventions, and there is a mountain of evidence showing that normal hormonal signaling is essential for everything from musculoskeletal maturity to neuromotor development, immune competence, and psychosexual development. What we are witnessing in this medical treatment is nothing less than human experimentation, performed on persons who could not possibly give informed consent. Even if they were legally competent, all that could rightly be offered in the way of pre-treatment counseling is "We don't know the long-term effects of these treatments."

Depending upon the age and desires of the person, surgeons may be consulted. Surgical interventions include a range of procedures, some of them comparatively simple and reversible, others very complex and irreversible. In the case of younger males who have entered into transgender clinics, the effects of puberty blockade and cross-sex hormones will have had varying degrees of success in preventing the development of secondary sex characteristics, such as facial hair and a deepening voice and more robust musculoskeletal development. If cross-sex hormones started later in development, or if the treatment has not been sufficiently effective, efforts will be made to feminize the face using various surgical procedures. The use of lasers to permanently destroy facial hair, surgery to "shave" the laryngeal cartilage (Adam's apple), nose surgery to feminize the nose, surgery to reduce the dimensions of the jaw, and hair transplantation to achieve a more feminine hairline are among procedures commonly done for males seeking to present themselves as females.

To this list we can add breast augmentation using implants. The cross-sex hormones will produce varying degrees of breast tissue development but rarely produces sufficient development to satisfy the desire to be unequivocally feminine in appearance.

In the case of females, puberty blockade in early development followed by cross-sex hormones will have had variable success in masculinizing the body, including the development of facial hair, deepening the voice, and suppressing breast development. Depending upon the age at which these measures are started, and the person's underlying genetics, the person may seek masculinizing interventions.

It is now a very common practice to refer girls who self-identify as transgender in mid-teens for surgical removal of their breasts. Subcutaneous mastectomies are increasingly being performed on girls who are not of the age of consent, based upon the recommendation of transgender clinics. This is not a reversible procedure. The operation results in the permanent loss of the girl's ability to breastfeed. The breast mound can be reconstructed, as we do for women who have undergone mastectomy for cancer care, but what is being reconstructed is a breast mound, not a breast gland. The construct is not capable of producing nourishment for a baby.

Decisions about genital surgery are highly variable, perhaps because they are related to a much more private aspect of the person's life. Whereas the "top" surgeries affect how the person is perceived by strangers, casual acquaintances, and co-workers, "bottom" surgery is about the private side of life. Additionally, transgenderism has great variability in terms of the "object" of sexual attractions, as well as the role that self-perception plays. Male-to-female transgenders who are attracted to men (androphilic) are more likely to transition early. Surveys of the age at which a person was first prescribed cross-sex hormones show that male-to-female subjects tend to be younger.[14] Male-to-female transgenders who are autogynephilic—that is, they are sexually aroused by the idea of themselves as women, but not particularly attracted to men—appear more likely to transition later in life.

Overall, female-to-male patients are more likely to have genital surgery than male-to-female patients are. The number of patients who undergo these surgeries has increased dramatically over the past several years. Statistics from the American Society of Plastic Surgery in the years 2016–2017 show an increase of over 280% for women seeking to present as men, and a more modest, but still startling, increase of 41% for men seeking to present as women.[15] This variability in motivation for genital surgery may stem from the fact that in the case of female-to-male, the ability to urinate standing up, or shower in the public

[14] Ian T. Nolan, Christopher J. Kuhner, and Geolani W. Dy, "Demographic and Temporal Trends in Transgender Identities and Gender Confirming Surgery," *Translational Andrology and Urology* 8, no. 3 (June 2019): 184–90, doi: 10.21037/tau.2019.04.09.

[15] American Society of Plastic Surgeons (ASPS), "2017 Plastic Surgery Statistics Report," https://www.plasticsurgery.org/documents/News/Statistics/2017/plastic-surgery-statistics-full-report-2017.pdf.

gym, makes what would otherwise be a private matter more public.

Clearly, the surgery is associated with a desire for a life in which the sexual self is visible to the patient and to the world in a particular way. Ironically, some sense of maleness and femaleness is surely acknowledged and is either desired or rejected, but not in its fullness. What we have here is typically a desire for a sexual self not for the sake of others but for the sake of oneself. The psychological literature is constantly re-writing the diagnostic criteria for transgender on the basis of these interior desires of the patient.

For example, a male-to-female transgender may be seeking sexual intimacy with a "heterosexual" male; he may be seeking to live as a woman among women, having "lesbian" sexual relations; he may be seeking to live as a highly feminized boy who is still in possession of functioning male genitalia, who lives in the company of homosexual men; or he may be seeking merely to see himself as a woman whose sexual life is solitary, or even celibate.

Similar examples can be found among female-to-male transgender persons. Sometimes the complexity of the paraphilias can be startling. Take the case of Dr. Richard Curtis, who at one time operated the largest private transgender clinic in the United Kingdom.[16] Dr. Curtis was born Vanda Zadorozny, the daughter of a miner from West Yorkshire. The doctor describes herself as "a gay man

[16] See David Batty, "Doctor Under Fire for Alleged Errors Prescribing Sex-Change Hormones," *The Guardian*, Guardian News and Media, January 6, 2013, https://www.theguardian.com/society/2013/jan/06 /transexualism-gender-reassignment-richard-curtis.

trapped in a woman's body." Curtis underwent the full surgical transition from female to male in appearance, thus
presenting as a "homosexual male."

In addition to the variability in the motivation for
surgery, there may be financial issues that affect decisions
concerning transitioning. Most of the surgeries are very
expensive and would therefore be out of reach for any but
the wealthy. As political pressure is applied to private
and public insurance companies, the financial barrier to
transitioning is being lowered. Aggressive pressure on
insurance companies and legislative bodies that regulate
health insurance has been a key part of the operation of
transgender clinics.

The Surgeries: Male-to-Female (MtF)

The most common "bottom" surgery, or genital surgery,
done to change a biological male into the appearance of a
woman involves the inversion of the penis.[17] In this technique, incisions are made on the underside of the penis,
and the erectile tissues (corpora) are removed, essentially
leaving only the skin of the penis, and the glans (tip). The
scrotum is opened, and the man is castrated. The incision

---

[17] For an overview of penile inversion, see R. Rossi Neto, F. Hintz,
S. Krege, H. Rubben, and F. Vom Dorp, "Gender Reassignment
Surgery—A 13 Year Review of Surgical Outcomes," *International
Brazilian Journal of Urology* 38, no. 1 (2012): 97–107, doi: 10.1590/
s1677-55382012000100014; and Sirichai Kamnerdnakta and
Nuttorn Boochangkool, "Five-Year Review Outcome of Microvas-
cular Free Flap in Siriraj Hospital," *Journal of the Medical Association
of Thailand* 98, no. 10 (2015): 985–92.

in the penis is closed, and the structure is pushed up into the pelvis and suspended from the sacrospinous ligament, essentially creating a receptive sleeve made from the skin of the penis. The skin of the scrotum is fashioned into labial structures, arranged around the neo-vaginal opening. The urethra is essentially shortened down to an opening at the upper part of the neo-vagina.

During this inversion operation, one of the goals is the preservation of tissue that produces erotic feelings. It is important that the skin of the glans, and the nerves that supply it, be protected from surgical injury, in the hope that future sexual activity will elicit sexual pleasure. The degree to which this succeeds varies, but in general one can expect a degradation in sensation coming from skin that has been subjected to radical changes in shape and position. It should also be noted that sensations coming to the brain from those areas have been "mapped" on the brain; that is to say that the brain understands that stimulation of those nerves means that the penis is being stimulated, even though the penis has been essentially removed. (This is akin to phantom limb phenomena, in which an amputee feels as though the missing hand is still there when the stump of the arm is bumped.) In time the patient will tend to "re-learn" to varying degrees, but very often MtF patients will describe sexual activity as if their penis is in the wrong place. Many report the capacity for orgasm significantly changed in certain respects from what they used to experience, often requiring very special circumstances to achieve and many times only as a result of masturbation.

It should also be noted that normally the skin of the penis achieves and maintains the dimensions associated with intercourse precisely because of the blood-filled erectile tissue that it envelops. Because those erectile tissues are removed during inversion surgery, there is no longer anything working to sustain the dimensions of the penile (now neo-vaginal) skin. For this reason, the MtF transgender needs to constantly mechanically dilate and elongate the neo-vagina; otherwise, it will shrink down to a small mass of empty skin.

An alternative operation, and one that is showing some signs of increase in frequency, is the use of a segment of colon to create the neo-vagina. This operation isolates a segment of the transverse, or rectosigmoid, colon, and rotates it down into the pelvis while keeping it attached to its native blood supply. The continuity of the gut is re-established in exactly the same way one would if you were removing a segment of colon in a cancer operation. The segment of colon is then sewn along the open edges of the scrotum, which itself was divided when performing the castration and which now becomes the labia. This operation has the advantage that the colon is a tube that wants to remain a tube, and it generally keeps its dimensions. Additionally, the colon is lined with cells that secrete mucus, which tends to provide protective lubrication. One of the reasons this operation is increasing in frequency is that we are now several years into the widespread use of puberty-blocking drugs in children. Those drugs massively inhibit the growth of the penis, and therefore there typically isn't sufficient tissue for any meaningful penile inversion operation.

Evaluation of success in such an operation is very difficult. Reports of collected cases from individual centers is typical, and they often show significant self-selection bias (the happy patients come back for follow-up, the unhappy ones don't). Most studies follow patients for only a few years. The initial motivation for surgery can be seen to be important in evaluating success. If the person just wanted to not have to look at a penis while getting dressed for the day, then "success" would be expected to be high, given the nature of the surgery. If the goal of the patient was to find and marry a "heterosexual man" and have frequent, satisfying marital relations without ever being reminded of once having been a normal man, this outcome would be in the "highly unlikely" category.

The Surgeries: Female-to-Male (FtM)

Most women seeking surgical transition will elect to have all internal reproductive structures removed with a hysterectomy (removal of the uterus) and bilateral salpingo-oophorectomy (removal of the Fallopian tubes and ovaries). Women seeking to present themselves as men will see varying degrees of effect from cross-sex hormones on the appearance of their external genitalia. Testosterone will tend to enlarge the clitoris—the clitoris in the female is the embryological analog of the penis in the male—but to a varying extent. One of the surgeries often chosen is called metoidoplasty. In this procedure, tissues are re-arranged on the undersurface of the clitoris to lengthen the urethra, so that it opens near the tip of the clitoris, enabling the patient to stand to urinate. Additionally, the labia majora (the embryological equivalent of the scrotum) can be modified and joined in the midline beneath the neo-phallus, to simulate a scrotum. Prosthetic implants can be placed in the neo-scrotum to simulate testicles. The overall result is of a small neo-phallus that retains erogenous sensation, but is generally incapable of penetrative intercourse.

Women seeking to present themselves as men who are capable of penetrative intercourse will generally opt for surgeries that produce a neo-phallus of sufficient dimensions into which malleable prosthetics can be placed that make the neo-phallus sufficiently rigid to permit penetration. These procedures are generally termed phalloplasties.[18]

The particular operations are varied, but all involve the importing of skin and soft tissue from the lower abdomen, the inner thigh, or the forearm. Efforts are made to preserve or establish the blood supply to sustain the tissue, and to preserve or establish sensory nerve supply that can be incorporated into local nerves. The skin is cut in patterns that when sewn together will produce an outer tubular phallus as well as an inner skin-lined tube that will serve as a neo-urethra that can be connected to the native

---

[18] For an overview of phalloplasty techniques and complications, see Aaron L. Heston, Nick O. Esmonde, Daniel D. Dugi 3rd, and Jens Urs Berli, "Phalloplasty: Techniques and Outcomes," *Translational Andrology and Urology* 8, no. 3 (2019): 254–65, doi: 10.21037/tau.2019.05.05; American Society of Plastic Surgeons, "Complications of Penile Reconstruction Surgery Differ for Transgender Patients," press release, January 30, 2018, https://www.plasticsurgery.org/news/press-releases/complications-of-penile-reconstruction-surgery-differ-for-transgender-patients; and Min Suk Jun and Richard A. Santucci, "Urethral Stricture after Phalloplasty," *Translational Andrology and Urology* 8, no. 3 (2019): 266–72, doi: 10.21037/tau.2019.05.08.

urethra at the base of the clitoris. The clitoral tissue is preserved and arranged at the base of the neo-phallus with the goal of preserving erogenous sensation. The malleable prosthesis can be placed within the constructed neo-phallus, producing what amounts to a permanent erection that can be pointed in any direction desired, depending on whether the person is dressing for the day, urinating, or attempting copulation.

Common Problems: Male-to-Female

In addition to the risks associated with any surgery, there are some complications that occur with some frequency in male-to-female plastic surgeries.[19] As described in the previous section, the neo-vagina does not have any intrinsic tendency to maintain its desired dimension and so must be maintained by frequent (sometimes daily) mechanical dilation. The suture lines along which the penile skin was closed during the construction are lines of comparative mechanical weakness. The best that one can hope for in terms of strength in a surgical scar is only 40% as strong as the native skin. Given the vigor of mechanical trauma that this skin might experience during penetrative intercourse, erosions of the skin are common. If the resulting wound develops into a full-thickness wound, it can lead to lower pelvic infections, and sometimes wounds that communicate with the rectum (recto-vaginal fistula).

If the neo-vaginal construct uses a segment of colon, although the lining is lubricated by the normal mucosal

[19] See Rossi et al., "Gender Reassignment Surgery—A 13 Year Review."

secretions, the colon itself is not structurally capable of resistance to repeated and vigorous mechanical trauma in the way that true vaginal lining is. The colon is lined with cells whose main function is the absorption of fluid from the fecal bolus, regulating the bacterial composition of the contents (gut flora), and providing an immunologic barrier to bacteria.

When the lining of the gut is subjected to chronic, repeated irritation and injury, as one would expect in penetrative sexual activity, it has a tendency to change in self-protective ways. As an illustration, consider the familiar problem of acid reflux in the esophagus. The esophagus is lined with cells that provide excellent mechanical protection from the sorts of rough textured things that people like to chew and swallow. The stomach, to which the esophagus connects, is a reservoir in which strong acids help in the initial breakdown of foods. The stomach is lined with cells that secrete acids and are capable of resisting the effects of those acidic fluids. The worlds of the esophagus and of the stomach are kept separated by muscles (lower esophageal sphincter) that keep those acids where they belong. But if the sphincter is unable to keep things separate, the acids will reflux into the esophagus (heartburn). Over time, this chronic reflux will cause the cells that line the esophagus to look less and less like esophagus cells, and start looking more and more like stomach lining cells. This process of change in response to chronic irritation and injury is called *metaplasia*. If you examine these tissues under the microscope, you will see esophagus cells, and you will see stomach cells, but you will also see cells that aren't really one or the other. The name for those cells is *dysplastic*, meaning that they lack some of the defining characteristics of either. Whenever you see dysplasia, you are seeing cell lines that have an increased likelihood of degeneration into cancer cells. There are many things that affect the likelihood that dysplastic cells will degenerate into cancer, including the vigor or the patient's immune system, the chronic nature of the irritation, and the specific nature of the irritation.

Dysplastic changes in the lining cells of the neo-vagina are being reported with increasing frequency. Among the dysplasias that often occur in the tissues of the neo-vagina are those associated with human papilloma virus (HPV)—the same virus that is associated with cervical cancers in women—as well as those that cause dysplastic growths such as condylomata. There are many case reports, and a growing body of epidemiologic studies on malignancies of varying aggression, including squamous cell carcinoma (sometimes called *erythroplasia of Queyrat* when it occurs on the penis, but simply referred to as squamous carcinoma in situ when found in the neo-vagina), as well as reports of more aggressive and widely spreading squamous cell cancer.

As explained earlier, the patient's ability to resist developing such cancers is affected by the general state of the immune system. Persons with repeated sexually transmitted infectious diseases and those who are habituated to the use of drugs, particularly drugs that have toxic effects on the liver (which includes the high-dose sex hormones used to maintain cross-sex appearance), would be expected to have some degree of immunosuppression, and so would be expected to have an increased likelihood of cancers, such as those described previously. At present these findings are still at the level of case reports, and small epidemiologic studies.

Common Problems: Female–to–Male

In FtM (female-to-male) transgender persons, a recurrent problem is the development of urinary strictures caused by scarring of the neo-urethra in FtM transgender persons.[20] These strictures can also be associated with fistulae, or leaking holes along the length of the neo-urethral construct, which would require re-operation.

Any time that a synthetic prosthetic device is used in plastic surgery, as in the use of a malleable implant that permits penetrative sexual activity, there is a risk of infection of the implant, and its subsequent eroding through the skin. This is a risk associated with the use of such implants, whether they are used in transgender surgery or in the care of men with erectile dysfunction.

There can also be problems associated with the "donor defect" in FtM transgender patients. For example, if the forearm is the donor area for the construction of the neo-phallus, in addition to the significant aesthetic deformity of the arm, there can be incidental injuries to nerves, muscles, and tendons of the arm that may produce functional losses of sensation and movement in the hand as well.

Virtually all of the problems discussed in these sections

---

[20] See Austin C. Remington et al., "Outcomes after Phalloplasty: Do Transgender Patients and Multiple Urethral Procedures Carry a Higher Rate of Complications?," *Plastic and Reconstructive Surgery* 141, no. 2 (2018): 220e–229e, doi: 10.1097/PRS.0000000000004061; also Jun and Santucci, "Urethral Stricture after Phalloplasty."

can truthfully be characterized as technical shortcomings. They will decrease in frequency and severity as the level of experience and training among transgender surgeons improves. This has been the consistent history of plastic surgery. There is no reason to suppose that "gender affirmation" surgery will be the exception.

VI. The Bigger Picture

Even though the problems associated with the various medical and surgical interventions described earlier are thought by many to be morally neutral technical problems, there is a larger question that cannot be so easily dismissed.

Transgender surgery has as its foundational principle the idea that it is legitimate to utterly destroy a human capacity, in this case the reproductive capacity, for the sake of producing a counterfeit structure in order to satisfy a subjective desire. The surgeon who performs such an operation is essentially saying that it is morally legitimate to destroy reproductive parts and replace them with structures that merely look like reproductive parts. A neo-phallus produced from forearm tissue is not a penis. It is a tube of flesh made to look like a penis. You have not turned a woman into a man. A neo-vagina produced by castration and mutilation, followed by inversion of the penile skin, is not female genitalia. It is a sleeve of soft tissue that can be used for receptive copulation. You have not turned a man into a woman.

These types of surgeries cannot be considered reconstructive surgery, because you are not restoring something that was missing at birth or lost through injury. These surgeries are producing counterfeit structures that were never a part of the nature of that person to begin with, and surgeons are doing it by actually destroying structures that were part of the nature of the person. Reflecting back on our discussion earlier, the "donor defect" from transgender surgery is total mutilation of the genitalia and loss of the reproductive capacity in order to produce a counterfeit structure.

The situation reminds me of a popular thought-problem that circulated around academic plastic surgery training programs. It was a thought-problem used to test the knowledge of plastic surgeons in training, challenging them to look into their total fund of knowledge of techniques and technology. As they did so, the attending surgeon would get to see how knowledgeable and inventive the surgeon-in-training was. Here is the thought-problem:

An otherwise perfectly healthy young man comes to your office seeking consultation. He has limitless money to make his desires a reality, and he has absolutely no health problems. He tells you, "Doctor, ever since I was a little boy I have had a recurring dream that I can fly. Almost every night, I dream that whatever else is happening in my dream, when I wish to, I can leap into the air, and by the movement of my arms, I can fly above the world. I am convinced in my soul that I am born to fly of my own power. Can you make my dream a reality? Can you turn my arms into wings?"

At this point in the thought-problem, the attending surgeon will ask the resident-in-training, "How would you use plastic surgery to turn a man's arms into wings?" And so the oral examination of the surgeon-in-training begins.

"Well," they might begin, "we would need to greatly lengthen the limbs to have sufficient span to lift the man. We could use Dr. Ilizarov's technique of bone lengthening using corticotomy and distraction osteosynthesis."

Another resident might chime in, "I think we would be aiming at a wing more like that of a bat rather than a bird. After lengthening the arm bones by distraction, we could use soft-tissue expansion along the back of the arm to create a broad, thin, soft tissue membrane. The blood supply would be enhanced by the expansion process, and the skin on that part of the arm is very pliant and smooth." To his satisfaction, the attending might reply, "Excellent! But what if he insists that he wants to be more bird-like; that he has a loathing for bats? What then?"

"Well, there is some interesting work being done at UC Santa Barbara that has isolated the gene sequence, common to all birds, that is responsible for differentiating skin cells into feathers. You could harvest the patient's adult stem cells, gene-splice the sequences from the bird, induce differentiation after micrografting them into the wing membrane that you created through tissue expansion, and your new wing would have feathers." The attending surgeon would now be very keen to hear more about this latest science that was not available when he was in training. "Tremendous! Do you think you could control the color of the feathers the same way?"

And so the thought-problem goes until the depth of

the trainee's knowledge has been tested. What is never discussed, because no one is particularly interested, is the life of the patient upon whom you have been working your plastic surgery wonders. Who is this young man who came to you with his persistent dream, and limitless money, seeking help? Even if all of the technical challenges of the transformation have been met, where is the patient now that he can fly whenever his spirit desires to rise?

Birds would certainly avoid such a flying man, and he would struggle to keep the company of people. His nature has been so changed that he is now alone with his dream. He can't feed himself with his hand, because it now serves to spread a wing. He must feed himself by placing his face in the bowl, and he will have to feed himself this way quite often because flying burns massive amounts of calories. He can't run the bath to wash himself; he must bathe in large outdoor pools. He can't use the bathroom. He can't even put on a pair of pants.

What was missing from our thought-problem, and what appears to be missing from the whole transgender surgery conversation, is the way in which the morality of medical and surgical care must rest upon the true nature of the person. Can a man dream that he is really a woman? That is not in question; that is a fact. Can he believe it to the depth of his soul? Clearly. Can the persistence of that thought affect his ability to live a happy and integrated life? Sadly, yes it can. Is plastic surgery able to make that man look just like a woman? Absolutely, and it's getting better at it by the minute. These, however, are all the wrong questions.

The Appeal from Sentiment

As all of the arguments against transgender medicine and surgery build, and as it becomes more and more apparent that the essence of transgender surgery amounts to a mutilation (the willful destruction of healthy structures of the body), and as we prepare to abandon such procedures, we are called back by a very powerful argument in favor of transgender surgery. It is an argument with so much power that you will find it presented whenever transgender medicine and surgery are discussed. This is how the argument goes:

People who experience gender dysphoria, that is to say, people who are distressed because their internal sense of their own gender does not agree with the gender they were "assigned at birth," have a very high incidence of self-harm. Transgender persons, regardless of where you find them, and as demonstrated by study after study, have a roughly 40% likelihood of suicide. That is an unimaginably high risk of death. There is nothing to compare with it. Returning war veterans with PTSD and rape victims each have about a 27% risk of suicide. It is startling to consider that the transgender person is suffering from emotional wounds that vastly surpass the effects of prolonged combat and rape.

Given the undisputed fact of a 40% suicide rate, it is then rightly argued that the condition of transgender demands action. Our squeamishness about the surgery is unimportant in light of that reality. Who cares if you choose to call the surgery a mutilation? If it saves the life of the person, it is morally justified, if not morally commanded. After all, a leg amputation is technically a mutilation. Cutting off a man's leg means the life-long compromise of the human power of walking, and it is obviously disfiguring, but if amputating a gangrenous leg saves his life, no one even raises an eyebrow. Isn't transgender surgery standing on exactly the same moral ground, given that it is a life-saving intervention? How could you possibly oppose it?

Study of the Studies

Understanding the medical literature is crucial. Before entering into that part of our discussion, I would like to reassure the reader that if your common sense is in stark disagreement with the opinions of experts, please do not abandon your common sense. The world is groaning under the weight of expert opinion, and it does not look to be in better order or a whit happier today than it was fifty years ago. Nonetheless, evaluating the power of a scientific study and the truth claims made by the researchers is not a simple matter. There is a whole area of investigation that literally amounts to the science of science. It is an area of study that looks into the way in which information is gathered, sorted, tabulated, and evaluated. It allows you to read a scientific paper and evaluate its ability to make claims about the nature of things. It is a very important part of the process of medical advancement because it allows you to separate the truth from the biased opinions that are the danger of every area of study and human improvement.

In the area of transgender medicine, this study of the studies is a very frustrating process because of the type of data presented and the startling certainty of the claims that are made. I would strongly recommend a document called "Sexuality and Gender: Findings from the Biological,

Psychological, and Social Sciences," by Lawrence Mayer and Paul McHugh.[21] It is available to read online, and for the layperson it is a tremendous help. It evaluates a total of five hundred scientific papers in epidemiology, genetics, endocrinology, psychiatry, neuroscience, embryology, and pediatrics. Dr. Mayer's specialty is in evaluating the power of scientific papers.

What they found is that the vast majority of transgender scientific papers in all these areas of study are of very low quality. They suffer from small sample sizes, ill-defined criteria for inclusion of patients, vague criteria of measurement, poor follow-up, short study duration, self-selection by the patients, and so on. The five hundred papers evaluated in this publication were the best that could be found. I will address their findings shortly.

In 2011 an important study was published in Sweden that looked into the long-term results of completed transgender surgery.[22] It is a crucial paper for several reasons. The first and perhaps most important strength of the article is that the findings are based on very long-term evaluations of data from a national database that is able to track patients throughout the whole of their lives. In

---

[21] Lawrence S. Mayer and Paul R. McHugh, "Sexuality and Gender: Findings from the Biological, Psychological, and Social Sciences," *The New Atlantis* 50 (Fall 2016): 90, https://www. thenewatlantis.com/wp-content/uploads/legacy-pdfs/20160819_ TNA50SexualityandGender.pdf.

[22] Cecilia Dhejne, Paul Lichtenstein, Marcus Boman, Anna L. V. Johansson, Niklas Långström, and Mikael Landén, "Long-Term Follow-Up of Transsexual Persons Undergoing Sex Reassignment Surgery: Cohort Study in Sweden," *PLoS One* 6, no. 2 (February 22, 2011): e16885, doi: 10.1371/journal.pone.0016885.

Sweden all medical treatment events from before birth until the end of life—whether in a small clinic, a prison infirmary, the military, an urban emergency room, or a psychiatric hospital—are recorded in the same database using the same criteria. The database is even aware of identity changes, which is important in transgender care. The database can be used to compare persons from the same demographic to see who is getting better, getting worse, or staying the same.

The second important strength of the article is that it is showing us the effects of transgender surgery in a culture that has been affirming of gender nonconforming persons for a very long time. For this reason, the findings from that study cannot be dismissed by claiming that the outcomes were affected by "transphobia" in the population, or "lack of inclusion of trans persons in society."

What the study shows is that persons who complete transgender surgery will indeed see the risk of suicide drop down to the level of the general population cohort. Transgender surgery appears to save transgender persons from self-harm and suicide. The effect, however, is short-lived. If you evaluate post-surgery transgender persons for only five or six years, things look very positive. At around eight years after surgery, the suicide rate begins to climb swiftly and by twenty years post-op is back to the alarmingly high levels seen without surgery.

Looking more deeply in the data, when you compare all sex-reassigned persons (male-to-female and female-to-male) with people who are matched to them by year of birth, and birth sex, you find that the transgender person has a risk of suicide that is 19.1 times higher than the control group. If you look only at persons who transitioned from female to male presentation, the risk of suicide is 40 times higher than in the control group. You also see the alarmingly higher likelihood of substance abuse, psychiatric hospitalization, and involvement in crimes of violence.

The findings of this study from Sweden go a long way toward helping us understand why so many doctors, therapists, and counselors have expressed support for transgender surgery. It is because these providers have seen only small case reports that follow the patients for just a few years. They do not have any airtight mechanism for tracking down all the patients, even the ones who disappeared from the study because of inability to travel, incarceration, withdrawal from society due to depression, and suicide after a period of living in obscurity.

But what about the "study of the studies" by Mayer and McHugh that we mentioned earlier? What does it show us about the effectiveness of transgender surgery as seen in those five hundred best papers? The study of the studies shows what common sense has been suggesting all along. Quoting directly from the paper, "The scientific definition of biological sex is, for almost all human beings, clear, binary, and stable, reflecting an underlying biological reality that is not contradicted by exceptions to sex-typical behavior, and cannot be altered by surgery or social conditioning."[23]

Looking specifically at the application of transgender medicine and surgery to young children, as we are now aggressively doing in pediatric centers all across the county,

[23] Mayer and McHugh, "Sexuality and Gender."

the authors sum up the science by saying, "The notion that a two-year-old, having expressed thoughts or behaviors identified with the opposite sex, can be labeled for life as transgender has absolutely no support in science."[24]

Having evaluated the scientific validity of pediatric transgender medicine, the authors offer a professional evaluation of the morality of these medical practices: "Indeed, it is iniquitous to believe that all children who have gender-atypical thoughts or behavior at some point in their development, particularly before puberty, should be encouraged to become transgender."[25]

Failure to Correctly Diagnose

These bad long-term results should come as no surprise, given what we know about the history of medicine and surgery. If you look at the great advances in surgical care over the last few centuries, you will see that advancements in diagnosis have been as important as advances in surgical techniques. Knowing how to do an appendectomy is very important. Doing the appendectomy on the right person is every bit as important. If I am a good diagnostician, I am more likely to find a sick appendix when I operate, and do the patient some good when I remove it. Objective findings (physical exam, blood tests, radiological scans) help aid accurate diagnosis, and correct diagnosis is foundational to good surgical results.

In the case of the transgender patient, the diagnosis is

[24] Mayer and McHugh, "Sexuality and Gender."
[25] Mayer and McHugh, "Sexuality and Gender."

being made by the patient rather than the doctor. Sometimes the diagnosis is being made by a child in adolescence, or even younger. There is no finding in the clinical exam, laboratory test, or radiologic study that can confirm or refute the diagnosis or that can predict who will benefit from the treatments. There is no other area of medicine in which the patient makes a diagnosis that leads to irreversible and massive surgical procedures that result in the loss of an essential human capacity. There is also no other area of medical care in which the power of the state is organized to command sterilizing, mutilating surgery based upon the feelings of an emotionally overwrought (consider the high suicide rate), adolescent child, especially when that suicide rate returns to pre-operative levels long after transition.

Summary

Self-identified transgender persons are a small but apparently growing population of persons who experience a severe dissonance between their sex (male or female) and their interior sense of themselves as men or women. It is a condition that is associated with a high rate of self-harming behavior, including alcohol abuse, drug abuse, sexual abuse, prostitution, and suicide. It is a condition that demands merciful care in every regard.

Care for transgender persons is presently being compromised by a distortion in our understanding of the human person. Whereas in times past the patient was seen as an intrinsic unity of body and spirit, today we are seeing large segments of the medical community tacitly accepting an understanding of the human person as a kind of spirit creature that may or may not be inhabiting the correct body. In all my seventeen years of training, and thirty-five years in medicine, I do not once remember a lecture, textbook passage, or peer-reviewed article that described humans this way.

In this idea of the human being, we see a contradictory mix of materialism and superstition. It is materialist because it proposes that man is nothing more than an evolved material thing that has a mind because the substance of the body is sufficiently complex. It is superstitious because it now suddenly proposes that the person is not linked to the substance of his or her body (chromosomes, genitals, etc.) but rather exists as a spiritual creature quite unconnected to physical nature. It is a view that utterly denies that the sexed nature of the human person is capable of producing new life precisely because humanity is binary and sexed. This worldview asks us to believe that "male" and "female," "masculine" and "feminine" are merely social constructs that inhibit our freedom to use our sexual nature in any manner we may find personally fulfilling. It is a most peculiar and often bewildering view of human sexuality that I have simplified into the form of an axiom. According to this neo-Gnosticism, "adult sexuality" is an endlessly variable, personal expression of individuality, the purpose of which is to produce joy for that person. It sometimes involves other people and, with alarming frequency, is known to produce other people.

This is a very lonely view of the human person. The sexual faculty, which in the order of nature is emblematic of intimate, life-giving, and life-long love, has been replaced with a view of sexuality that is entirely self-referential (what I like, what excites me, what brings me joy) and utterly lifeless, separating itself from the generative aspect of the sexual embrace. It defines itself by whom it can use to satisfy itself. You can see this perverse view of sexuality in the teaching materials being distributed in schools, which are used to initiate children into this sense of themselves (see the "Gender Unicorn"[26]). This worldview is employing the sorrows of transgenderism in order to somehow teach us all that our embodied selves, male and female, are nothing more than an illusion that can be manipulated to our own satisfaction. This view of sexuality is willing to sterilize itself in order to satisfy a vague and mysterious interior life that is subject to change.

This transgender worldview does not stand on scientific truth. There is no scientific or clinical finding that can confirm the diagnosis or predict the outcome of care. Thousands of children are now being conscripted into a lifelong dependence on medical support, including hormonal treatments and repeated surgery. Their physical, psychological, and sexual development is being arrested with drugs, hormones, and pornographic exploration of "their true self." They are being made sterile in the vain hope of saving them from suicide, when there is proof that these interventions do not change that variable. This is antithetical to all of the fundamental principles of the practice of medicine and surgery. We are headed for a medical scandal never before seen in human history. Whole medical institutions will be bankrupted by the legal consequences of this disaster.

[26] http://www.transstudent.org/gender.

In the beginning of this chapter, I suggested that this examination of the truth of transgender surgery would lead us to the most profound question. I said that "we know that the Truth is actually a person, the God-Man Jesus Christ, and thus it is to him that this conversation must ultimately lead."

At Caesarea Philippi, Jesus asked his disciples, "Who do you say that the Son of Man is?" (see Matt 16:15). They saw a man, but he wanted to know if they saw his divinity. He was asking them if they could accept the mystery of the Incarnation, that Jesus could be fully man and fully God. Were his human and divine natures separable from the body they saw before them, or was that inseparability the necessary condition for making his sacrifice on the cross efficacious? In the end, the question of transgenderism might be stated as "Who do you say that man is?" Is he merely a spirit creature that inhabits a body that isn't really him, but is useful to him? If you believe that children can, in truth, look at themselves in a mirror and say, "That isn't really me," then those same children will look at Christ hanging on the cross and say, "That isn't really God. God merely used that body. God never really became one of us." In the final analysis, the transgender view of the human person is an attack on the revealed truth of the Incarnation, an attack that makes us unable to answer the most important question that we will ever hear, and the question is put to us by Christ himself: "Who do you say that I am?"

REVIEW

1. Good surgery involves knowledge of human nature and especially of the ordering of form (anatomy) to function (physiology).

2. A good surgical plan takes into account both the objective nature of the parts to be restored and the subjective truth of the particular patient's circumstances.

3. Plastic or reconstructive surgery is really an embracing of the true (in the part's form and function), the beautiful (in the harmony within the part and its relation to the whole), and the good (in the part's service to the person's own flourishing).

4. What is affirmed in "gender affirmation" surgery is a subjective feeling or belief without correspondence to any biological reality.

5. Most children who identify as cross-sex will naturally grow out of it in adolescence.

6. The diagnostic tests for gender dysphoria (sadness or distress over one's biological sex) are based on fairly superficial cultural forms and can't well predict who will benefit from surgery.

7. "Transitioning" typically involves pubertal blockade drugs, cross-sex hormones, and encouragement from family, friends, and community.

8. The World Professional Association of Transgender Health does not view transgender identity as a psychological problem but as suffering based on "wrongly assigned" birth gender.

9. No body of evidence supports the safety of pubertal blockade. It is essentially human experimentation on people too young to give informed consent.

10. Male-to-female (MtF) procedures include lasers to destroy facial hair and surgeries to shave the Adam's apple, feminize the nose, reduce the dimensions of the jaw, and augment the breasts.

11. Female-to-male (FtM) procedures include hormones to develop facial hair, deepen the voice, and suppress breast development. Often breasts are surgically removed, which permanently destroys the capacity to breastfeed.

12. MtF genital surgery results in sterility, involving castration, removal of erectile tissues from the penis, and inversion of the penis skin or use of a colon segment to create a neo-vagina. Sexual sensation and orgasm are often compromised. Other problems can include skin erosion, infection, dysplasias, and risk of various cancers.

13. FtM genital surgery usually results in infertility because it often includes hysterectomy and removal of the fallopian tubes and ovaries. Usually there is also

the construction of a neo-phallus, sometimes with the help of prosthetics. Problems include urinary strictures, fistulae, infection, and injury to the donor area.

14. Transgender surgery is based on the principle that it is legitimate to destroy a human capacity (reproduction) in order to produce a counterfeit structure to satisfy a subjective desire.

15. Transgender persons have a dramatically high rate of suicidality, at 40%. Reliable studies have shown that while surgery drops this rate in the short-term, suicidality begins to rise again after eight years, and the rate is back to its previous level by around twenty years post-op.

16. In no other area of medicine does the patient make a diagnosis that leads to irreversible medical procedures resulting in the loss of a human capacity.

17. The transgender view, in being an attack on the truth of the human person, is ultimately an attack on the truth of the Incarnation.

Further Reading

Anderson, Ryan T. *When Harry Became Sally: Responding to the Transgender Moment.* New York: Encounter Books, 2019.

Mayer, Lawrence S. and Paul R. McHugh, "Sexuality and Gender: Findings from the Biological, Psychological, and Social Sciences," *The New Atlantis* 50 (Fall 2016): 90, https://www.

thenewatlantis.com/wp-content/uploads/legacy-pdfs
/20160819_TNA50SexualityandGender.pdf.

Sex Change Regret. A website presenting personal stories and scientific, medical, psychological, and legal resources for those who have undergone or are considering undergoing "sex change" procedures: https://sexchangeregret.com.

Shrier, Abigail. *Irreversible Damage: The Transgender Craze Seducing Our Daughters.* Washington, DC: Regnery Publishing, 2020.

CHAPTER 5

Metaphysics: A Note on Soul, Body, and Sexuality

John D. Finley, PhD

As PART OF AN EFFORT to legitimize the transgender identity, talk of the human soul has resurfaced in some quarters of our largely secular culture. The soul, or "spirit," in such contexts is referred to as one's true self, the real "I," in contrast to one's body, which is experienced as wrongly sexed. In this view, the human person at its core is held to be something other than bodily, something sheerly bound up with consciousness and feeling. One might well wonder what this non-bodily human self is, and whether consciousness, thought, and desire are even conceivable apart from bodiliness. Moreover, this non-bodily self is held to possess an independent sexuality of some kind under the ambiguous name of "gender," a view whose incoherence has been discussed in chapters 1, 2, and 4.

Still, the notion that humans possess a soul can be found across the globe and throughout history, in many religious traditions and non-religious schools of thought that have nothing to do with the transgender conversation. Particularly for our purposes, the Christian tradition holds that we are composed of body and soul. In light of the transgender phenomenon, the question arises more pointedly for Christian thought: just what connection, if any, does sexuality have with the human soul? There may be a tendency among some Christians to see sexuality as ultimately belonging to the soul, since otherwise it could be seen as basically animal, which does not seem appropriate for us, who are made in God's image and likeness. How ironic it would be if both transgender ideology and certain forms of traditional Christianity were to agree in placing human sexuality in the soul! The underlying premise, of course, would be that the human person finally *is* a spiritual, or non-bodily, being, linked in some way with materiality.

Here I will briefly explain the Catholic tradition's understanding of the human person as a unity of matter and soul. While accepted by the Church, this articulation bases itself on reason, not revelation: it purports to make sense of common human experience. In examining ourselves as body-soul unities, we are considering human nature in its most fundamental structure or way of being. Such discourse has traditionally been called metaphysics. The account given here is based on Thomas Aquinas' view of human nature, which in its essentials has been adopted in the language of Catholic teaching.[1] The following pages will give an overview, explaining the most relevant points without arguing for them in detail. After discussing the human soul and its union with the body, I will consider sexuality's place in the soul-body unity.

---

[1] See Thomas Aquinas' *Summa theologiae* I, questions 75–76.

I. THE HUMAN SOUL AND ITS UNION
WITH MATTER

The Catholic tradition holds that the human soul is the *form of the body* and is *spiritual.*[2]

Soul as Form of the Body

The notion of the soul as "form of the body" goes back to Aristotle.[3] He begins with an everyday understanding of "soul" as the animating principle: that which gives life, whether it be in the form of an oak tree, a falcon, or a human. The word "soul" still possesses the connotation of that which animates, or gives life, to something physical. All things in the world around us are bodily, but some are living and some aren't. Bodiliness itself can't account for life, since bodiliness is precisely what living and non-living things have in common. Consequently, some principle other than materiality must be at work in living beings, and this principle is called "soul" (*anima* in Latin, *psyche* in Greek).

But *what is* soul? Many of Aristotle's predecessors, and many after him, held the soul to be its own independent reality, a different kind of thing from the body it animates. Perhaps it is a distinct kind of material energy, perhaps it is something spiritual, but whatever it is, it comes to a body and gives it life, making it do living sorts of things. This

[2] CCC, §§362–65.
[3] See Aristotle's *De anima*, bks. 1–2.

view of soul and body as ultimately two distinct beings in their own right can be called radical *dualism* and can be found in different forms throughout the history of human thought.

Aristotle does not hold to this dualism. Such a view, he argues, leads to absurd consequences. It would mean that each living being in our world is in fact not a unified thing at all but a mere conjunction of two things: a soul and a body. Accordingly, it would be only by chance that any given soul and body exist together. There would be no reason why souls and bodies always appear *together*, or why only the *same kinds* of soul and body appear together. For example, if souls and bodies are really separate things in their own right, then we ought to find *some* falcon bodies with falcon souls, but others without them. And we ought to find different kinds of souls coming to different kinds of bodies: falcon souls in crow bodies, fish bodies, or even flower bodies. Moreover, we ought to find bodies existing as themselves both before the soul enters (i.e., conception), and after the soul departs (i.e., death).

But of course we encounter none of these situations. We always find that the same kind of soul (life-principle) accompanies the same kind of body: a falcon life-principle is always and only found in a falcon body. More fundamentally, we don't even get a falcon body in the first place unless the falcon life-principle is present. This, after all, *is* conception: the beginning of life, yes, but as the beginning of a new living body of a certain kind. Which is to say that we don't get a falcon *soul* unless and until the new embryonic falcon body has come to be. At the other end of life, as soon as the falcon life-principle is gone due to death, not only is the falcon body non-living; it is also no longer a falcon body at all, strictly speaking. The corpse is in fact not one thing but literally a decomposing thing: a number of inanimate substances like oxygen, hydrogen, and nitrogen, still physically connected but quickly reverting back to their own distinct modes of being.

In a word, there is no evidence that soul and body are two separate things in their own right. They come and go together, they entail each other and are responsible for each other, and they form one thing: a living being, whether a sycamore, a swordfish, or a human.

Aristotle concludes that a living being is truly one substance, as experience attests, composed not of two *things* but of two *principles*: soul and matter. In defining soul as the "form of the body," Aristotle maintains that the soul first and foremost *actualizes* matter: it gives it being, in the first place, and forms it to be a body of a certain kind— namely, a living organism belonging to the species from which it came.

Notably, in this view, the fact that plants and animals have souls means nothing ghostly, spiritual, or eternal. It simply means that their bodies can be what they are— living bodies of a certain kind—only on account of some principle in them that actualizes and structures their materiality in a distinctive manner. This soul, while not a body itself, is *something of* a body. It is the body's actuality: that which makes bodiliness exist and act as a certain kind of living, unified thing. Soul and matter, in this view, are necessarily one. You can't get a living body without a principle of life and unity that actualizes matter into a living organism; and it wouldn't make sense to speak of a soul, or animating principle, without some matter for the principle to animate.

Consequently, we should not so much think of souls or bodies existing in their own right. What exists first and foremost is a unified, living substance, *composed of* soul and body. Parent falcons give rise to their offspring, and *in so doing* they give rise to falcon matter and falcon soul. As belonging to this particular species, a falcon soul actualizes and structures its matter so as to possess capacities characteristic of falconhood: a certain shape and range of size, the ability to fly, to hunt, to dive at great speed, and so on. One can see what kind of soul, or life principle, is present precisely by attending to the organism's structure, its shape and approximate size, and especially its distinctive capacities, marked by organ systems oriented toward the particular tasks they enable the organism to perform.

We can now better understand what it means to say that the human being is a soul-body composite. We are not primarily spirits, souls, or non-bodily selves. Nor are we simply materiality: a random collection of particles and fields that happen to exist near each other for a while. We are human substances: bodies actualized and structured by a distinctive sort of soul that enables us to possess human capacities.

Soul as Spiritual

Soul, for humans, does not primarily mean self-awareness, consciousness, or feeling. It means something deeper: that which enables our bodiliness to exist as a human organism in the first place. This *includes*, over time, capacities for the various living activities found also in plants and animals: growth, nutrition, self-repair, locomotion, sensation, feeling, and desire. But it also includes two remarkable capacities not found in other animals: reason and free will. As rational beings, we are not limited to sensing the realities around us through vision, hearing, and touch. More than this, we are able to know *what* things are, as evidenced by our abilities to name them, talk about them, study them, and make art that imitates them. Reason allows us to know ourselves and to know, at least in principle, the entire spectrum of reality, from the lowest physical particles to something of God himself. We also have a will, by which we are not limited to instinctive pursuit of proximate sensory pleasures. Instead, we thoughtfully seek happiness, discern what is good for us, and freely choose that good. Reason and free will enable self-knowledge and self-governance within us. They are capacities that transcend the physical and sensory, not by leaving it behind but by seeing more deeply into it and attending to it in light of what is truly good.

As particular human capacities, reason and free will reveal the human soul to be unique among souls. It is the form of the human body and, at the same time, a spiritual reality, transcending the realm of matter. The human soul, as form of the body, can hardly be separate from bodiliness, but neither is it completely subject to bodily limitations, as evidenced by our rational and volitional abilities. To say the soul is spiritual means that its existence is not fundamentally physical or dependent upon the physical. A spiritual reality is immaterial, and thus it cannot break, get sick, or die. It is immortal.

As form, the human soul is radically one with the body it animates. They come into being together as the embryonic human person, and naturally exist as one being throughout the person's life. Yet, as spiritual, the soul cannot *depend* on matter for its existence. It comes into being at the time of human procreation but can be directly sourced only by a spiritual maker, God himself. Similarly, when the person has died, the body corrupts but the soul continues to exist on account of its spiritual being. (Even then, such an existence is incomplete and unnatural for the soul, which is by definition the form of the human body. From this standpoint, how fitting—even necessary—is the Christian teaching on bodily resurrection!)

The human person, then, is a microcosm of reality, as the early Church Fathers put it. We are the border of the spiritual and physical realms in creation. As actualized by the spiritual soul, everything about our physicality, sexuality included, is granted a degree of nobility beyond other bodily substances in our cosmos.

Still, throughout human history, the dualistic tendency recurs and presents the soul as an invisible consciousness existing inside the body and making it move and do things, like a ghost in a machine. At times we identify with our "soul" or consciousness, and regard our bodies as effectively foreign to us; we see this in eating disorders or gender dysphoria. At other times we identify with our bodies and effectively regard our mind as alien; think of hedonistic pursuits. But these views of ourselves are false. Ironically, the fact that we humans can be disunified in, say, psychological disorder does not mean that our selves and our bodies are separate. Rather, we're so unified that an issue in one dimension of ourselves causes the whole self all the more pain and frustration.

II. Sexuality and the Soul

We have seen in preceding chapters that human sexuality is a whole-person reality. Biologically, it characterizes the male and female organisms at the anatomic, genetic, and molecular levels. It affects behavior, typically entailing a host of psychological tendencies. It naturally marks one's self-identity and self-expression, calling for thoughtful choice in the realms of personal presentation, encounter, and sexual activity. The depth of sexuality is only confirmed by the physical and personal ordeals suffered by those who experience some trauma pertaining to their maleness or femaleness (often in the form of a violation, a serious intersex condition, or gender dysphoria). Most dramatically, the surgical and hormonal attempts to actually change one's sex not only can't achieve what they promise; they also typically leave a patient infertile, resulting in loss of a human capacity, not in gain.

This is all to say, in metaphysical terms, that sexuality is a matter of *soul and body together*.[4] It clearly involves one's bodiliness: organ systems, hormones, genes, tissues, body shape, and so on. And it involves soul precisely because the soul is the *form of* the body. The soul actualizes matter as human, structuring it over time into a mature organism possessing various living capacities, one of which is

---

[4] For affirmation of this point in the *Catechism of the Catholic Church*, see §2332.

the reproductive. Male and female are the two ways in which this capacity is manifest in the human species. The human soul, we could say, naturally seeks to form maleness or femaleness in the body, just as it naturally seeks to form eyes for seeing, ears for hearing, and legs for walking. If such capacities are not developed, then human nature is present in a deficient manner.

In this sense, sexuality is a metaphysically deeper reality than our other individual traits, like specific eye color, height, vocal tone, temperament, or native athleticism. Such characteristics are not demanded by human nature (soul and body) itself; they do not involve distinct organ structures to enable capacities and purposes requisite for the mature human substance. Instead, they manifest more superficial variations within the organs and structures that the nature entails. Being man or woman, then, while not as fundamental as being human to begin with, is more fundamental than any other individual aspect of ourselves.[5]

From the beginning of life, sexuality belongs to the whole person in the manner we have described: soul and body together. Sexuality's relation to consciousness, self-identity, and self-expression comes later in life and *presupposes* the fundamental soul-body connection. From the perspective of the soul as form of the body, it makes no sense to speak of one's soul as female and one's body as male, or vice-versa. All "soul" could mean in such a context

---

[5] I deliberately use the word "fundamental" here because I do *not* mean that one's sexuality is simply the most important personal characteristic in one's life, across the board. For example, one's particular state of virtue is more important, inasmuch as it pertains to our ultimate fulfillment.

is consciousness: one's own self-perception, or self-feeling. To divorce consciousness from the bodily realm is a very tenuous move: it leads right into the terrain of radical dualism mentioned earlier. In fact, virtually everything in our consciousness has some dependence on the world of physicality. And as we remarked in chapter 1, to speak of one's consciousness alone as possessing gender—or indeed, as one's very self—is highly problematic.

Conclusion

Seeing ourselves as soul-body unities in the manner described does justice to our experience. It entails a vision of the person that ennobles physicality and grounds spirituality. It makes of us one thing—a human substance—that cannot exist or be understood without materiality *and* spiritual soul. Human sexuality, like the person itself, possesses physical and spiritual dimensions from the beginning. This will become more manifest over time, as sexuality contours the organism biologically and naturally enters the realms of rational self-awareness and free choice.

There is something striking about the fact that in human beings, a *spiritual* principle is significantly responsible for capacities like digestion, vision, and sexuality. While these powers and their corresponding activities properly belong to the whole person and not to the soul, they would seem to possess a kind of transcendent significance inasmuch as the human soul itself is immortal. What do we make of this? And what about those who deliberately choose not to exercise their sexual capacities? They are no less man or woman than others, and yet are we to think that their sexuality somehow exists in a superfluous manner? Here we are close to the limits of natural reason's power. For deeper insight into the human story, we need to move beyond science, medicine, and philosophy. Let us turn to divine Revelation concerning the Creator and his creation.

Review

1. The human being is neither a disembodied spirit nor a random collection of materials. We are unified substances, foundationally composed of two principles: soul (animating principle) and matter.

2. The soul is not its own thing, independent of the body. It is the very *form* of the body, actualizing and unifying matter as a certain kind of living thing.

3. The soul is not consciousness, feeling, or desire. These are capacities possessed by the *person*, and so they *presuppose* the kind of thing we are: a human composite of form (soul) and matter.

4. As form of the body, the soul structures matter into a mature organism of its parent-species. This entails the appearance of distinctive *capacities*, which are marked by particular configurations of anatomy and organ systems.

5. Among other capacities, the human being possesses intellect and free will. These transcend physicality,

thus displaying the human soul itself as spiritual. Although it is the form of the human body, the soul does not *depend* on matter for its existence and so is incorruptible.

6. Strikingly, the human person is the microcosm of reality, uniting the physical and spiritual in one being.

7. In the human and most other animals, one capacity central to the mature organism is the reproductive (sexual), manifest as either male or female. It is the *person* (soul and body) that is sexed, not the soul or matter in their own right. The soul naturally seeks to form matter into maleness or femaleness. Human sexuality possesses a spiritual and physical dimension.

8. After human nature itself as a body-soul unity, sexuality is the most fundamental attribute of the person. Maleness and femaleness are integral to human nature. Other individual traits, like eye color, native intelligence, or temperament, do not involve their own capacities and organ systems. They are superficial variations within the distinct structures entailed by our nature.

Further Reading

Allen, Prudence. *The Concept of Woman*. 4 Vols. Grand Rapids, MI: Wm. B. Eerdmans, 1997–2017.

Finley, John. "The Metaphysics of Gender: A Thomistic Approach." *The Thomist* 79, no. 4 (2015): 585–614. (See also the insightful response by William Newton in *The Linacre Quarterly* 87, no. 2 [2020].)

Fortin, Timothy. "Finding Form: Defining Human Sexual Difference." *Nova et Vetera* 15, no. 2 (2017): 397–431.

Jensen, Steven J. *The Human Person: A Beginner's Thomistic Psychology.* Washington, DC: The Catholic University of America Press, 2018.

Schindler, D. C. "Perfect Difference: Gender and the Analogy of Being." *Communio* 43 (Summer 2016): 194–231.

CHAPTER 6

Man, Woman, and Creation: A Theological Account

Lawrence J. Welch, PhD

ON SEVERAL OCCASIONS, Pope Francis has reflected on the meaning of human sexual difference in the relationship between man and woman.[1] In the course of these reflections, he has voiced a concern about an ideology of gender and why it seeks to cancel out sexual difference.[2] In this chap-

[1] General Audiences of April 15 and 22, 2015, http://w2.vatican.va/ content/francesco/en/audiences/2015/documents/papa-francesco_ 20150415_udienza-generale.html and http://w2.vatican.va/content /francesco/en/audiences/2015/documents/papa-francesco_ 20150422_udienza-generale.html.

[2] Francis, Apostolic Letter on Love in the Family *Amoris Laetitia* (March 19, 2016), §56: "Yet another challenge is posed by the various forms of an ideology of gender that 'denies the difference and reciprocity in nature of a man and a woman and envisages a society without sexual differences, thereby eliminating the anthropological basis of the family.'" The pope here quotes *Relatio Finalis*, §44, from the 2015 Synod on the family. See also Address to the Participants in the General Assembly of the Members of the Pontifical Academy for Life, October 5, 2017, §3. See his strong remarks to Polish bishops on the occasion of his visit to Poland: Dialogo del Santo Padre con i Vescovi della Polonia, Kraków, July 27, 2016, https://press.vatican.va/content/salastampa/it/bollettino/pubblico /2016/08/02/0568/01265.html#en: "In Europe, America, Latin America, Africa, and in some countries of Asia, there are genuine forms of ideological colonization taking place. And one of these—I will call it clearly by its name—is [the ideology of] 'gender.' Today

ter, I will explore how the pope situates these reflections in relationship to the ecology crisis, which he speaks about in his encyclical *Laudato Si'*. While Pope Francis intends to make his own distinctive insights about human sexuality, he draws on the thought of his predecessors John Paul II and Benedict XVI. I will also indicate briefly how their thought is helpful to what Pope Francis proposes in *Laudato Si'* about human sexuality.

I. The Context: Integral Ecology or the Technological Paradigm

In chapter 3 of *Laudato Si'*, Pope Francis gives a penetrating analysis of the human roots of the ecology crisis. He maintains that "there can be no ecology without an adequate anthropology."[3] Everything is connected and interlinked. Hence the pope speaks of an "integral ecology." Humanity's relationship with nature cannot be renewed apart from renewal of humanity itself. The pontiff is quick to point out that if humanity is regarded to be the product of pure chance or the result of a kind of physical determinism, then it is very difficult for people

---

children—children!—are taught in school that everyone can choose his or her sex. Why are they teaching this? Because the books are provided by the persons and institutions that give you money. These forms of ideological colonization are also supported by influential countries. And this is terrible!"

[3] Francis, Encyclical Letter on Care for Our Common Home *Laudato Si'* (May 24, 2015), §118, http://www.vatican.va/content/francesco/en/encyclicals/documents/papa-francesco_20150524_enciclica-laudato-si.html (hereafter cited as LS).

to perceive, let alone feel, a responsibility for the environment.[4] The second chapter of the encyclical already proposed that the human responsibility for the environment can best be grounded by an understanding of creation as the product of love, the love of God the Father, who alone owns the good creation.[5]

Pope Francis quotes his predecessor Benedict XVI, stating that since "the book of nature is one and indivisible" and includes the environment, life, sexuality, the family, social relations, and so on, it follows that "the deterioration of nature is closely connected to the culture which shapes human coexistence."[6] Both popes believe that closely linked to the deterioration of nature is the culture that conditions and shapes our human coexistence. Irresponsible behavior has damaged the natural environment and the social environment. Pope Francis adds that both injuries stem from the mistaken ideas that there exist no indisputable truths to guide our life and therefore that human freedom is limitless. Quoting his predecessor again, he remarks that we have forgotten that "man does not create himself. He is spirit and will, but also nature."[7] Pope Francis takes this analysis a step further. He believes there is a globalized cultural understanding of human life and activity. He proposes that we turn our focus to "the dominant technocratic

---

[4] LS, §118.

[5] LS, §76.

[6] LS, §6, quoting Benedict XVI, Encyclical Letter on Integral Human Development in Charity and Truth *Caritas in Veritate* (June 29, 2009), §51: *Acta Apostolicae Sedis* [AAS] 101 (2009), 687.

[7] LS, §6, quoting Benedict XVI, Address to the Bundestag, Berlin, September 22, 2011: AAS 103 (2011), 664.

paradigm and the place of human beings and human action in the world."[8]

The pope is no luddite. Far from it. He acknowledges that technology has improved the quality of human life and even given us beautiful things. It is right to rejoice in technological advances, especially those that have removed evils that have harmed human beings. For "science and technology," the pontiff observes, "are wonderful products of God-given human creativity." Technology with its modification of nature for useful purposes even manifests something spiritual in man because it "expresses the inner tension that impels man to overcome material limitation."[9]

The pope also says we should recognize that science and technology have given humanity a tremendous power over itself at a level it has never had before. He mentions the two atomic bombs dropped in World War II and the technological means that Nazism and Communism used to murder millions of innocents. There is also our own situation today with its massive buildup of arsenals for modern warfare. The pontiff claims that it is very risky for this power to eventually lie in the hands of only a small part of humanity. Echoing the argument of the Second Vatican Council in the document *Gaudium et Spes*, he maintains that our enormous advance in technological development has not been followed by "a development in human responsibility, values and conscience."[10] We have not been prepared to use power well. So, there is a great risk that humanity will not use power as

[8] LS, §101.
[9] LS, §102.
[10] LS, §105.

it should in the face of the challenges of today, for we lack a culture and spirituality that can enable humanity to set limits and teach self-restraint.

According to *Laudato Si'*, the basic problem lies even deeper:

> It is the way that humanity has taken up technology and its development *according to an undifferentiated and one-dimensional paradigm*. This paradigm exalts the concept of a subject who, using logical and rational procedures, progressively approaches and gains control over an external object. This subject makes every effort to establish the scientific and experimental method, which in itself is already a technique of possession, mastery and transformation. It is as if the subject were to find itself in the presence of something formless, completely open to manipulation. Men and women have constantly intervened in nature, but for a long time this meant being in tune with and respecting the possibilities offered by the things themselves. It was a matter of receiving what nature itself allowed, as if from its own hand. Now, by contrast, we are the ones to lay our hands on things, attempting to extract everything possible from them while frequently ignoring or forgetting the reality in front of us. Human beings and material objects no longer extend a friendly hand to one another; the relationship has become confrontational.[11]

[11] LS, §106. Pope Francis argues that such a confrontational approach

The pope points out that the method and aims of the technological paradigm tend to become an epistemological paradigm in an unconscious or unreflective way in the minds of people today. This means that the way our culture predisposes us to act tends to seep into our way of understanding the truth, if we do not think carefully about it. The technological paradigm can become a model imposed on the whole of reality. It has a tremendous power to globalize and absorb things in its logic. Therefore, it becomes very easy to view most things we interact with as good insofar as they are useful. Pope Francis says that we must become aware that even technological products themselves, far from being neutral, shape our way of living and our way of looking at things in the world. The products of technology strongly influence and, often enough, condition social possibilities according to the interests of power groups. Decisions about technological means may appear to be purely instrumental, but they are really choices about the kind of social order we are building.[12]

What is needed, according to Pope Francis, is the creation of a resistance "to the assault of the technocratic paradigm." He believes this will require a distinctive way of thinking and of looking at things—particular life styles and spiritualities, as well as policies and programs of education—that together can work against the globalized logic of this paradigm.[13]

---

makes it seem like there can be unlimited and infinite growth and an inexhaustible supply of the earth's goods. Within this approach is also the false notion that the negative effects and impact of the exploitation of the natural order can be easily outlasted and overcome.

[12] LS, §107

[13] LS, §111.

The Technological Paradigm and Modern Anthropocentrism

Resistance to the technocratic paradigm, however, is complicated by modern anthropocentrism, which marks modernity and which the pope describes as being excessive. It supposes the self to be sovereign and independent from reality. The self of modern anthropocentrism behaves with an absolute dominion.[14] About its effects, the pope writes,

> Modern anthropocentrism has paradoxically ended up prizing technical thought over reality, since "the technological mind sees nature as an insensate order, as a cold body of facts, as a mere 'given,' as an object of utility, as raw material to be hammered into useful shape; it views the cosmos similarly as a mere 'space' into which objects can be thrown with complete indifference." The intrinsic dignity of the world is thus compromised. When human beings fail to find their true place in this world, they misunderstand themselves and end up acting against themselves: "Not only has God given the earth to man, who must use it with respect for the original good purpose for which it was given, but, man too is God's gift to man. He must therefore respect the natural and moral structure with which he has been endowed."[15]

---

[14] LS, §117.

[15] LS, §115; Pope Francis quotes first Romano Guardini, *The End of the Modern World* (Wilmington, DE: ISI Books, 1998), 55 (first

The sovereign self, in its ever increasing will to power, uses the technique of the technological paradigm to acquire control over an external object in order to possess and transform it.[16] As Reinhard Hütter has observed, what Pope Francis alerts us to is that modern anthropocentrism creates the illusion that the world, indeed, the entire created order, is an instrument in the service of the pursuit of self-fulfillment and self-realization.[17] The idea that we might use our bodies and all of nature as instruments of self-expression and self-realization is nothing less than the appearance of the sovereign self, behaving with an absolute dominion.[18] We could say that the hormonal and surgical attempts at gender transition, described in chapter 4, illustrate the technocratic paradigm in service of radical self-realization. They also show tragically how through such activities, "human beings . . . end up acting against themselves."[19]

In a crucial passage in *Laudatio Si'*, Pope Francis connects again with Benedict XVI's teaching. Both popes appeal to the indivisibility of nature. They argue that if human persons approach their own natures, their own bodies, as being raw instruments of self-realization and self-expression, then it becomes very easy to believe we

published in 1965 as *Das Ende der Neuzeit*); and then John Paul II, Encyclical Letter on the Hundreth Anniversary of *Rerum Novarum*, *Centesimus Annus* (May 1, 1991), §38: AAS, 83 (1991), 841.

[16] LS, §106.
[17] Reinhard Hütter, "We Are Not God: Reflections on the Theology of *Laudato Si*," *Nova et Vetera* 17, no. 3 (Summer 2019): 647.
[18] Hütter, "We Are Not God," 648.
[19] LS, §115.

have absolute power over creation as well. Pope Francis writes,

Human ecology also implies another profound reality: the relationship between human life and the moral law, which is inscribed in our nature and is necessary for the creation of a more dignified environment. Pope Benedict XVI spoke of an "ecology of man," based on the fact that "man too has a nature that he must respect and that he cannot manipulate at will." It is enough to recognize that our body itself establishes us in a direct relationship with the environment and with other living beings. The acceptance of our bodies as God's gift is vital for welcoming and accepting the entire world as a gift from the Father and our common home, whereas thinking that we enjoy absolute power over our own bodies turns, often subtly, into thinking that we enjoy absolute power over creation. Learning to accept our body, to care for it and to respect its fullest meaning, is an essential element of any genuine human ecology. Also, valuing one's own body in its femininity or masculinity is necessary if I am going to be able to recognize myself in an encounter with someone who is different. In this way we can joyfully accept the specific gifts of another man or woman, the work of God the Creator, and find mutual enrichment. It is not a healthy attitude which would seek "to cancel out sexual difference because it no longer knows how to confront it."[20]

This claim that respect for all creation includes respect for the "gift" of our own bodies and for other men and women deserves to be investigated further, since the pope sees an integral ecology as connected to the acceptance of our own biological sex and the embodied differences between men and women.

An Ontology of the Gift

Against the self-determining and sovereign subject and its use of the technological paradigm, Pope Francis proposes the ontology of the gift.[21] The totality of human existence in its natural and moral constitution is a gift. It is not a product of chance. It did not have to exist, but it does exist, because of the creative love of God the Father. For us to accept the gift of human nature and existence is "to accept the natural and moral structure with which it has been endowed."[22] We cannot accept it if we think of the human person as completely self-constituting in the sense of transcending his nature and his body through technological means. As embodied spiritual creatures, we are created as sexually differentiated and complementary.

[20] LS, §155; Pope Francis quotes Pope Benedict, Address to the German Bundestag, Berlin, September 22, 2011: AAS 103 (2011), 668; and Francis, Catechesis of April 15, 2015: *L'Osservatore Romano*, April 16, 2015, p. 8.

[21] I owe this turn of phrase to Hütter, "We are Not God," 648.

[22] See previous quote, LS, §115.

Previous chapters have shown that this complementarity—and the beauty of it—is indisputable biologically, psychologically, and philosophically. What the Church affirms in her preaching of the good news is that this complementarity is true of the whole human being, because the human person is a unity of body and soul. As chapter 5 explained, we are composites of the corporeal and spiritual. We are not spirit creatures or souls who inhabit a body. This means that we cannot think of our true selves or real selves apart from our bodies. In the anthropology of the Bible and the Gospel, a human person does not "have" a body but is a body animated by a soul, which is the spiritual principle of a man or woman.[23]

"There can be no ecology without an adequate anthropology," *Laudato Si'* insists.[24] Connecting his thought to that of his predecessors, Pope Francis proposes that accepting one's masculinity or femininity is necessary for any genuine human ecology and therefore for an integral ecology in which everything is connected. The acceptance of one's masculinity or femininity is part of our respect for the natural and moral structure with which we have been endowed. As we have seen, Pope Francis cites John Paul II on this very point.

---

[23] It is true that the Catholic Christian tradition speaks of the soul separating from the body at death and remaining immortal, but this is an unnatural state for the soul, which God created to be united with the body of the person. Thanks to the resurrection of Christ, the soul will be reunited with the body, and human persons will be made whole again.

[24] LS, §118.

Is this understanding of the natural and moral structure available to all men and women, or is it limited only to people of faith? In other words, is what the popes propose based on reason or on revelation?

On the one hand, this appeal by Francis and his predecessors is made to people of all good will, because we can know from reason and experience something of the natural and moral structure with which our humanity has been endowed. The heightened awareness of the environmental crisis is a new opportunity for people to perceive the indivisibility of the book of nature, which includes the environment, sexuality, marriage, the family, and social relations. Today we are more profoundly aware than in the past of the harmful consequences that result when the design, laws, and structures of the environment are not respected. How can we come to respect environmental goods if we do not respect human goods as well? How can we avoid thinking that the goods of the environment are raw material for us to manipulate for our own purposes if this is how we approach human sexuality? Here the pope's proposal about the connection between an acceptance of one's femininity or masculinity and an integral ecology appeals to reason and does not require faith.

On the other hand, the popes propose that the full meaning of this indivisible book of nature is disclosed in divine Revelation and in Christ, who is the fullness of that revelation. In *Laudato Si'*, Pope Francis tells his readers,

> In the Christian understanding of the world, the destiny of all creation is bound up with the mystery of Christ, present from the beginning:

"All things have been created though him and for him" (Col 1:16).[25]

and,

The creatures of this world no longer appear to us under merely natural guise because the risen One is mysteriously holding them to himself and directing them towards fullness as their end.[26]

This means that the acceptance of our masculinity and femininity as persons, and the natural and moral structure with which it has been endowed, has a meaning and a fulfillment in Christ that we cannot fathom on our own. So, in addition to reason (not in contradiction to it), the Christian's faith enables a deeper, more exalted understanding of masculinity and femininity.

St. John Paul II engaged in profound meditations on the meaning of the embodied sexuality of the person during his Wednesday audiences on Genesis, which have come to be known as the Theology of the Body. It is helpful to our consideration of the proposal Pope Francis makes about the ontology of the gift and his call for a resistance to the technological paradigm to recall some key elements of his predecessor's Theology of the Body.

The Theology of the Body is governed from the start by the theme of the giftedness of creation and humanity's very existence. Fundamental to the revelation of God

---

[25] LS, §99.
[26] LS, §100.

as Creator, in the Book of Genesis, is that he creates the world from nothing and sees that it is very good. Nothing forces God to create. He creates freely. St. John Paul II observes,

> As an action of God, creation thus means not only calling from nothing to existence and establishing the world's existence as well as man's existence in the world, but, according to the first account [*bereshith bara*] it also signifies *gift*; a fundamental and radical gift, that is, an act of giving in which the gift comes into being precisely for nothing.[27]

Man's very nature, his being in the world, is qualified by an ontology of giftedness. It is important to be aware of the context of Pope St. John Paul's study of biblical anthropology. He turns to the Book of Genesis in order to study the meaning of the human person as man and woman in response to the invitation of Jesus in his encounter with certain Pharisees over the question of marriage and divorce. In this passage in the Gospel according to Matthew, chapter 19, Jesus refers to both accounts of the creation of humanity: Genesis 1:27 ("he who made them from the beginning made them male and female" [Matt 19:4]) and Genesis 2:24 ("'For this reason a man shall leave his father and mother and be joined to his wife, and the two shall become one'" [Matt 19:5]). Pope St. John Paul

---

[27] John Paul II, *Man and Woman He Created Them: A Theology of the Body*, trans. Michael Waldstein (Boston: Pauline Books and Media, 2006), 180 (hereafter cited as TOB).

says that the repeated reference Jesus makes to the beginning invites his listeners to reflect upon the way in which humanity was formed in creation as male and female. He observes that the chapters in Genesis to which Jesus directs his questioners tell of not just past events but an ongoing narrative that expresses the deepest reality of the human person. The early chapters of Genesis, John Paul claims, depict original, archetypal human experiences that have deep theological content and that serve as a foundation for a Christian anthropology.

Pope John Paul II reads the first two chapters in Genesis together in light of one another. The first account in Genesis defines human beings in distinction from the rest of creation according to their special relationship to God. Humankind is created in the image and likeness of God as male and female. This establishes the dignity and equality of each person before God. It also follows that both man and woman are unique and equally personal insofar as they are created in the image of a God, who is a person. John Paul writes, "Man, whom God created 'male and female,' bears the divine image impressed in the body 'from the beginning'; man and woman constitute, so to speak, two ways of 'being a body' that are proper to human nature in the unity of this image."[28]

The second creation account in Genesis gives a more subjective definition of the human being. It tells the story of Adam's self-awareness, the human dialogue with God, the dissimilarity with the animals, the human longing for a companion, the creation of woman, the unity of the two,

[28] TOB, 179.

and their self-determination, whereby they are faced with a choice with respect to the tree of good and evil. This second account sheds light on the meaning of the divine image. John Paul says it agrees with the content of the first account; moreover, the second account enables us to deduce that man and woman are in the image of God in a full and perfect way through a communion of persons, in which man and woman become a mutual gift for each another. This is a key element in the Theology of the Body, and I will return to it later.

In the second creation account, before the creation of woman, Adam is not specified as male. Adam does not have an awareness of being male, because he still is not in the presence of the other sex. Adam discovers his dissimilarity to the animals and finds no other creature like him. Adam is alone. This aloneness is "not good" (Gen 2:18). It is then that "the LORD God caused a deep sleep to fall upon the man, and while he slept took one of his ribs and closed up its place with flesh; and the rib which the LORD God had taken from the man he made into a woman and brought her to the man" (vv. 21–22). In the presence of the woman, Adam "wakes up" male, exclaiming, "'This at last is bone of my bones and flesh of my flesh; she shall be called Woman, because she was taken out of Man'" (v. 23). This account of woman coming from the rib of Adam contains some important anthropological and theological truths.

The second chapter of Genesis does not present the first man or the first woman having his or her own human sexual identity established independently of the other. On the one hand, man and woman share a common humanity:

"bone of my bones, flesh of my flesh." On the other hand, Adam becomes aware of himself as man, as masculine, only in the presence of the woman. For Adam to say "I" as man, he must look to Eve as woman. Likewise, the woman appears only in relation to man, having come from his rib. She finds her femininity in the presence of man. As woman she must look to Adam as man. John Paul notices that even the Hebrew words of the text express something of this truth, as man is *is* and woman *issah*. Neither man nor woman is intelligible apart from the other. Neither man nor woman is, taken alone, the whole of humanity. What the biblical text discloses is that the search for human identity must pass through the presence of the other way of being an embodied person. St. John Paul writes,

> In light of this text we understand that the knowledge of man [read: humanity] passes through masculinity and femininity, which are, as it were, two incarnations of the same metaphysical solitude before God and the world—two reciprocally completing ways of being a body and at the same time of being human—as two complementary dimensions of self-knowledge and self-determination and at the same time two complementary ways of being conscious of the meaning of the body. Thus, as Genesis 2:23 already shows, femininity in some way finds itself before masculinity, while masculinity confirms itself through femininity. Precisely the function of sex (that is, being male or female), which in some way is "constitutive for the person" (not only as an attribute of the person), shows how

deeply man, with all his spiritual solitude, with the uniqueness and unrepeatability proper to the person, is constituted by the body as "he" or "she."[29]

There are two ways of being a body that at the same time complete each other. Thus, John Paul speaks of an original unity of man and woman. "In the 'unity of the two,' man and woman are called from the beginning not only to exist 'side by side' or 'together,' but they are also called to *exist mutually 'one for the other.'*"[30] The human body, whether male or female, expresses this meaning that John Paul calls spousal. God called the first man to accept the woman as willed "for her own sake," and reciprocally woman is called to accept man as willed for "his own sake" by the Creator.[31] Sexuality here is not a mere attribute of the embodied person, the way that ethnicity or race is, but a constituent part of the person because of how femininity and masculinity are determined in the presence of each other.[32]

---

[29] TOB, 166. I have added "humanity" to be clear to the reader about the meaning of the word "man" as it is used here. The rest of the parentheticals are original to this text.

[30] John Paul II, Apostolic Letter on the Dignity and Vocation of Women *Mulieris Dignitatem* (August 15, 1988), §7 (hereafter cited as MD).

[31] TOB, 187.

[32] Joseph-Marie Verlinde, *L'ideologie du gender: Comme identite reçue ou choisie?* (Mesnil Saint-Loup, FR: Editions Le Livre Ouvert, 2012), 101–2. Yves Semen observes, "It is remarkable that in the Bible sexual difference is announced just after the affirmation that man is in the image of God. This signifies that sexual difference is inscribed in this image and is blessed by God" (Yves Semen, *La sexualit selon*

It is important to understand the kind of complementarity that St. John Paul believes the chapters in Genesis disclose. Cardinal Angelo Scola's writings on the nature of this complementarity of sexual difference can be helpful. Scola has observed that sexual difference is not a mere complementarity in the sense that the one sex is a missing part of the other sex. The sexual reciprocity that is at the heart of human existence is "asymmetrical," to use the words of Cardinal Scola.[33] There is a complementarity between the sexes, to be sure, but not in the sense that the sexes are understood as two fractional parts that can somehow be overcome in a kind of higher unity. Sexual difference in humanity and the orientation to the opposite sex is not about a frantic seeking of the other half of one's self and the recovery of a lost whole. Such a view would involve an androgynous understanding of humanity. Common human experience shows this to be false. Sexual difference is not

Jean-Paul II [Paris: Presses de la Renaissance Sexual, 2004], 80.) On this point, Verlinde remarks: "The sexual difference is therefore to be interpreted as a fact of nature infused with spiritual intentions. This is indicated in the seven days of creation; the animals are not presented as sexed beings. What characterizes them is not the difference between the sexes but the difference of orders and, within each order, the differences among species: There are the fish of the sea, the birds of the air, the beasts of the earth, etc. All living beings are produced, according to the refrain, 'after their kind' (Gen. 1:21). In the same account, sexuality is mentioned only in the case of man, for it is precisely in the communion of love, which includes the sexual act by which man and woman 'become one flesh,' that both fulfill their proper end: to be in God's image" (Verlinde, *L'ideologie du gender*, 99–100. Translations are mine).

[33] See Cardinal Angelo Scola, *The Spousal Mystery*, trans. Michelle K. Borras (Grand Rapids, MI: Eerdmans, 2005), 92.

transcended in our basic human relationships. A woman's feminine "I" is a point of reciprocity when she relates to persons of the opposite sex, every one of whom has a different status in relation to her. So, for instance, a woman is immediately related as a woman to her father, her brother, her male friend, and so on. Every man or woman lives in a plurality of relationships with different persons of the opposite sex, and in doing so we are not at all on a quest to find "the other half" of ourselves.[34]

An androgynous view of humanity, which understands the highest form of unity to be one in which sexual difference is transcended and eliminated, is actually a very old temptation. Some Christians have understood Galatians 3:28 ("There is neither Jew nor Greek, there is neither slave nor free, there is neither male nor female; for you are all one in Christ Jesus.") to mean that the Risen Christ has overcome sexual differences and that there will be an absence of sexuality in heaven. However, the good creation in Genesis speaks of something entirely different. The reciprocity between man and woman is not some sign of cosmic alienation but is at the center of the good creation and therefore is not some negativity or fracturedness to be overcome. Far from meaning that man and woman are two fractional halves of humanity, sexual reciprocity means that there are two ways of being an embodied human person, two ways that complete each other and therefore do not overcome each other. Writing on this subject, Cardinal Angelo Scola helps us to understand the point:

[34] Scola, *The Spousal Mystery*, 92.

My existence as a sexual being means, in some sense, that I am placed from the beginning in relation to another. The other is present to me as being identical in her own being as a person, but at the same time, because of sexual difference, she reveals to me a radical difference that distinguishes her from me at all levels. Thus, if my way of embodying the identity of the person is masculine, the feminine that stands before me is a different way of being a person. The reciprocity that springs from sexual difference thus shows that the "I" emerges into existence from within a kind of constitutive polarity.[35]

Peter Henrici comments in a similar vein, emphasizing the connection between sexual difference and the experience of transcendence:

As soon as a person becomes conscious of her sexual identity, she is confronted with a kind of transcendence. She is required to think beyond

---

[35] Scola, *The Spousal Mystery*, 93–94. Scola continues on p. 121: "Anthropologically speaking, human sexuality is the 'high road' along which man experiences differences as internal to the 'I' itself. This is so not because the 'I' lacks its own autonomous ontological consistency, made up, as Maritain writes, of constitutive elements and necessities. Rather, the polarity of the other at the same time constitutes the 'I'; There is not *first* a wholly autonomous 'I' which *then* enters into relation with another. The relation is not extrinsic and accidental, but intrinsic and constitutive." Scola cites J. Maritain, "La personne et le bien commun," in Maritain, *Oeuvres 1940–1963* (Paris: Desclée de Brouwer, 1978), 287ff.

herself and recognize the existence of an inaccessible other—that is of him who is essentially related and desirable yet never totally comprehensible. The experience of sexual difference becomes the model for all experiences of transcendence, which designates an indissoluble relation with an absolutely inaccessible reality.[36]

So, for example, from the man's perspective, a woman is more than just an "other"; she is the "other" sex that makes the masculine "I" grow and become. In the presence of the "other" sex, who is different yet like me, there is a movement toward a greater possession of my own humanity. God created a sexual reciprocity in which the opposite sex, the other sex, always remains "the other" for me. It is in this way that sexual complementarity is understood to be "asymmetrical."

As Scola says, "Sexuality always presents itself in terms of difference. *Sexuality is sexual difference.*"[37] The otherness of the opposite sex can never be overcome or transcended, and seeking to do so would harm one's own identity as man or woman, which is naturally, as it were, polarized toward the opposite sex. As Cardinal Scola observes, to try to overcome the duality of the sexes would involve

---

[36] Peter Henrici, "Les deux sexes: Vers un dépassement de l'anthropologie," *Communio* (September–December 2006): 16–17; translation mine. On one level, Henrici's point hearkens back as far as Plato's *Symposium*, in which sexual difference and erotic love are discussed as earthly analogues to man's relationship to the divine, the transcendent Good itself.

[37] Scola, *The Spousal Mystery*, 119.

necessarily a refusal to accept the opposite sex for what he or she is as a person.[38] It could also jeopardize, suggests Henrici, one's experiences of transcendent (ultimately divine) reality.

Joseph-Marie Verlinde, a commentator on the Theology of the Body, remarks that the complementarity of the first man and woman in the second creation story expresses a double finitude in humanity: "I am not everything; I am not even all that is human; and I do not know all that is human. The other sex always remains partly unknowable to me. This means that self-sufficiency is impossible for man. This limitation is not a privation but a gift that allows for the discovery of the love born from the wonder of difference."[39]

John Paul II observes that after the words in Genesis 2:23 expressing the joy of Adam discovering the woman, the other sex who is "bone of my bones and flesh of my flesh," there follows verse 2:24, which speaks of their unity ("they become one flesh").[40] These verses, according to St. John Paul, allow us to speak of a spousal meaning of the body in the mystery of creation. The spousal meaning of the body means that the body expresses the truth that man and woman are ordered to one another, and each person is called to be a gift for the other through one's masculinity or femininity. As Verlinde observes, sexual difference in human persons is a fact of nature infused with spiritual intentions.[41]

---

[38] Scola, *The Spousal Mystery*, 119.
[39] Verlinde, *L'ideologie du gender*, 101–2; translation mine.
[40] TOB, 164–65.
[41] TOB, 100.

II. The Spousal Meaning of the Body and the Image of God

The spousal meaning of the body, John Paul II explains, is ordered to an end: the communion of one flesh. This communion is a matter of choice and freedom because it involves the reciprocal self-gift of persons. The pope writes,

> We read, in fact, "A man will leave his father and mother and unite with his wife." While the man, by virtue of generation, belongs "by nature" to his father and mother, "he unites," by contrast, by choice. The text of Genesis 2:24 defines this character of the conjugal bond in reference to the first man and first woman, but at the same time it does so also in the perspective of man's earthly future as a whole.[42]

Man and woman were created for communion, and neither man nor woman fully find themselves apart from a sincere gift of self. The body of the person has a spousal meaning independently of any subjective act affirming it. Welcoming this call is another matter. A person may perceive something of the spousal meaning and choose to reject it or subvert it or overcome it. The gift of the other person can be welcomed or rejected. The spousal meaning of the body can be denied. These choices are not uncommon after the Fall of Adam and Eve. It is the religious and spiritual response that will welcome the call and accept

[42] TOB, 168.

the design of it. It understands the spousal meaning as open and accepting of the other and not closed in on itself. Before the sin of Adam and Eve, there was a freedom and deep capacity for the gift of self and the communion of persons.

St. John Paul maintains that in the realization of the spousal meaning of the body through the communion of persons, we find the fullness of the divine image in humanity. The revelation that God is the loving communion of the Father, Son, and Holy Spirit sheds much light on human persons created in the image of God. St. John Paul writes,

> *Man became the image of God not only through his own humanity but also through the communion of persons,* which man and woman form from the very beginning. The function of the image is that of mirroring the one who is the model, of reproducing its own prototype. Man becomes an image of God not so much in the moment of solitude as in the moment of communion. He is, in fact, "from the beginning" not only an image in which the solitude of one Person, who rules the world, mirrors itself, but also and essentially the image of an inscrutable divine community of Persons.[43]

The first man and woman's creation in the image of God means not only that each of them individually is like God, as a rational and free being. It also means that man and

---

[43] TOB, 163; emphasis in the original.

woman, created as a "unity of the two" in their common humanity, are called to live in a communion of love, and in this way to mirror in the world the communion of love that is in God, through which the Three Persons love each other in the intimate mystery of the one divine life.[44] In other words, the communion of persons in love as man and woman, who as man and woman share a common nature but differ from each other in their personal sexual identity, reflect the communion of love in the three persons of the one God, who are one in substance but distinct persons. Here again, we see how constitutive sexuality is for being a person created in the image of God. We stand in relation to others not in a generic way but as a woman or man. Sexuality specifies our relationality. The Triune God, who exists as a communion of three related divine persons, does not create a divine image that thrives in solitude. To speak of Adam and Eve as existing in the image and likeness of God means, of course, that human persons are called to exist "for others, to become a gift."[45] Sexual difference in its giving and receiving belongs to an ordered communion that is iconic of the Triune God, a communion of divine persons, in perfect love.

A Limit on the Spousal Meaning of the Body

The spousal meaning of the body has a limit placed on it because of the Fall of our first parents. The words of Jesus in Matthew 19:8, "from the beginning it was not so,"

---

[44] MD, §7.
[45] MD, §7.

instruct both the Pharisees and us that something changed for the worse. The consequences of the tragic disobedience of Adam and Eve include not only death and corruption but also the burden of lust for them and their descendants. The First Letter of the Apostle John (2:16) tells us, "For all that is in the world, the lust of the flesh and the lust of the eyes and the pride of life, is not of the Father but is of the world." Adam and Eve found themselves naked and ashamed, which manifested the "uneasiness of conscience connected with lust." Fearing that they might be looked on by the other as an "object" rather than as a creature willed for their own sake, Adam and Eve hid their nakedness, removing from one another's sight their genitalia, the clearest bodily expression of the sexuality that affects the whole being of their persons.[46] Now, ironically, the first couple find themselves alienated from one another on account of their sexuality. Genesis 3:16 testifies to this break and threat to the "unity of the two" with the words "your desire shall be for your husband, and he shall rule over you."

Here is a fundamental loss, John Paul II explains, in the communion of persons. Through the entrance of concupiscence, or disordered desire, into humanity, Adam and Eve and their descendants bear within themselves the

---

[46] John Paul II, Audience of May 28, 1980; TOB, 242–46. The pope observes that man's original spiritual and somatic unity is ruptured. The body has ceased drawing on the power of the spirit, which raised him to the level of the image of God. The body is no longer capable of expressing the person as man or woman as it had been created to do. The body could now obscure the person as well as reveal him or her. Now the body could play into the selfish desire to consume and manipulate as well as to give oneself away in love.

constant "inclination to sin," the tendency to go against the natural and moral structure that corresponds to the truth of the body as persons called to communion. Reflecting on the meaning of concupiscence, John Paul observes that it involves the loss of an interior freedom to give, to make a gift of self, because concupiscence reduces the other person to an object of satisfaction:

> Concupiscence brings with it the loss of the interior freedom of the gift. The spousal meaning of the human body is linked exactly to this freedom. Man can become a gift—that is, man and woman exist in the relationship of the reciprocal gift of self—if each of them masters himself.[47]

In other words, genuine freedom requires that a person has the spiritual maturity to be master of him- or herself; for only persons in possession of themselves can freely give themselves in love. It is precisely this kind of freedom that is lost in the Fall. With the loss of this freedom, it becomes difficult to look upon the otherness of masculinity or femininity as gift, but it becomes quite easy to see it as a threat to be reined in or dominated: "Sexuality is no longer freshly surrounded by the powers of the soul, which allow the body to radiate the beauty of the person, but can become an expression of the will to power, of the one human being's domination over another to the point of making the other a thing."[48]

---

[47] TOB, 259.
[48] Scola, *The Spousal Mystery*, 77.

The relationship between man and woman is distorted. The human heart now becomes a battlefield between lust and love. In this way, the subjection of man and woman to lust puts a limit on the spousal meaning of the body. This meaning is not just a conceptual reality. It is, at the same time, the way of living in the body in concrete interpersonal relations. It remains true objectively that the body manifests the truth that man and woman are created for one another and are called to communion; however, in the fallen state, the interior spiritual condition of man and woman make it difficult for them to live according to this objective truth. Essential to this communion is the freedom for it, which is nothing less than the freedom for love.

St. John Paul recalls in his writings that freedom has been understood for centuries by the Christian tradition to be an outstanding manifestation of the divine image. Because of sin, this freedom, while not completely lost, is reduced and diminished. This in turn diminishes the divine image in Adam and Eve in the communion of persons in love. In his encyclical *Veritatis Splendor* John Paul says,

> Reason and experience not only confirm the weakness of human freedom; they also confirm its tragic aspects. Man comes to realize that his freedom is in some mysterious way inclined to betray this openness to the True and the Good, and that all too often he actually prefers to choose finite, limited and ephemeral goods. What is more, within his errors and negative decisions, man glimpses the source of a deep rebellion, which leads him

to reject the Truth and the Good in order to set himself up as an absolute principle unto himself: "You will be like God" (Gen 3:5). Consequently, *freedom itself needs to be set free. It is Christ who sets it free:* he "has set us free for freedom" (cf. Gal 5:1).[49]

III. Christ the New Adam, His Church the New Eve

It is, of course, the condition of humanity after the Fall that the Son is sent by the Father to reverse and overcome. In becoming man, the Son assumes our human condition, which is burdened by sin and death. His perfect self-giving obtains for us the forgiveness of sins and our freedom. In *Veritatis Splendor,* John Paul II points out that true freedom is won and disclosed for us on the cross: the Crucified Christ reveals the authentic meaning of freedom; he lives it fully in the total gift of himself and calls the disciples to share in his freedom. Moreover,

> contemplation of Jesus Crucified is thus the high-road which the Church must tread every day if she wishes to understand the full meaning of freedom: the gift of self in service to God and one's brethren. Communion with the Crucified and Risen Lord is the never-ending source from which the Church

---

[49] John Paul II, Encyclical Letter on the Splendor of Truth *Veritatis Splendor* (August 6, 1993), §85, http://www.vatican.va/content/john-paul-ii/en/encyclicals/documents/hf_jp-ii_enc_06081993_veritatis-splendor.html (hereafter cited as VS).

draws unceasingly in order to live in freedom, to give of herself and serve.[50]

True freedom is the ability to make a sincere gift of self in service to God and one's brothers and sisters. Christ is the New Adam, who gives himself up out of love for the sake of the humanity that he gathered to himself in the form of the Church, the new Eve. The communion of love of the new Adam and new Eve is the restoration of the fullness of the divine image and likeness that was defaced and diminished by the first Adam and the first Eve. In Christ's union of communion with his Bride, the Church, the call of humanity—as a unity of the two, living in a communion of love and mirroring that communion of love that is in God—is realized in a way that is even greater than was possible in the first Adam and Eve. The Father's intention for man and woman from the beginning is fulfilled in Christ, the second Adam, and the Church, the second Eve. It is fulfilled in a way that is permanent and can never be lost, because Christ, the Son of God made man, has perfectly given himself to the Church, and he has made his Bride holy. The spousal meaning of the body is realized and its full meaning is revealed in the one-flesh union of Christ, the Bridegroom, with the Church, his Bride.

This reconstitution of the Trinitarian divine image in humanity involves a conformation to Christ, who restores us to full freedom and communion. This conformation is communicated to us in the gift of the Holy Spirit, whose first fruit is charity. Pope John Paul affirms that through

[50] VS, §87.

the Spirit of truth, freedom, and love, we are enabled "to interiorize the law [of love] and live it as the motivating force of freedom."[51] Conformed to Christ in his crucified gift of self, we are empowered to love and to look upon the other as man or woman, as willed by God for their own sake, and as such, accepted in their otherness.[52] This freedom for love is a movement away from the sovereign self of the technological paradigm, which finds it difficult to receive things as they exist for their own sake and seeks rather to control, possess, and refashion.

The participation in the freedom that Christ offers and the renewal of the divine image in the communion of persons takes place in us gradually, but it has a tremendous power to resist the sovereign self of the technological paradigm. Christ, the new Adam, is to be followed step by step. The way to freedom, the way ultimately to the communion of love, is by entering into the one sacrifice of Christ in the Church's worship, especially in the Eucharist. This gift of Christ, the new Adam, is, in the words of Pope

---

[51] VS, §87.

[52] This invites a sharing in the communion of the second Adam and the second Eve. It does not mean, of course, that a person must be in the married state of life to realize the spousal meaning of the body. It can be lived in the state of celibacy and virginity or the devoted single life. Living the full truth of the body by the sincere gift of self as man or woman is made possible by the grace of Christ and is a participation in his union of communion with the second Eve, the Church. The ordained pastors have the vocation of representing Christ before the Church, offering himself most especially in the celebration of the Eucharist. To be sure, the ordained are baptized Christians too, and as such they must be actively receptive of Christ's grace as members of the Church.

Benedict, "like inducing nuclear fission in the very heart of being—the victory of love over hatred, the victory of love over death. Only this intimate explosion of good conquering evil can then trigger off the series of transformations that little by little will change the world. All other changes remain superficial and cannot save."[53]

REVIEW

1. Popes Francis and Benedict XVI hold that an "integral ecology" demands a right understanding of the "one and indivisible book of nature," including the human person, environment, life, sexuality, the family, and social relations.

2. According to Francis, in modern society a "technocratic paradigm" has come to dominate, in which human beings view reality fundamentally as something to be used.

3. Further, modern anthropocentrism creates the illusion of the "sovereign self," who sees the entire created order, including our bodiliness and sexuality, as the raw instrument of self-expression and self-realization. This strikes at the dignity of nature and of ourselves.

---

[53] Benedict XVI, Homily at World Youth Day, Cologne-Marienfeld, August 21, 2005, http://www.vatican.va/content/benedict-xvi/en/homilies/2005/documents/hf_ben-xvi_hom_20050821_20th-world-youth-day.html.

4. All of creation is a gift, and to accept it we have to accept the truth of it, including our nature as soul-body unity, male or female. In rightly seeing our bodiliness and sexuality, we can better approach all of physical creation and others who are different from us.

5. The full meaning of the book of nature, including our physicality and sexuality, is found in Christ, the fullness of divine Revelation.

6. Pope John Paul II writes that man and woman in their unity of nature are equally made in the image of God. They are human nature's "two ways of being a body."

7. In Genesis man and woman's sexual identity is established in view of each other. The other way of being an embodied person is central in the search for human identity. Thus, sexuality is not a mere attribute but a more constituent part of our personhood.

8. Far from meaning that man and woman are two fractional halves of humanity, sexual reciprocity mean that there are two ways of being an embodied person, and these ways complete each other and therefore do not overcome each other.

9. According to Cardinal Angelo Scola, the experience of sexual difference is significant as the "model for all experiences of transcendence."

10. As Verlinde says, the individual human being is not

the whole of reality or the whole of humanness: the other sex to some degree eludes us. "This limitation is not a privation but a gift that allows for the discovery of love born from the wonder of difference."

11. As indicated by the spousal meaning of their bodies, neither man nor woman can fully find themselves apart from a sincere gift of self. In this communion of persons, we find the fullness of the image of the Trinitarian God in humanity.

12. As a result of the Fall, the first couple is alienated from each other on account of their sexuality. Concupiscence reduces the other person to an object of satisfaction, thereby diminishing the communion of persons and the interior freedom to make a gift of self.

13. The perfect self-gift of the Crucified Son of God obtains for us true freedom. God's intention for man and woman from the beginning is surpassingly fulfilled in Christ, the new Adam, in his communion with the Church, his bride and the new Eve.

14. Conformed to Christ through the charity of the Holy Spirit, we can look upon the other as man or woman, as willed by God for their own sake and, as such, to be accepted in their otherness.

15. Freedom for love opposes the sovereign self of the technocratic paradigm, which does not receive things

in their own right but seeks rather to possess and refashion. We gain such freedom by entering into Christ's perfect self-gift, especially in the Eucharist.

Further Reading

Francis. *Laudato Si'*. Huntington, IN: Our Sunday Visitor, 2015. The Holy See's version is at http://www.vatican.va/content/francesco/en/encyclicals/documents/papa-francesco_20150524_enciclica-laudato-si.html.

Hütter, Reinhard. "We Are Not God: Reflections on the Theology of *Laudato Si.*" *Nova et Vetera* 17, no. 3 (Summer 2019): 639–52.

John Paul II. *Man and Woman He Created Them: A Theology of the Body*. Translated by Michael Waldstein. Boston: Pauline Books and Media, 2006.

———. *On the Dignity and Vocation of Women:* Mulieris Dignitatem. Boston, MA: Daughters of St. Paul, 1988.

———. Apostolic Exhortation on the Formation of Priests *Pastores Dabo Vobis*. March 15, 1992. http://www.vatican.va/content/john-paul-ii/en/apost_exhortations/documents/hf_jp-ii_exh_25031992_pastores-dabo-vobis.html. (See especially §22, on the priest as image of Christ, Bridegroom of the Church, his Bride.)

Scola, Angelo. *The Spousal Mystery*. Translated by Michelle K. Borras. Grand Rapids, MI: Eerdmans, 2005.

About the Contributors

JOHN D. FINLEY, PHD, is a professor of philosophy at Kenrick-Glennon Seminary in St. Louis, Missouri. He received his doctorate at the University of Dallas. He has taught at Thomas Aquinas College in California and is a member of the Aquinas Institute at Blackfriars Hall, University of Oxford. Dr. Finley has lectured and published on the nature of the human person, sexuality, phenomenology, and the thought of Thomas Aquinas. In 2017 he was awarded a grant from the John Templeton Foundation to pursue interdisciplinary research on philosophy, science, and gender. He and his wife, Hilary, have three children.

CARA BUSKMILLER, MD, received her bachelor's degree in liberal arts from Thomas Aquinas College in 2011. She earned her medical degree from Texas A&M University in 2015 and completed a residency in obstetrics and gynecology in 2019 at Saint Louis University. She is presently a fellow in maternal-fetal medicine at the University of Texas Health Science Center in Houston, Texas. Her research and clinical interests include the ethics of maternal-fetal and fetal-fetal vital conflicts, grief in reproductive loss, contraception, and ectopic pregnancy. She is a board member of the American Association of Pro-Life OB/GYNs, and the founder and current chair of the board of Conscience in Residency, which advises medical students and residents on conscience-based decisions.

PAUL W. HRUZ, MD, PHD, is an academic pediatric endocrinologist (hormone specialist) and tenured physician scientist with faculty appointments in both Pediatrics and Cellular Biology and Physiology. Dr. Hruz has over twenty years of clinical experience in caring for children with disorders of sexual development. He has received certification in Healthcare Ethics from the National Catholic Bioethics Center and is a regular contributor to his university's course on research ethics for graduate students. He has authored over sixty peer-reviewed manuscripts, scientific reviews, and book chapters. Together with his wife, Anne, he has raised his five children in St. Louis, Missouri.

DEACON PATRICK W. LAPPERT, MD, has been a physician and surgeon for almost forty years. He received board certification in General Surgery and later Plastic and Reconstructive Surgery. He served in the United States Navy for twenty-four years, first as a Flight Surgeon, then as a General Surgeon, and finally as a Reconstructive Surgeon. He founded a major wound care center as well as a cranio-facial reconstructive team for congenital deformities at what was, at the time, the largest military hospital in the world. He was also the specialty leader for reconstructive surgery for the Office of the Surgeon General USN. He was in the private practice of plastic surgery for seventeen years and is now retired. Deacon Lappert was born into a Jewish family but lived as an ardent atheist for most of his adult life. He had a conversion in his last year of training in reconstructive surgery. He was baptized and received into the Catholic Church at the Easter Vigil in 1995. He has been married to Patrice Ann for thirty-nine years. Together they have raised six children. Deacon Lappert was ordained to the permanent diaconate by Bishop

Robert Baker of Birmingham in Alabama in 2013. He has lectured on the subject of transgender surgery since 2014.

Andrew Sodergren, PsyD, is a Catholic clinical psychologist and director of psychological services for Ruah Woods, a Theology of the Body ministry in Cincinnati, Ohio. He earned his Master's and Doctoral degrees in Clinical Psychology from Divine Mercy University's Institute for the Psychological Sciences. Dr. Sodergren also holds a Master's degree in Theology from the John Paul II Institute for Studies on Marriage and Family in Washington, DC, where he has taught as an Adjunct Professor. He regularly speaks to lay and professional audiences on topics related to the integration of psychology and Catholic anthropology, attachment, marriage, and sexuality. He and his wife, Ellie, have been married twenty-two years and have five children.

Lawrence J. Welch, PhD, is professor of Theology at Kenrick-Glennon Seminary, where he has taught since 1994. For the last twenty-six years he has taught courses in theological anthropology, the sacrament of marriage, and ecclesiology. He has published articles in the *Thomist*, *Nova et Vetera*, *Theological Studies*, *New Blackfriars*, and other journals. He is active in the Academy for Catholic Theology and served on its Board for two terms.